CONSERVATIVES AND THE UNION

A Study of
Conservative Party Attitudes
to Scotland

Conservatives and the Union

A Study of Conservative Party Attitudes to Scotland

JAMES MITCHELL

EDINBURGH UNIVERSITY PRESS

Edinburgh University Press
22 George Square, Edinburgh

Set in Linotron Palatino and
printed in Great Britain by
Redwood Press Limited,
Melksham, Wilts

British Library Cataloguing
in Publication Data
Mitchell, James
Conservatives and the Union:
a study of Conservative Party
attitudes to Scotland.
1. Scotland. Policies of the
Conservative party
I. Title
324.2410409411

ISBN 0 7486 0123 6
0 7486 0176 7 pbk

Contents

Introduction

After the 1987 General Election, only ten Conservatives out of seventy-two MPs in total had been elected from Scotland. The party had suffered its worst performance since 1910, or 1880 if the Liberal Unionists are not included in the pre-World War One figures. But the Conservatives won an overall Commons majority which was the size of the total representation of Scotland in the Commons. Following the Election the two vice presidents of the Scottish Conservative and Unionist Association (SCUA) produced a report for their executive. The report's central comment was that the party was perceived in Scotland to be 'English and anti-Scottish'. The authors went on to argue that this was a 'feature of (let's admit it) an over-centralized London-dominated country and of Scots having very sensitive nerve endings'.[1]

The conclusion that the party was perceived to be anti-Scottish was significant. It recognised that a political party had to be seen as having a Scottish dimension, that being a British party, even one that had revived a sense of British patriotism, was insufficient in contemporary Scotland. Support for some measure of Scottish devolution has, historically, been the most obvious means by which political parties have presented themselves to the electorate as pro-Scottish. For over a century, the Conservatives had succeeded in this by supporting the passage of an Act to establish the Scottish Office and subsequently by their association with the Office's development. Occasionally, during this period the Conservatives portrayed their opponents as anti-Scottish. The nationalisation programme of the post-war Attlee Government was presented as taking control of Scottish industries out of Scotland and placing them in the hands of London bureaucrats.

By the late 1980s the appearance of Scottish control of Scottish affairs had been created with a structure of administrative devolution based in Edinburgh. This inevitably led to frustration when Scots found that this proved to be more apparent than real. For the Conservatives to turn round and argue that Scotland was a part of Britain and had to accept British policies was bound to be unpopular after a century when the notion of some kind of Scottish control of Scottish affairs had developed. Ironically, the Conservatives had played a major part in developing this notion.

The political component of Scottish identity during the twentieth century has most obviously been related to institutional structures, but has also had a more nebulous content in the form of a Scottish political culture. Political culture attempts to 'make explicit and systematic much of the understanding associated with such long-standing concepts as political ideology, national political psychology, and the fundamental values of a people'.[2] It is a contestable, but useful concept. Scots often recite a litany of separate or distinctive institutions as evidence of uniqueness or, more accurately, of being different from the English.

INSTITUTIONAL DISTINCTIVENESS

Scottish political distinctiveness has its origins in the historic evolution of separate traditions in administration, laws and social ethics. Though no Scottish Parliament has existed since 1707, these traditions have ensured that distinctiveness in the provision and administration of public services exists today. Time has lessened the differences but Scotland retains a unique position within the United Kingdom. The political institutions which have evolved in Scotland, as much as in Western Europe generally, followed that pattern described by T. H. Marshall in his evolutionary conception of citizenship.[3] Marshall defined citizenship in terms of rights which began with civil rights, followed by political rights before social rights, particularly embodied in the welfare state established by the Attlee Government.

Subsequent debates on Marshall's approach have concentrated on the rôle of conflict in this evolutionary process, whether citizenship integrated the working-class into society, whether one set of rights ineluctably led to the next, to what extent this evolution was reversible or entrenched, and the role of the state.[4] These are all important questions in discussion of Scottish politics and society, but central to the question of the Conservatives and the Union is the effect development of citizenship had on perceptions of Scottish national identity amongst Scots. Contrary to what might be expected this process did not create a homogeneous British political identity, though a fairly uniform British citizenship evolved. The importance of the artefacts of political life – in this case of Scottish central administration – must be taken into account. While Scottish civil, political and social rights during the twentieth century have been comparable, if not identical, with those south of the border there developed alongside this process a belief that Scotland was *politically* distinct and that Scots should control distinctively Scottish affairs.

In Scotland, as in England, the civil and political rights which predated and served to influence the nature and institutional form of social rights of the twentieth century were quite distinct. Civil rights had been enshrined in laws which were unusually systematic, dating from Stair's *Institutes* written shortly before the Union of 1707. A distinct Scottish jurisprudence was to have important consequences for future developments in the political and social spheres. Even today, civil rights remain different in Scotland from those south of the border.

Political rights in Scotland, in Marshall's sense, resembled those of the south but differed in detail. Parliamentary representation was based on a similar, but not exactly replicated, franchise in Scotland as England before universal adult suffrage was instituted. Before 1884 Scotland's share of seats in the House of Commons was lower than that which would have been accorded using a strict population calculation. Between 1884 and 1948 Scottish representation in the House of Commons approximately reflected the population distribution in Britain. However, from 1948 Scotland has had a higher proportion of seats than her population merits though, of course, other considerations including distance from Westminster and territorial distribution of population must also be accounted for.

But it has been the institutions of government which have been most obviously distinct in political terms. Scottish local government grew out of the parochial system of the Church of Scotland and the central administration of these local authorities – developing particularly from the early Exchequer grants in the mid nineteenth century – inevitably took on distinct characteristics in light of the local administrative and legal arrangements. The Scottish Office, established in 1885, was unique in being a territorial Department of State rather than a functionally based Department until 1964, when the Welsh Office was set up, at least if Colonial Departments such as the India Office are ignored.

Social rights, the third and crucial set of rights in Marshall's view of citizenship, have not differed markedly in Britain during the latter part of this century, though the social ethics and policies of earlier periods did. Uniformity in the principles of social rights throughout Britain (the case of Northern Ireland has to be excluded from this statement) has been a hallmark of the modern welfare state. However, this has not meant a uniformity in the mechanisms of allocation, nor has it prevented some differences in detail or degree.

The social ethics and administrative machinery of the Poor Law, rudimentary health and educational provision in past centuries had been dominated by the Church of Scotland. Before the twentieth century the role of the Church of Scotland in Poor Law administration, for example, meant that payments were disbursed on criteria and through mechanisms quite different from those south of the border. For example, no payment was made to the able-bodied unemployed in Scotland.[5] As one historian has recently suggested, the

myth of Scots thrift, incidentally, may be partly explained by the
exceptional harshness of the Scottish Poor Law which fostered a
disposition to save.[6]

The Disruption of 1843, when the Church of Scotland split, was a
crucial watershed in Scottish history, marking not simply an ecclesiastical controversy in a narrow theological sense, but a dispute affecting educational and Poor Law provision. Though the 'presbyterian
inheritance' remains, the Disruption facilitated the already evident
movement of the secular state to take a more direct involvement in
social welfare provision as was happening elsewhere in Europe. The
divided Church was no longer in the same position to administer
parochial relief and services. Two years after the Disruption the Poor
Law Amendment (Scotland) Act was passed, which set up parochial
boards, statutory bodies for the administration of the poor law in each
parish. Though this secularization process was already evident, the
Disruption played a part in its development.

As the state's social welfare increased, so too did the tendency of
centralization in decision-making and administration. The 'centre'
was ambiguous; sometimes it was London, on other occasions it
meant Edinburgh, but increasingly, particularly from the First World
War, the ascendant Treasury in London meant that in the all-import-
ant area of finance, the centre meant London. The period between
1843 and the establishment of the modern welfare state under the
Attlee Government witnessed a major move away from social welfare
being disbursed and its finances raised in the local parish to the state
at the centre – again recognising the amibiguity of the term – taking
responsibilities for these functions. Field administration was needed
but the local offices of the welfare state were stripped of the powers
while disbursing far larger sums than the old, disparate and frag-
mented structure of the nineteenth century.

The development of citizenship in Scotland was similar to that of
England, and other European countries for that matter, inasmuch as
social rights followed on from civil and political rights. However, the
different base from which the social rights developed ensured that
uniformity was not to exist throughout the United Kingdom. Of
course, pressures towards uniformity were at work, most notably the
single Parliament, which legislated for the diverse state and the
dominance and centralizing influence of the Treasury.

Nonetheless, the basis of Scottish distinctiveness had been established. It is conceivable that the Scottish Board system might have
been swept away, that the Scottish Office might not have been established and Scotland would have been more fully integrated into the
British state. But this was not to be and Conservatives were at least as
important as others in ensuring that a distinctive Scottish institutional
order existed into the twentieth century.

It would be mistaken to suggest that citizenship in Scotland developed entirely along class lines. A crucial dimension distinguishing Scotland from England was that of religion: the importance of the Kirk in Scottish history is difficult to avoid. Related to this was the position of the growing Catholic population of Scotland in the late nineteenth and early twentieth century. Coming from Ireland, the Catholic population faced the same antipathy as other subsequent waves of immigrants, and in many respects suffered greater discrimination. Equal rights to education for the Catholic community only came about with the passage of the Education (Scotland) Act, 1918. Prior to that date, Catholics were given no state support for their own schools while, effectively, Protestant education was provided in the state sector. This dimension of the uneven development of citizenship within Scotland did have its equivalent in England. Scotland had tackled the problem around the time of the First World War while R. A. Butler faced considerably greater problems with the religious dimension to the 1944 Education Act than Tom Johnston had with his comparable piece of legislation for Scotland.

Though the development of the social dimension of citizenship was often British based, clearly Scottish aspects became evident. Housing, for example, had a distinctive Scottish basis. Though the Scottish Office was not able to develop different policies from those developed for England, it acted as a pressure group for additional resources and for extending English legislation, thus ensuring a peculiarly Scottish situation in housing. The vast size of the Scottish public sector in housing was remarkable, as were its problems. As in so much public policy, the problems and solutions were only quantitatively different from those of England, but so much so as to create an impression of a qualitatively different situation. Consequently, the perception of citizenship in Scotland, though perhaps not always viewed as a coherent or clear idea, has undoubtedly included a Scottish dimension during the twentieth century.

Essentially, the distinctive facets of Scottish citizenship in themselves would probably not have been sufficient to develop a sense of Scottish national identity in political terms as has occurred. The crucial additional factor was the perception that Scotland had a distinct 'political system'.[7] Though this term is open to criticism,[8] the fact that it is used at all signifies the existence of a Scottish political identity and a belief that something more than the appearance of Scottish political autonomy exists or, if it does not exist, that it ought to. This has proved to be one of the most persistent aspects of Scottish political culture.

SCOTTISH POLITICAL CULTURE

Political culture has been described in one standard textbook as 'essentially psychological; it refers to what people think about politics – to their beliefs, values and emotions. It does not refer to actual political behaviour'.[9] Whether founded in fact or fantasy, political culture can be potent. Political culture is a disputed notion and surveys and polls will tell little about it, and may even be misleading. The extent to which a British political culture exists and whether it can be compatible with a Scottish political culture is very important.

In Scotland a number of potent aspects of political culture can be identified. Examples serve to illustrate a body of ideas which distinguish Scottish political culture from that south of the border. These are not necessarily equally potent, valid or mutually compatible but each in its own way has some importance.

The idea of Red Clydeside is one example which has resulted in historical dispute. Some historians would argue that Red Clydeside was real; the revolutionary potential of Clydeside workers towards the end of the First World War was evidenced by rent strikes and industrial unrest. Others maintain that this is fanciful, that the peculiar circumstances of wartime permitted and encouraged these disturbances which were misinterpreted by a Government in London fearful of a Bolshevik-type rising and have been exaggerated subsequently by romantic politicians.[10]

A comparable emotive myth relates to the Highland Clearances. The enforced emigration of Highlanders in the last century to make way for sheep has been a powerful and equally disputed aspect of Scottish history which has reverberated down through a number of generations. The Sutherland family's part in the Clearances and thereby its attack on the Gaelic culture was the reason why the Duchess of Sutherland had to resign as president of the Mod in the 1970s. Furthermore, the analogy of the Clearances with modern de-industrialisation has been used frequently during the twentieth century. In the 1970s the play, *The Cheviot, the Stag and the Black, Black Oil* developed a theme comparing the discovery of oil and its opportunities with the Clearances. Recently a balad entitled 'Letter from America' sung by The Proclaimers held the number one position in record sales for a number of weeks with a theme which compared industrial closures under the Thatcher Government and lack of opportunities for Scots in Scotland with the Highland Clearances.

Another example is the idea of the 'democratic intellect', which has been eloquently articulated by the philosopher George Elder Davie. The notion that Scotland once possessed an educational system which permitted all classes of children to overcome their background has come to be widely believed though historian Robert Anderson provides ample evidence to suggest that this golden age never existed.[11] The idea that Scotland 'above all other countries is essentially educational', as Sir Lyon Playfair maintained during a debate on the Bill setting up the Scottish Office in 1885,[12] has been a potent Scottish myth. Conservatives have played a considerable part in propagating the myth. Walter Elliot is particularly notable for his references to the 'democratic intellectualism' of Scottish education, though he had a somewhat different meaning from George Davie.[13] Despite the conservatism and generally repressive nature of traditional Scottish primary and secondary eduction, Scots – and others – still cling to the myth that education is a national commodity for which they should take great pride.

Centralization, collectivism and corporatism are recurring themes in the discussion of Scottish political institutions. Michael Fry in *Patronage and Principle* has argued that after the reorganization of the Scottish Office in 1939, patronage to the collectivist, corporate institutions largely at the instigation of wartime Secretary of State Tom Johnston has been an all too familiar facet of Scottish politics. The notion that centralization, as compared with England, has emerged consequent on these developments is also suggested. However, as the comprehensive study of educational policy since the war, Mac-Pherson and Raab's *Governing Education*, has argued, it is too simplistic to make the centralization charge. A far more complex situation has existed. Nonetheless, a distinct policy style with distinct policy communities have been identified by Keating and Midwinter in *The Government of Scotland*.

In Scotland today a myth has gained credence that Scots are anti-Conservative. Opposition politicians adopt the obverse of this idea to attack the Conservatives by arguing that the Conservatives are an anti-Scottish party. The Liberal hegemony in the nineteenth century and Labour hegemony today seem to prove this. Yet, neither the Liberals in the nineteenth century nor Labour in recent years, and far less so in the latter case, has dominated Scottish politics as much as they would have us believe. It is notable that the only party ever to achieve a clear majority of the popular vote in Scotland this century was the Unionist Party in 1955. On the other hand the notion that Scotland suffers from a dependency culture – a poltiical myth in the making – as an explanation for Conservative failure is based even less in fact but has a potency which cannot be ignored and feeds into the political culture of Scotland.

These ideas, notions and myths are not comprehensive. Indeed, perhaps the most valid statement on Scotland's political culture is rarely made. The true nature of Scottish political culture encompassing each of the ideas outlined above is the idea that Scotland is a conservative country with radical pretensions. A view similar to this was made by an editor of the *Scotsman* almost ninety years ago when he wrote that the Scottish people were 'conservative in their customs, in their institutions, in the Radicalism of their politics'.[14] Scotland's politics display conservative features, but conservatism should not to be confused with Conservatism; facts which are unpalatable to the left and frustrating to the right.

These ideas all flow together to form the political culture of Scotland

and at different times with different force are influential in the politics of Scotland. Sometimes some aspect may have the effect of gaining support for an idea while at another it may have the opposite effect. A myth may be more potent on Clydeside than in rural Buchan or may have equal but opposite force. The case of the referendum on Scottish devolution in 1979 is a case in point. The myth of Red Clydeside was used, however indirectly, by elements on the left of Scottish politics in Clydeside to encourage voters to vote for an Assembly in order to attain socialism, while it was used by right-wing politicians in North-East Scotland to frighten voters of the consequences of Socialist Home Rule. There is no evidence that the promise of socialism aided the 'Yes' side in the referedum – but the prospect of West of Scotland Labour domination seems to have harmed the devolution cause elsewhere.

The prospectus on which Scottish politics is based seems bound to favour Conservatives so long as it is replete with unsubstantiated and unsubstantiable myths. The Red Clydeside myth benefits the Tories more than any others. There is no more powerful argument in the Tory armoury than to concede distinctiveness but warn of the dire consequences of this distinctiveness. Red Clydeside is the means by which Tories make Scots frightened of themselves. The Tories are, however, as much victims as they are beneficiaries of Scottish political culture. They have played no small part in developing Scottish institutions – those associated with or consequent on the development of citizenship – and the political culture. In doing so they have made their own position as the Unionists *par excellence* often difficult to sustain.

Acknowledgements

This book began as an undergraduate dissertation on Conservative attitudes towards Scottish Home Rule while I was a student at Aberdeen University. I would wish to thank the staff of the Department of Politics and International Relations in Aberdeen, and particularly to Michael Dyer and Grant Jordan for their support and advice. Alistair Smith, a former President and Vice Chairman of the Scottish Conservative and Unionist Association must be thanked for his enormous assistance in helping arrange meetings with a number of Conservative politicians as well as supplying me with much valuable information himself. Without his support it would have proved impossible to gain access to serving Cabinet Ministers.

My time at Nuffield College, Oxford allowed me to read more widely on the subject and meet others with an interest in the subject. There, I was fortunate to have the comments of Nevil Johnson and Vernon Bogdanor on an early draft of this work. The chapter on Scottish Administration and references to Walter Elliot in the book are based on research for my doctoral thesis on Scottish central administration completed at Nuffield. The pressure of work on other projects meant that I did not complete the final draft until I was fortunate to be awarded a Post-Doctoral Fellowship by the Royal Society of Edinburgh. This has allowed me to include references to *dependency* and *enterprise* cultures.

Many very busy people gave generously of their time in meetings with me and I would wish to acknowledge this support from across the entire spectrum of the Conservative Party. Former Prime Ministers Lord Home of the Hirsel and Edward Heath agreed to discuss events and episodes which must have appeared fine to the point of being trivial amongst the world affairs in which they had been involved. Government Ministers gave up some time in busy schedules to be interviewed: Michael Ancram, Alick Buchanan-Smith, Sir Russell Fairgrieve, Francis Pym, Malcolm Rifkind, Iain Sproat, George Younger. Many other politicians, including those in other parties, either answered queries in letters or gave brief interviews.

Iain Lawson very kindly agreed to read and comment upon a chapter and explained a great deal about a period of his political life he probably now finds painful to recall. Another person whose views changed dramatically should be mentioned: the late Jim Shearer was not only a friend but someone who taught me to respect those I may disagree with. I did not know Jim when he was a Tory but do not doubt that his anti-devolutionist beliefs then were as principled and sincere as was his passionate support for Scottish Home Rule during the period I knew him.

A number of other people gave me considerable support. Elizabeth Allan, Alison Crook, Linda Watt and Julie Fogg helped with typing or gave other valuable support. Kevin Gibbon's encyclopaedic knowledge of Scottish electoral history and general interest in this work were very much appreciated. William Maloney read through and commented on the proofs. I must also thank Martin Spencer and the staff of Edinburgh University Press for their patience and help.

Of course, while many people aided me in producing this book none bears any responsibility for its contents. The interpretations and opinions expressed will run contrary to many, if not most, of those to whom I am grateful. This does not diminish the value I attach to their help.

                                                                    J.M.

Conflicts within Conservatism
in Scotland

In the preface to his recent book on Conservatism, Robert Nisbet noted that the one overriding objective for a serious political party was victory.[1] Rigid adherence to a political doctrine is not to be expected of politicians, and merely surveying the actions and statements of political practitioners would serve only to confuse anyone attempting to discover the ideology of a party. A political party's ideology will be discovered in the 'pre-political' stage, as T. S. Eliot referred to the theoretical underpinning to policies, the 'stratum down to which any sound political thinking must push its roots, and from which it must derive its nourishment'.[2] For this reason it may be necessary to focus on the ideas of individuals other than politicians. This is particularly the case when considering Scottish Conservatism. Few Conservative politicians have articulated their political philosophy in a Scottish context. This in itself may be important. Perhaps it is explained by the conflicts which appear to be inherent in any attempt to do so. It is these conflicts which will be the basis of this chapter.

Certain central ideas recur in the writings of conservative thinkers. From Edmund Burke to Michael Oakeshott themes such as tradition, change, organicism, authority and scepticism are discernible which, though with different emphases, suggest the existence of a Conservative *Weltanschauung*. Of course, these may seem arbitrary or academic themes with little relevance to the practical world of party politics. One political scientist castigated Teddy Taylor, once the quintessence of Scottish Conservatism, as representing a 'know-nothing populist version of Conservatism whose connection with any of the historic tenets of the party remains obscure'.[3] This criticism seems harsh in that populism has played a considerable part in the Conservative Party's policy-making and presentation. Nonetheless, it is an understandable comment and in this chapter it shall be assumed that there is more to Conservatism than an appeal to base instincts. While consideration must be given to Conservative views of tradition, organicism and change, it will also be important to consider Unionism, given the centrality of its place in Scottish Conservative thinking before finally turning to the 'New Right' which has been seen as an important influence on contemporary Conservatism.

TRADITION

In 1947, Quinton Hogg, as he then was, wrote that the principles of patriotism, constitutionalism, continuity and tradition were those of Conservatism. However much the Scottish Conservative may agree with Hogg in this identification of principles, there will not necessarily be common agreement as to the artefacts meant. No doubt Hogg had in mind the Church of England, Parliamentary sovereignty, English Common Law, as well as the Boat Race, cricket and the Tudors. He would not have been thinking about the Church of Scotland, popular sovereignty, Scots Law and the Democratic Intellect, the Old Firm and William Wallace. But what would a Scottish Conservative think of when listing the artifacts of his or her conservative principles?

Sir Walter Scott has been described as the 'purest of instinctive Tories'[4] and was recognised as a classic example of a Conservative Romantic by the American Conservative philosopher Russell Kirk. Kirk devoted a chapter in his book on Conservatism to the conflict between the romantic and the utilitarian using Scott as his prime example of the former.[5] Scott's nephew and biographer tells the story which Kirk cites:

> At a debate of the Faculty of Advocates on some of these propositions, (reforms in the Scottish legal system) he made a speech much longer than any he had ever before delivered in that assembly; and several who heard it have assured me, that it had a flow and energy of eloquence for which those who knew him best had been quite unprepared. When the meeting broke up, he walked across the Mound, on his way to Castle Street, between Mr Jeffrey and another of his reforming friends, who complimented him on the rhetorical powers he had been displaying, and would willingly have treated the subject-matter of the discussion playfully. But his feelings had been moved to an extent far beyond their apprehension: he exclaimed, 'No, no – 'tis no laughing matter; little by little, whatever your wishes may be, you will destroy and undermine, until nothing of what makes Scotland shall remain.' And so saying, he turned round to conceal his agitation – but not until Mr Jeffrey saw tears gushing down his cheek – resting his head until he recovered himself on the wall of the Mound. Seldom, if ever, in his more advanced age, did any feelings obtain such mastery.[6]

However, in his classic work on *Scott and Scotland*, Edwin Muir highlighted the dilemma inherent in Scottish Conservatism. As a Conservative, Scott believed in the established order and tradition. The established order was the Union of 1707 which he accepted as it was,

> rooted in history and sanctified by the past. But at the same time he saw this established order gradually destroying another estab-

lished order, that of Scotland. That order was equally old, equally rooted in history and sanctified by the past, and moreover it was the order to which he was most intimately bound by birth, early memory and the compulsion of his imagination. From this inward conflict he never escaped.[7]

Allan Massie, remarkably, described this piece from Muir's book as one of the critic's 'brilliant flashes'.[8]

Again for the student of politics, another critic offers an alternative and interesting view; in a bicentennial study of Scott's work, David Daiches suggested ulterior motives:

> What we have here is a case of Scott drawing on Scottish national feeling as a means of preventing the development in Scotland of liberal democratic measures.[9]

Whatever may be the case with respect to Walter Scott, Daiches has surely touched on an important point. The romantic inclination may merely be a contrived covering for a Conservatism devoid of philosophical content but may merely be opposition to progress. Such an argument is particularly relevant when considering the rhetoric of Conservative politicians.

An alternative view of Sir Walter Scott is provided by P. H. Scott who has argued that Sir Walter was the author of the 'first manifesto of modern Scottish nationalism'.[10] Written in 1825, *The Letters of Malachi Malagrowther* were letters written by Sir Walter in a campaign against an attempt to prevent Scottish banks issuing their own notes, an issue of economic significance and not simply a symbolic matter. Additionally, P. H. Scott has questioned the uncritical assumption that Sir Walter Scott was a strong supporter of the Union.[11] The importance of this view is the primacy given to the older of the 'established orders' and the acceptance of change in order to conserve. However, it would be incorrect to imply that this view is reactionary, as P. H. Scott views Sir Walter's politics in a more sophisticated manner encompassing a social component involving a fairly well developed conception of citizenship and not simply as some crude atavism.[12]

Another Conservative who combined literary and political aspirations was John Buchan. Buchan's Conservatism, though he preferred to be known as a Tory or a Unionist, was probably less ambiguous than was Scott's. Both as a writer and as a politician Buchan claimed to draw inspiration from Scott. Buchan's conception of his Conservatism was undoubtedly linked to his idea of Scott's politics and in his biography of Scott marking the centenary of the earlier novelist's death, Buchan described Scott as

> a poet who loved the old ways, and as a practical man would conserve them, however logically indefensible, so long as they serve their purpose.[13]

In almost exactly the same words, Buchan defined his own Conservatism in his maiden speech in a debate on the reform of the House of Lords in July 1927.[14] But despite his defence of Scottish traditions and his interest in Scottish matters, Buchan appears to have been less concerned with the possibilities of 'lowering and grinding down all those peculiarities which distinguish us as Scotsmen' of which Scott had warned. Scott's fears were being acquiesced in even by some of those who claimed him as their mentor.

The difficulty which many Scottish Conservatives in the twentieth century have had in placing Scottish history and traditions into the atriculation of their political outlook can be seen most clearly in the case of Walter Elliot. Elliot could be determinedly Scottish, writing under headings such as 'We like being un-English',[15] and would attack the Labour Party in Scotland for the number of English candidates it fielded north of the border, as well as threaten to become a Scottish Nationalist in opposition to Bevan's National Health Service Bill 'if England remained Socialist'.[16] Obviously, most of this was the rhetoric of a robust political practitioner. No more was it genuine than the equivalent oppositional neo-nationalist noises emanating from the Labour Party in the 1980s.

It is to Elliot's book, *Toryism and the Twentieth Century*, written in 1927, that one must go in order to discover the other side of this most ambitious politician. In this book there is an appreciable absence of Scottish references and notable uses of examples from English, not even British, history. In the second chapter, Elliot's observations of the period prior to 1707 are an example of how this otherwise 'proud Scot' could be thought to have been unaware of the very existence of Scotland; it is peculiarly *English* history to which Elliot makes reference. At the very beginning of the book he writes:

> The thesis of the book is simple. It is that in England the beliefs of the Right are descended from the beliefs of a great mass of people held for hundreds of years, based on the observation of life and not *a priori* reasoning.[17]

As a Conservative statement this would be unremarkable but for the fact that Elliot was a Scot. In the same book, in words replete in unintended irony, this Janus-faced politician stated that,

> History shows the extraordinary strength and persistence of national characteristics, and the success of policy based on these.[18]

In his book Elliot was, of course, referring to England, not Scotland, not even Britain.

It would seem that tradition has a part to play in Conservative thinking in Scotland only so long as it can be used as a device to defend the status quo. During those years when Scotland was brought to the forefront of British politics by the SNP's electoral successes, Conservatives would attempt to draw on Scottish traditions, but this appears to have been related to electoral politics rather than Conservative ideology.

ORGANICISM

In the Conservative mind attitudes to authority and legitimacy relate closely to those concerning organicism. As Quinton has argued, the Conservative

> takes a society to be a unitary, natural growth, an organism, living whole, not a mechanical aggregate. It is not composed of bare abstract individuals but of social beings, related to one another within a texture of inherited customs and institutions which endow them with their specific social nature.[19]

Authority for the Conservative will be rooted in historic traditions, institutions and values. Those who deny this would be seen as crude rationalists by Conservatives. The constitution of the United Kingdom is, in this respect, very much in the Conservative tradition. Lacking an entrenched, formal, written element and consisting of written laws and unwritten conventions – at least as seen by Conservatives[20] – it was characterized by its 'evasive fluidity'[21] according to the Scottish Unionist MP, Henry Craik in 1922. This 'evasive fluidity' suggests that the constitution should be well capable of accommodating Scottish distinctiveness. Conservatism's recognition of the claims of entities and institutions other than and as well as the individual and state ought to lend credence to Scottish national institutions. The traditions and institutions which are familiarly listed distinguishing Scotland from England do not, however, always have a great deal of autonomy.

Scotland, as a community below the level of the state, should, in the Conservative mind, be accepted as a fairly significant entity permitted a substantial existence. In reality, this is not permitted except in a most superficial way. The artefacts remain but the autonomy has long since disappeared, if it ever existed. The Scottish Office fulfils a role as British central government's means of administering Scotland, and is inappropriately described as administrative *devolution* if by that it is intended to suggest the capacity to innovate and diverge from governmental policies South of the border. Furthermore, the Scottish local government structure – particularly under recent Conservative Governments – has had its scope for initiative and autonomy reduced. There is little doubt that Scottish education has lost much of its distinctiveness, whether or not one accepts entirely Davie's thesis.[22] Nothing has replaced the central position of the Church of Scotland as the real focus for Scottish distinctiveness during its continuing demise over the last century and a half since the Disruption.

Without the institutional arrangements to cater for Scottish distinctiveness, the authority of the state at the centre has ensured that the Conservative faith in decentralization and entities below the state has become hollow. Revivifying existing institutions or creating a new arrangement would be implausible or unthinkable. The Kirk has had its day. The educational structure, legal paraphenalia and structure of local government all present the same problem to the Conservative. To vest any meaningful authority in such entities it would be necessary to permit a degree of autonomy which might act against Conservative interests. Quite simply, Conservatives fear that institutions whose existence may be expressions of their faith might, in their actions and attitudes, run contrary to the interests of Conservatives.

CHANGE

Michael Oakeshott has defined the conservative 'disposition' as:

> warm and positive in respect of enjoyment, and correspondingly cool and critical in respect of change and innovation: these two inclinations support and elucidate one another. The man of conservative temperament believes that a known good is not lightly to be surrendered for an unknown better. He is not in love with what is dangerous and difficult; he is unadventurous; he has no impulse to sail uncharted seas; for him there is no magic in being lost, bewildered or shipwrecked. If he is forced to navigate the unknown, he sees virtue in heaving the lead every inch of the way.[23]

Change, for Conservatives, is viewed with suspicion and without relish, but will be conceded when necessary. This is related to the Conservative reverence for continuity and tradition. Sir Ian Gilmour identified two different attitudes to change within conservatism; these he associated with two former Conservative Prime Ministers, Sir Robert Peel and Benjamin Disraeli. The former was wholly responsive, accepting the inevitable at the very last moment 'and occasionally even later'. The latter's attitude to change was anticipatory. 'Where Peel usually accepted the inevitable, Disraeli tried to forestall it.'[24]

In the Scottish context there are instances of both the Peelite and Disraelian forms. The establishment of the Scottish Office in 1885 is an instance of Disraelian conservatism while opposition to legislative devolution, excepting the brief flirtation of the Heath years, exemplifies the Peelite form. That a Conservative should support or work towards the establishment of a democratically elected forum suggests that it would be a *pis aller*, something preferable to some more radical alternative. Just as Robert Michels recognised the nature of conservative support for social reform as being motivated with a view to preventing radical reform rather than meeting a need, so too might we view Conservative support for the establishment and development of the Scottish Office and brief support for a Scottish Assembly.[25]

A feature of Conservatism which prescribes attitudes to change is the opposition to rationalism. The trust which Burke had in 'prejudice' is reflected in Oakeshott's essay on rationalism. Modern European history is 'littered with the politics of Rationalism', according to Oakeshott.[26] Accordingly, devising schemes, initiatives, and radical departures from the present takes one from the familiar into the unknown however detailed and rational the planning and forecasting may be. Indeed, the scepticism of Conservatism leads to doubts concerning the ability to plan with any precision. Thus the status quo is the preferred option.

Yet in practical politics Conservatives have felt it necessary to adopt a course which leaves behind the known and gamble on the unknown. In the late 1920s, the Conservative Government radically reformed the structures of local government in Britain. The reform-minded Minister of Health Neville Chamberlain produced a more systematic, indeed rational, structure. In Scotland, the Conservative Secretary of State had no choice other than to follow his English counterpart, though the reform of Scottish local government on rational lines met with strong opposition from within and outwith his party. The abolition of the parish as the basis of the old structure and the creation of larger entities would not seem to have been very popular and, as we shall see later, helped foster support for the nascent National Party of Scotland. Here was an example of a reform imposed upon Scotland against its wishes and which ran contrary to conservative tenets but which was implemented by a Conservative Secretary of State. In this case, as in the case of the reform of the Scottish Office, which will also be considered further later, those who expressed strongest opposition in Parliament to the reforms and invoked the classic arguments and language of Conservatism were Labour Members, particularly the 'Red Clydesiders'.

Change, for the Conservative, should be organic and gradual, not radical. In the Scottish context this will prove difficult if this does not fit into the larger British structure. Worse than this, the change which may be imposed will often have little relevance to Scotland. The rationale behind a change which is motivated by some perceived need in England may run contrary to Scottish traditions as well as give credence to the conservative view of rationalism as

> the politics of the felt need, the felt need not qualified by a genuine, concrete knowledge of the permanent interests and direction of movement of a society, but interpreted by 'reason' and satisfied according to the technique of an ideology: they are the politics of the book.[27]

What may pass as a *pis aller* in England, conforming to the Disraelian attitude to change, may be of no relevance in Scotland and if imposed constitute a radical, unnecessary and undesirable change. Even if the change is necessary and desirable the perceived impulse for the change, coming from England rather than domestically, will remove an element of legitimacy from it.

Likewise, necessary change which may be of the Disraelian sort – anticipatory, even progressive – may well be opposed because it does not conform with the rest of the state. While not lacking authority in Scotland for a particular change, the overriding authority in Britain as a whole will stand in the way. Consideration of the idea of authority or legitimacy in Conservatism in the Scottish context demonstrates further the conflict within Conservatism in Scotland.

UNIONISM

Unionism is central to any understanding of Conservatism in Scotland. Unionism in its Scottish context has three distinct meanings; as a social and cultural meaning, as expression of Scotland's constitutional position within the United Kingdom, and a jurisprudential meaning as the sovereignty of Parliament. A strong link exists between each of these, with the 'Irish Question' forming that link. That Scottish Unionism should be derivative is remarkable given that the Anglo-Scottish Union of Parliaments predated the Anglo-Irish Union of Parliaments by almost a century. The explanation lies in the transformation of politics in Scotland in the late nineteenth century.

As the Irish Question came to dominate Westminster in the 1880s fundamental realignments took place in politics which had important consequences in Scotland. Liberalism's Scottish hegemony between 1832 and 1914 has been attributed to the strength of Presbyterianism by both historians of the Scottish Liberal Party and the Unionist Party of Scotland.[28] Pryde describes a combination of factors which aided the Liberals:

> The evil memory of the unreformed borough corporations, the genuine national aspiration for a 'Christian democracy', the dissenters' distrust of authority and repression, the general adherence to free trade doctrines, and the influential support of the leading newspapers . . . combined to make Scottish Liberalism irrepressible.[29]

Another feature noted by Kellas was the conservatism of Scottish Liberalism; it was 'conservative of historic traditions in Scottish institutions and Scottish society'.[30] The dominance of Liberalism in nineteenth century Scotland was abruptly shaken with the Gladstonian conversion to the cause of Irish Home Rule. The emergence of a split in the Victorian Liberals, with Gladstonian and Unionist wings emerging, offered the Conservatives an opportunity.

The split in the Liberal Party caused by Gladstone's acceptance of Irish Home Rule benefited the Conservatives though, at least at first, they were

merely recipients, and contented themselves with accepting

their new supporters (in some areas not without suspicion), and with searching means to retain them.[31] The issue of disestablishment of the Church of Scotland coincided with the Home Rule issue to further alienate many Liberals from Gladstone. The extended franchise of 1867 and 1884–85, the embryonic Labour movement, the process of urbanization and the growing Irish community meant that by 1900 the Liberals were 'fumbling for a policy that would reconcile their old market-oriented philosophic basis with the new needs, especially those of welfare.'[32] Though the Liberals performed well, and spectacularly so in 1906 and both 1910 elections, they were heading for eclipse.

The opportunity which Irish Home Rule offered the Conservatives was grasped. Links with Ulster Unionists were forged, close ties with the Grand Orange Order were developed and in 1912 the party abandoned the name 'Conservative', which had proved so unattractive during the previous century, to adopt the name Scottish Unionist Party. This was to remain the party's name until 1965 when 'Conservative' was re-incorporated into the name. From the outset the Union referred to was that with Ireland and even after the establishment of the Irish Free State the title remained. In 1927, Lord Balfour explained why he preferred the term Unionist, even though he was willing to be called a Conservative or Tory. For him it was a 'mere question of personal prejudice . . . partly because so much of my life was spent in attempting to preserve in its full sense the union with Ireland' and partly because a 'very large fraction of the future felicity of the world depends upon the union of classes within the Empire'.[33]

Electoral considerations cannot be ignored. Opposition to Irish immigration provoked fears amongst the indigenous population that they would be swamped and these fears were, ironically, potent campaign themes of the party calling itself Unionist. The close, often familial, links between Ireland and Scotland meant that Scottish Unionists could easily play on already existing prejudices and fears. Unionism also, as Balfour made clear, referred to a notion of British Empire. While Balfour's comments regarding the Empire should not be taken at face value, neither should they be completely disregarded. Implicit in the notion of Unionism lay the belief in British Greatness – a notion challenged by Irish secession, later by decolonization, and by Scottish nationalism still later.

It is significant that following the Suez debacle, the most severe blow to the notion of British greatness since 1945 calls for changes in the party in Scotland, as elsewhere in Britain, were made. Attempts by progressive, modernizing elements in the party were made not only to change its name but to inject new blood and to restructure its organization. A motion to change the party's name to 'The Scottish Conservative and Unionist Association' was passed by a small majority in May 1956 at its Scottish conference, but was not accepted by the executive committee of the Central Council. It was asserted that 'Unionist' had lost much of its original significance and that literature and propaganda produced by the English Central Office could not be used because the term 'Conservative' appeared in it. This demand cannot be attributed to a reaction following a poor General Election result. It occurred following what remains the party's best perform-ance in a General Election – the 1955 Election when the Unionists succeeded in becoming the only party to achieve over 50 per cent – 50.1 per cent in fact – of the vote.

But Unionism retained a social and cultural appeal. Though the links with Orangeism declined during the secular century, they played an important part in the party's ability to win support amongst working-class protestants, at least into the 1960s. Explicit links such as the Grand Orange Lodge's seat on the Western Division of the Unionist Party, its influence in candidate selection and active cam-paigning for selected candidates[34] were most evident in the inter-war period, when the Scottish Presbyterian civil and ecclesiastical estab-lishment in the 1920s was 'more profoundly anti-Catholic and anti-Irish than at any point in modern times'.[35] Calls for tight immigration controls were made by the Established and United Free Churches during this period. Amongst the press cuttings kept by leading Scot-tish Unionist politician Walter Elliot were reports of a sermon deliv-ered in January 1927 by a leading Churchman, Rev Dr Mackintosh Mackay. Mackay had argued that Scotland was 'being Anglified on the upper strata and Irishised on its lower strata' and that if Roman Catholics gained 'mastery' in Scotland they would 'very much impair our intellectual and political freedom, and Scotland would lose one of the noblest qualities of Scottish character, her civil and religious freedom.'[36] Mackay was no eccentric nor even on the fringes of the Church, but Moderator of Glasgow United Free Presbytery, Con-vener of its Education Committee and after the union with the Kirk became Convener of the Church of Scotland's Education Committee.

The post-1945 period has been marked by a sharp decline in sec-tarianism in Scotland. Nonetheless, there remained a tendency amongst a sizeable section of the protestant working-class to vote Unionist. In a study published in 1966, it was found that religious affiliation distinguished Scottish voting behaviour from that south of the border. In Cathcart in Glasgow a significant correlation appeared between religion and voting behaviour. 'Catholics voted dispropor-tionately for the Labour Party, while among Protestants there was a less marked tendency to support the Unionists.' The same tendencies were apparent in Scotland as a whole.[37] In 1968 a similar conclusion was reached from a survey into voting behaviour in Dundee.[38]

With the adoption of the name 'Conservative,' the Unionists were only responding to an increasingly secular society. Additionally, by the late 1960s the primary source of information for the electorate was television and this was a centralizing force requiring the Scottish Party to integrate with their Southern neighbour. It was a *Conservative* Party leader not a *Unionist* Party leader who appeared or was reported on television – if the Scottish party was to gain from this exposure it had to be more clearly associated with the English party. The Scottish Conservatives' connection with Unionism in its social and cultural aspects was shown to be largely a thing of the past when Michael Ancram, a member of a leading Scottish Catholic family, became Scottish Party Chairman in the 1980s, and in the 1982 Glasgow Hillhead by-election when a Catholic, Gerry Malone, was adopted as candidate. The Heath Government's prorogation of Stormont in 1972 led to the Ulster Unionists breaking with the Conservative Party in Westminster. Though occasional demands have been made to reforge the links, there appears to be little appetite for what leading Conservatives perceive to be a link leading to far more trouble than benefits. Nonetheless, as Anna McCurley noted after her defeat as Tory MP for Renfrew West in 1987, the Conservatives lost something

> when Unionism lost its significance in Scottish politics. The days of being able to count on solid support from those whose profound belief in the Protestant ethic and the empire transcended economic and social divisions have vanished.[39]

In contemporary Scotland, the remnants of this socio-cultural Unionism are notable in two settings – in the sublimated form of support for football teams and in small town politics on the fringes of Glasgow. In the latter case, Unionism and its opposite appear as sectarian equivalents of the Kailyard – narrow, atavistic and becoming a parody of itself.

Unionism as the expression of Scotland's constitutional position was most succinctly defined by Sir Henry Craik, the first Secretary of the Scotch Education Department and later Unionist MP. In his two volume work, *A Century of Scottish History* (1901) Craik maintained that after a century of Union with England, during which time much resentment existed

> Scotland had, in fact, settled for herself a convenient compromise between her own national existence and that history which she shared as the partner of her southern neighbour.[40]

Craik pointed to those Scottish Whigs who, he argued

> fancied themselves superior to the more marked peculiarities of the national temperament. They had affected a thin veneer of English sentiment, had sought to break down the barriers of Scottish idiosyncrasies, and had, even in the minor matters of dialect and of manner, striven to efface what they thought to be marks of provincialism, only because these marks had been rigorously maintained by their political opponents.[41]

This determinedly Scottish aspect to Unionism was to find echoes in the twentieth century in the writings and statements of John Buchan and Walter Elliot, as mentioned earlier.

However, as was noted in the section on tradition, conflicts can occur and the Union is ultimately given. The Scottish dimension of Unionism has taken on institutional form most significantly in the establishment of the Scottish Office. The problem for Unionism has been that, in maintaining a distinctive Scottish aspect, the danger always existed that a demand to incorporate a democratic component would be made or even that the Union should be abandoned. The defence of the Union comes first, before the retention of the Scottish aspect whenever the question is put – a fact only fully appreciated in the last twenty years.

The Irish Question looms large when considering Unionism in its jurisprudential form. The most significant Unionist writer, influencing both the debate on Ireland a century ago and current debates on the Scottish Question, was the English legal theorist Albert Venn Dicey, who lived from 1835–1922. Dicey's early works posited a liberal theory of the state. In his two classic works, *Introduction to the Study of the Law of the Constitution* (1885) and *Lectures on the Relation between Law and Public Opinion in England during the Nineteenth Century* (1905), he defined a state in which the greatest possible freedom could be permitted for the individual. Dicey's Liberalism remained central to his philosophy throughout his life but he broke with Gladstone's Liberal Party over Irish Home Rule. Like many of his contemporaries, the Union was to transform his political outlook or, at least, to bring out a facet which had lain dormant.

Dicey's most important contribution to the debate on Ireland was his book *England's Case Against Home Rule*, first published in November 1886, only months after the defeat of Gladstone's first Home Rule Bill. There were remarkable similarities in the arguments deployed by many Unionist politicians involved in debates on the Scottish Question in the 1970s. One of the sharpest criticisms of the Kilbrandon Royal Commission's Report on the Constitution, advocating a measure of legislative devolution in 1973, was written by D. G. Boyce, an authority on Irish politics. In an article published in 1975, Boyce rehearsed the arguments used by Dicey and applied them in the Scottish context and concluded his piece by asking 'Have you read your Dicey?'[40]

Dicey's arguments were aimed at proponents of Home Rule, rather than at Nationalists who wanted independence. While a chapter is devoted to 'Separation', which he strongly opposed, it is the anomalies of legislative devolution, particularly as they affect England, which concerned him. His trenchant criticisms of various schemes to provide Ireland with a legislature were based on his conception of Parliamentary sovereignty. In a later work co-authored with R. S. Rait, *Thoughts on the Union between England and Scotland* (1920), Dicey turned his attention to what he regarded as the 'greatest achievement of British statesmanship'.[43] Though he maintained that the Anglo-Scottish Union was based on a federal basis, his articulation of sovereignty made it abundantly clear that the Union in his eyes was far from federal in conception.

Debate on the nature of sovereignty has been the essence of debate about Scotland's constitutional position. Whether the Union of 1707 merely incorporated Scottish representatives into the English Parliament with English traditions being retained or whether the Union was a fundamental law bringing into being a new state is a crude but largely accurate description of the debate. Scottish conceptions of popular sovereignty contradict English conceptions of Parliamentary sovereignty. Though Parliamentary sovereignty has been a post-Union development in English constitutionalism, the doctrine of the Royal prerogative was more prominent in England than in Scotland prior to the Union. Blackstone's account of unlimited Parliamentary sovereignty which from the late eighteenth century gained acceptance within English legal philosophy – with notable doubts expressed on grounds of natural law and the ambiguous relationship between both the Crown and Parliament and the Irish Parliament during the nineteenth century. The question of sovereignty, unresolved at the time of the Union, lies at the heart of the debate on Scotland's position within the United Kingdom. State mergers by cession have been the norm in international politics but the 'supercession of *two* existing States by their incorporation in a third'[44] is highly unusual. The 'identity' of the Scottish legal system, and by implication the Scottish 'political system', is therefore problematic.[45]

The notion of a legal system has only been given attention by legal theorists in recent times, certainly after Dicey was writing. If a legal system is considered to consist only of legal norms this fails to address the conundrum which conflicting conceptions of sovereignty throws up. However, if an 'historically first' constitution is conceived to the basis of every system of law, as Kelsen argued,[46] then the starting point would, as Dicey would himself accept, be the Treaty of Union. But as T. B. Smith has argued, this conception of the Treaty would mean that the new state which came into being cannot simply be assumed to have adopted the norms or traditions of *either* of the pre-existing states.[47] Dicey and Rait maintain that the Act of Union was the

> most conservative of revolutionary measures. To put the matter shortly, it repealed every law and custom of England or of Scotland inconsistent with the political unity of the new state, but it did not make or attempt any change or reform which was not necessary for the creation of the new United Kingdom.[48]

A contradiction becomes apparent in this statement when sovereignty is considered and it is possible only to speculate as to how

Dicey would have responded to suggestions that a distinct Scottish conception of sovereignty existed. The contradiction in Dicey's thinking is most obvious in his description of the Treaty as both 'conservative' and 'revolutionary' unless, wittingly or otherwise, Dicey assumes that it was conservative in its implications for England while it was a revolutionary measure in respect of Scotland.

Fundamental to the Unionist conception of the British state is this notion of sovereignty. Whether articulated in legal theory or otherwise, the central position of Parliament has been of paramount importance in Unionist thinking. This, more than anything else, appears to have been the touchstone of Conservative Party politics in Scotland.

THE NEW RIGHT

Any consideration of contemporary Conservatism in Britain must include a passage, at least, on the New Right. The New Right is a term used to describe the heterogeneous ideas which have influenced certain Governments during the 1980s, including that of Margaret Thatcher. Opponents have made much of the eclectic nature of New Right philosophy and stressed contradictions between Classic Liberalism and Conservatism. The mutual antipathy of Hayekian dogma and the Oakeshottian anti-rational disposition is evident in the former's essay, 'Why I am not a Conservative', appended to later editions of *The Constitution of Liberty* and the latter's comments in *Rationalism in Politics*. These are the works of political thinkers not political practitioners and, as was noted earlier, a disjunction between political theory and practice is to be expected.

The Classic Liberal's acceptance of political principles is challenged by the caution and scepticism of Conservatism. The certainty of Classic Liberal principles seem out of place in a party so doubtful as the Conservatives and explains why reference is made to the hijacking of the party by the New Right.[49] On the other hand, Norman Barry's sympathetic account sees less contradictions and more agreement in the ideas which make up the New Right. For Barry, Oakeshott's connection with the Conservative Party is 'quite erroneous' and the trend of 'almost all official conservative thinking in the post-war period would be alien to his thought'.[50] This statement in itself is an admission of the differences between Classic Liberals and Traditional Conservatives, if Oakeshott is recognised as the leading articulator of the latter view. While Barry would refute the existence of an ideological underpinning to Oakeshott's writings there are too many similarities with the scepticism and traditionalism in the work of Lord Hailsham, presumably allowed to be a Conservative by Barry, to allow the differences to be passed over so easily. Hailsham's chapter on the 'Liberal Heresy' in *The Case for Conservatism* is as much a refutation of Hayekian Liberalism as anything that has been written by Michael Oakeshott.

Nonetheless, the significance of the theoretical differences is that the New Right is essentially a collection of ideas rather than a coherent ideology. Most pertinent to this study will be those aspects of this set of ideas which have most affected Scotland in the 1980s. From this perspective, the most significant issue concerns nationalism and social values in the ideas of the New Right. Though conservatism is not explicitly nationalist and is particularly unwilling to support separatism, Conservatism has much sympathy for entities lying between the individual and the state. Roger Scruton, who has Barry's seal of approval as offering a 'more robust conservatism',[51] is explicit on the question of nationalism in his statement that 'it is only an unfortunate society that cannot lay claim to nationhood'.[52] Though Scruton appears unaware of the existence of a separate Scottish nationality,[53] his views in abstract at least give credence to claims for distinctive treatment, if not independence, for Scotland.

Classic Liberalism has no room for such emotions and dispositions which would permit the recognition of entities between the individual and state. The existence of a distinctive Scottish administrative apparatus and the distinctive origins and traditions of the social rights component of citizenship noted in the earlier chapter are unlikely to appeal to Classic Liberals. Indeed, the social rights component in the New Right conception of citizenship hardly exists.[54]

The importance of the social rights component to citizenship and the distinctive Scottish dimension – in terms of political culture and institutions – was noted earlier. If there is any meaning to Scottish distinctiveness, allied with the perception that New Right policies are being imposed from outside, it is possible to conclude that Scottish identity acts as a bulwark against these changes. However, if Scottish politics in the final analysis amounts to little more than a combination of radical rhetoric and political inertia, then a declining Conservative Party may continue to pursue its policies against a verbal onslaught from a substantial but impotent opposition.

CONCLUSION

Robert Michels identified two meanings of the term conservative. These were the technically political, which meant a 'tendency to maintain the status quo regardless of what may be' and the philosophical idea of conservatism which implied

> a particular *Weltanschauung*, such as love of authority and tradition (monarchical, ecclesiastical or liberal in oligarchical form), which may in turn be but a reflection of particular psychological conditions, although they may appear as wholly rational conceptual preferences.[55]

The extent to which the philosophical idea prevails in the Scottish context seems conditional, if not subservient, to the technically political idea. In essence, conservatism is about the defence of the status quo, belief in tradition is a mere trapping to be dispensed with whenever necessary but to be used whenever possible. As Samuel Huntington has observed in his situational definition; conservatism is the

> rationalization of existing institutions in terms of history, God, nature, and man . . . In any society, there may be institutions to be conserved, but there are never conservative institutions. The lack of a conservative ideal necessarily vitiates the autonomous definition of conservatism.[56]

Alternatively, the view might be adopted that support for recognized traditions are vitally important for conservatism to prosper. If this view was accepted then it might explain the apparent weakness of conservatism in Scotland. One writer has suggested that the relative weakness of a Burkean form of conservatism, that is one based on support for established traditions, in France, Germany and Italy compared with England, is because, amongst other reasons,

> there has not been sufficient agreement among the men of the Right as to what institutions and values they want to conserve.[57]

This might also explain the relative weakness of Scottish Conservatism. The lack of agreement or confusion as to which institutions are the established traditions, to which values should Scots owe their ultimate allegiance, have been the hallmarks of debates on Scotland's constitutional position. As Scots' attention has turned away from Ireland and Empire, the need to come to terms with their position in the United Kingdom has created problems for Conservatives.

Conservatives and Scottish Administration

Contrary to what might be expected, Conservatives have played a considerable part in developing a distinctive Scottish central administration, even if, on the other hand, they have greatly reduced the distinctive nature of Scottish local government. Over the years from the establishment of the Scottish Office in 1885, Conservative Governments have initiated the most important reforms and encouraged the development of the Office's functions and scope. The reasons behind this have usually been of two sorts; either they have been responding to political pressure – appeasing Scottish nationalism, or for reasons of administrative efficacy. In the process, they have determinedly opposed the creation of a Scottish Parliament. However, their actions in developing a distinct Scottish central administration have helped lend credence to the view that Scotland has a political system in all respects apart from a Scottish parliament and, thereby, aided the cause of Scottish self-government by default.

ESTABLISHING THE SCOTTISH OFFICE AND ITS EARLY DEVELOPMENT

Hanham identified three groups who were involved in the developing Nationalist movement, and significantly involved in pressure leading to the establishment of the Scottish Office. There was the radical element with the slogan 'Scotland arise', who saw social and economic changes coming from a revived Scottish national consciousness; there were the practical reformers and businessmen in Glasgow who thought that Westminster was neglecting Scottish affairs; and finally there was the Scottish Tory literary establishment.[1] The Tory elements in the movement tended to view their goals in cultural rather than political terms but their opposition to the anglicization of Scottish society, as they saw it, led them to lend support from 1853 and the establishment of the Society for the Vindication of Scottish Rights to support the establishment of a Secretaryship of State for Scotland, which had appeal for cultural nationalists as it involved the revival of an old office; the Secretaryship of State for Scotland had existed after the Union, until its association with the Jabobite cause led to it being abolished.

The Tories' association with the corrupt and unpopular system of Managers had undoubtedly done the party great harm. As late as 1867, Sir Grahame Montgomery outlined the reasons for Liberal dominance in Scotland and the weakness of the Conservatives with this enduring association:

> Before the passing of the Reform Bill of 1832 Scotland had no real representation . . . This state of things has never been forgotten by the people and they are continually being reminded of it, consequently they can't tolerate the supremacy of a Party that opposed the Reform Bill of 1832 and tried to keep them out of power in the constituencies which they now possess.[2]

The Conservatives would want to divorce themselves from their opposition to reform, and the opportunity to lend support to a measure which seemed likely to to be enacted in only a matter of time may have been viewed as an opportunity to shake off their image as obstinate obstructors of reform in Scottish Administration.

In 1878 the Conservatives introduced a Bill to create an Under-Secretary for Scotland but it was not proceeded with. By the 1880s, however, a large majority of Scottish MPs supported the establishment of a Scottish Secretary. The Liberal peer Lord Rosebery was the major protagonist, and as Under Secretary of State at the Home Office from 1881 set up an office in some spare rooms in Parliament House in Edinburgh from which to conduct specifically Scottish administrative work. Gladstone was initially hostile to the idea of a Scottish Office, but as cross-party pressure mounted, came round to the idea. The Liberal Government presented Bills attempting to create a Scottish Office. The defeat of one such in the Lords in 1883 and the blocking of another in the Commons the following year did not stem the pressure from Scotland.

At an important meeting organised by the Convention of Royal Burghs in Edinburgh in January 1884, all shades of political opinion expressed support for the establishment of a Secretaryship of State for Scotland. The meeting was chaired by the Conservative Marquess of Lothian and was addressed by, amongst others, Arthur Balfour and Lord Balfour of Burleigh. As Hanham has noted, Lothian and the two Balfours lobbied Lord Salisbury, so that when a Liberal Bill setting up the Scottish Office was introduced that year Salisbury gave it his support.[3] When Gladstone's Government fell before the Bill had been passed into law and Salisbury became Premier – no Election was called – he invited the Liberal peer, Lord Rosebery to continue steering the legislation establishing the Scottish Office through the Lords. The Conservative Prime Minister had taken the most unusual course of permitting a Bill introduced by the Liberal Government to continue on its way through Parliament led by a member of the opposing party.

It is difficult to ascertain which individuals or party should be given credit for the creation of the Scottish Office, and simply suggesting that Gladstone had to be bullied into supporting it while the Conservatives 'pressed for it' is without foundation.[4] Rosebery was undoubtedly a leading force in the passage of the measure towards which the Liberal Government had been lukewarm but did after all introduce. The Convention of Royal Burghs had played a significant part in campaigning in Scotland for the Office and suggested that Lord Lothian was mainly responsible for the Secretary for Scotland Act. His public support and private canvassing was a notable factor in convincing the Conservative leadership. All in all, both Liberal and Conservative parties seem to have viewed the measure cynically, and individuals, some equally motivated by cynical reasons,[5] may best be credited with the establishment of the Office.

There had been growing concern in Scotland at the treatment of Scottish affairs in Parliament. Something had to be done which would have the appearance of taking Scottish grievances seriously but which would, in fact, amount to very little. As Salisbury stated, with the cynicism for which he was celebrated, in a letter inviting the Duke of Richmond and Gordon to accept the newly created office:

> The work is not very heavy – the dignity (measured by salary) is the same as your present office – but measured by the expectations of the people of Scotland it is approaching the Archangelic . . . Lothian's health would not be up to it – and Balfour of Burleigh or Dalrymple are too insignificant. The Scotch people would declare we were despising Scotland – and treating her as if she was a West Indian Colony. It really is a matter where the effulgence of two Dukedoms and the best salmon river in Scotland will go a long way.[6]

Later, Salisbury was even more explicit. The Prime Minister explained to the first Scottish Secretary that the 'whole object of the move is to redress the wounded dignities of the Scottish people – or a section of them – who think that enough is not made of Scotland'.[7]

Once established, the Scottish Office was soon to find a substantive role for itself. It was not to be for long that the primary role of the Secretary for Scotland was 'to make himself visible'.[8] Within two years, amendment legislation was passed which extended the Office's functions to include matters of law and order. By 1900 the staff of the Scottish Office numbered twenty-two, including the Permanent Under-Secretary and an Assistant Under-Secretary. But the Office was not growing as fast as other departments of state or, indeed, the Scottish Boards which remained in being even after 1885. The result was that despite real administrative responsibilities the Office was relatively stagnant. The Secretary's powers were limited to such an extent that innovation was unlikely, and had not really been intended anyway. The undefined and uneasy relations with the Lord Advocate and the House of Commons, with four out of the six holders of the Office up to the turn of the century sitting in the Upper House, meant that far from appeasing Scottish grievances, the Scottish Office had served as a focus for disquiet. However, the Secretary for Scotland was a member of the Cabinet continuously after 1892 and the gradual increase in central government responsibilities offered the Scottish Office opportunities to expand its functions further.

Apart from its primary responsibility for education, granted in the initial legislation of 1885, responsibility for agriculture was vested in the office in 1912 and following the Great War the responsibility for health became a Scottish Office function. Conservative opposition to the 1912 legislation had been concerned with the Small Landholding aspects of the proposals rather than the establishment of a Scottish Board of Agriculture. Conservatives, of course, served in the post-war Lloyd George Government which established the Scottish Board of Health.

Tied up with the issue of Scottish central administration was the nascent issue of Scottish Home Rule. Debates on Home Rule inevitably involved criticism and defence of the existing administrative apparatus. But the critics of the Scottish Office during these debates were not always those who supported the establishment of a Scottish Parliament but were often Conservatives who called for reforms of the Office and maintained that administrative deficiencies were one reason for 'misguided' support for a Scottish Parliament. Conservatives would propose reforms in the Scottish central administration which they believed would dissipate the agitation for Home Rule.

A notable example was the argument of Sir George Younger, Unionist Member for Ayr Burghs, during a debate in 1914. Younger argued at the second reading of the Government of Scotland Bill, which aimed to establish a Scottish Parliament, that the Scottish Office was overburdened, as the Home Rulers maintained, but that what was needed was a reorganization of the Scottish Office, not Home Rule. According to Younger, the Scottish Office was 'four Cabinet Ministers rolled into one', with sixteen departments plus the Board of Agriculture under his charge. He saw the need for Secretaries in the different departments, each responsible to the Commons under the control of the Scottish Secretary rather than a Home Rule Parliament in Edinburgh.[9] Inasmuch as administrative reform was advocated in preference to a Scottish legislative forum, this resembles the line adopted by his grandson George Younger (also member for Ayr Burghs) when in the office of Secretary of State between 1979 and 1986.

From a purely administrative point of view the Office had failed to replace the existing structure of appointed Boards – the 'lawyer government'. In 1914 the Royal Commission on the Civil Service, the MacDonnell Commission, criticised the Boards and listed three major objections: they had no clear line of command from central government, despite the existence of the Scottish Secretary; appointments were made on political and other criteria rather than by administrative and organizational meritocratic criteria; and they brought little or no expert understanding to the problems they had to deal with which Administrative Class officials would provide.[10]

THE REFORMS BETWEEN THE WARS

During the course of the First World War there were two important developments affecting the government of Scotland: a growth in the activities and functions of government, and simultaneously, control and administration became more centralized. The Haldane Committee on the machinery of Government met, and amongst its conclusions were some criticisms of Boards which were not dissimilar to those made by the MacDonnell Commission,[11] In 1919, Lloyd George's Coalition Government, which included Conservatives, passed the Scottish Board of Health Act which created a Parliamentary Under-Secretary for Health for Scotland which was at least a step in the direction which Sir George Younger had advocated five years before. The establishment of a separate Scottish Board of Health, responsible for housing, might not have occurred had there not already existed a distinctive Scottish central administration. Whatever the explanation for its establishment it meant that the work of the Scottish Secretary had greatly increased, necessitating the appointment of the Under-Secretary.

During the inter-war period there were three Acts of note passed by the Conservative Administrations which related directly to Scottish central administration. In 1926 the office of Secretary for Scotland was upgraded to that of a Secretaryship of State. Periodic demands for the upgrading of the office from 1885 intensified after the First World War until, eventually, the Secretaries of State Act was passed. In 1921 the Conservative Lord Chancellor Lord Birkenhead announced that the Government intended to introduce a Bill immediately which would raise both the status and salary of the Scottish Secretary. However, the measure was deferred when it was realized that there was considerable opposition in Parliament and the chances of its passage seemed slim, or perhaps that opposition from English backbench Conservatives might prove embarrassing.

It was a further five years before the Secretary of State Act was passed which upgraded the office of Secretary for Scotland to that of Secretary of State and simultaneously upgraded the Under-Secretaryship to an Under-Secretaryship of State. The 'of State' was a superficial change and did not affect the Office's powers. But traditionalists clearly regarded it as significant. In strict constitutional terms there is only one Secretary of State, hence legislation referred to the Secretary of State rather than to any specific office. The post derives from the Sovereign's Secretary though by the twentieth century it had come to refer to senior Government Ministers with special privileges such as membership of the Cabinet and direct access to the Sovereign. Of course, in step with British constitutionalism this is a convention and it is therefore not a definitive statement; in Geoffrey Marshall's memorable phrase, British constitutional conventions are 'somewhat vague and slippery – resembling the procreation of eels'.[12]

Traditionalist English Conservatives opposed this measure, though without going so far as to cause a division at second reading. Maidstone's Conservative Member and the Oxford historian Commander Bellairs had assigned to themselves the role of guardians of the historic English constitution. Bellairs gave a potted history of the Secretaryship of State from the time of Henry VIII and cited Edmund Burke's successful motion abolishing the office of Secretary of State for the Colonies in 1782. In similar pompous vein, Marriot maintained that Parliament had been

> light-heartedly, or I would rather say, airily multiplying individuals among whom the ancient and honourable office is now distributed, with perhaps some little dissipation of its ancient dignity.[13]

In this case of conflict over very little, the demands of Scottish dignity won out over English traditionalism. Scottish Unionist MP Sir Henry Craik referred to 'those prolific-of-dispute-brains which are concerned with minute and erudite constitutional points'[14] in his contribution. It was once more a case of shadow boxing. The 'upgraded' office did not even carry with it an increase in salary. The Scottish Secretary's remittance remained at a lower rate than was paid to others of similar Cabinet rank until 1937. Nonetheless, the Act of 1926 was warmly welcomed by those who had campaigned for an increase in the 'dignity' of the office, and the Scottish Unionists made much of the change.

Two years later, in 1928, the Conservatives embarked on a major reform of the Scottish central administration. During the debates on the 1928 reforms the Unionists were not slow to point out that it was their party which had raised the status of the Scottish Secretary and maintained that while others talked about Home Rule the Unionists had acted in defence of Scottish dignity. The Reorganization of Offices (Scotland) Act, 1928 aimed to rationalize the central administration which had been developing over the years in a fairly haphazard manner. Scottish administration had once been organized on the basis of central Boards operating from Edinburgh; from 1885 these had become the responsibility of the Scottish Secretary, but as each Board had its own internal organization and practices there was little consistency or coherence in the apparatus of Scottish central administration.

The Board structure was the traditional Scottish manner of administration, with Board members appointed from amongst Scotland's 'great and good'. Ironically, it was a Conservative Government which set out to rationalize the administrative structure and a Labour Opposition which defended the old traditional – and notably nepotistic – Boards. One Conservative Member, Noel Skelton, who became Under-Secretary of State for Scotland from 1931 to 1935, opposed the changes on solid Conservative grounds. His father had been successively Secretary and Chairman of the Board of Supervision and Chairman of the Local Government Board over a period of 31 years. Thus Skelton was fully aware of the continuities of the Board structure as were few others, including Conservatives.

Skelton warned against rationalizing the administrative structure and replacing the Boards with civil servants, which might, he suggested, result in the appointment of an Englishman as head of the Department of Agriculture.[15] Whatever their failings, the Boards were seen as *Scottish*:

> The Secretary of State for Scotland is really either a Scottish Cabinet, or, if you like to put it a little lower, he is a Scottish Prime Minister with a Cabinet consisting of his Law Officers and his Under Secretary of State . . . That being so, there appears to me to be real administrative value in having these Departments not under individual civil servants, who perhaps know little about Scotland, but under a body of representative Scotsmen who can convey to the Secretary of State, who is much occupied in London, a kind of general Scottish view upon topics.[16]

The Labour Party defended the Boards with great fervour. Using arguments which might appear founded in Conservative thought, Willie Adamson, senior Labour Scottish Member, praised the Boards in an earlier debate as consisting of an 'excellent body of men', and stated that the change would 'remove from Scotland practically the last vestige of independent Government and nationhood, and to have its centre in London'.[17] The Labour Member for South Ayrshire declared that 'We are the Conservatives'.[18] At the second reading of the Reorganization of Offices (Scotland) Bill, Tom Johnston warned that abolishing the Boards was part of a gradual tendency 'towards the bureaucratization and the concentration in Whitehall of the administration of Scottish affairs'.[19] Even more vociferous statements were made by the 'Red Clydesiders'. The spirit of Sir Walter Scott was alive – on the Labour benches.

A decade later, a further reform of the Scottish central administration occurred under the Conservatives. Not all of the Scottish Boards had disappeared in the 1928 cull, and the Reorganization of Offices (Scotland) Act, 1939, continued the process which had begun in 1928. The remaining Boards were brought under the Scottish Office structure as civil departments on the model of other Whitehall departments. On this occasion the opposition was relatively muted, largely because the Opposition were involved in consultations from an early stage.

The later piece of legislation undoubtedly involved an element of reaction to the revived Home Rule movement of the 1930s. Political reasons as well as administrative reasons were involved. Even the expression 'administrative devolution' was intentionally coined in order to suggest that the reforms involved some kind of transfer of responsibilities to Scotland, and that Scottish distinctiveness was being catered for. Those Unionists who were most vehemently opposed to Scottish Home Rule were supporters of this process.

Sir Robert Horne, the former Chancellor of Exchequer and Unionist Member for Glasgow Hillhead, had argued against Scottish Home Rule in a debate in November 1932 and suggested two improvements in Scottish administration. He wanted the appointment of a second Under-Secretary of State, and the various Departments in Edinburgh to be concentrated in a single building. Concerned that Scots did not appreciate the 'amount of dignity which is accorded' to the Secretary of State, he argued that a new building in Edinburgh at that time of distress

> when people are out of work, is a suitable opportunity for building that accommodation which Scotland undoubtedly requires.[20]

To what extent Horne saw his proposals as placating national sentiment at a time of Nationalist activity and economic depression or as a necessary reform of a branch of British Government is difficult to judge. What is clear is that the reform process had only begun in 1928.

The Secretary of State who initiated the reforms was Sir Godfrey Collins, who was probably largely motivated by a desire to improve the administrative efficacy of the Scottish central administration. Though it was his successor who formally announced the establishment of the Committee of Inquiry set up to propose changes, Collins had begun the process but died before the formal announcement of its establishment.[21] Sir John Gilmour was appointed chairman of the Committee on Scottish Administration which reported in October in 1937. Gilmour had been Scottish Secretary from November 1924 to June 1929, during the time of the upgrading of the Office and the first reform. Unusually for a Scottish Secretary, Gilmour had gone on from the Scottish Office to a senior Cabinet post. He had served as Minister for Agriculture and Fisheries and then as Home Secretary. Tom Johnston, former editor of the left-wing paper *Forward*, served on the Gilmour Committee, which seems to have spiked the Opposition's guns.

Gilmour's recommendations rested on three points: the Scottish people wanted to see Scottish administration in Scotland; the process of administration reflected a 'picture of considerable diversity and haphazard growth revealing no underlying or consistent principle'; and the construction of a new building would facilitate the consolidation of responsibilities to the Secretary of State.[22] The recommendations were translated into legislation in 1939 and St Andrews

House was opened that year. Sir Reginald Coupland has suggested that the reforms were simply an 'appeasement of Scottish nationalism'.[23] Christopher Harvie agrees with Coupland, and added that the 'obsession that "the bomber will always get through" was probably as influential as political nationalism in securing administrative devolution'.[24]

However, both Coupland and Harvie underestimate the importance of the administrative aspects of the reforms. They were certainly presented in language suggesting that Scottish nationalism was important (and indeed it had been to some extent) but the need to consolidate and reorganize the administrative apparatus which had been developing since before 1885, particularly from the MacDonnell Commission, was pressing. The idea that the obsession with 'German bombers' encouraged the devolution of the Scottish Office from London to Edinburgh is based on a misconception. Very little was moved from London to Edinburgh. The vast bulk of movement of staff took place within Edinburgh. Indeed there was for a period some concern that concentrating the administrative offices under one roof might make St Andrews House a target, and that one bomb was all that would be necessary. However, air defence was of the opinion that German bombers would be unlikely to view Edinburgh as a target unless by chance they happened to pass over it on their way to Clydeside.

The Scottish Office which resulted after the 1939 reforms was certainly a Ministry with a remit defined territorially and was clearly Scottish. However, Scottish central administration was no longer the distinctive structure of Boards which had existed prior to the Acts of 1928 and 1939. Hanham identified a number of implications of the 1939 reforms,[25] including the breaking of the Whitehall tradition with the abandonment of the idea that the administrative class should be confined to Whitehall, the Scottish Secretary was 'now an overlord over an empire whose character could be changed from time to time by administrative fiat',[26] and a structure capable of becoming the administration for a self-governing Scotland had been created.

But the break with the Whitehall tradition had come long before 1939 – administrative class civil servants, and not simply the Board members, who were arguably of a comparable rank to such a class of bureaucrats, had long been based in Scotland. The head of the Scottish Education Department, which had never been part of the Board structure, had been based in Edinburgh from shortly after the First World War. Also, the Scottish Secretary's position as 'overlord' had long existed. What changed in 1939 was that he became an overlord over a more administratively efficacious and rationally organized bureaucracy.

In effect then, the Conservative reforms of the inter-war period were presented as maintaining or even enhancing the distinctiveness of the Scottish central administration but, in reality, they had the opposite effect. This is not to diminish the importance of the reforms with respect to Scottish nationalism; appearances can have real effect.

THE WARTIME SCOTTISH OFFICE

The peculiar circumstances of wartime and the particularly good personal relations between Churchill and the Labour Secretary of State, Tom Johnston, ensured that the Scottish Office during this period of Coalition Government probably had a greater degree of autonomy than at any time before, or since. Johnston established a Scottish Advisory Council of ex-Secretaries, commonly known as the Council of State. The surviving former Scottish Secretaries served on this body. The Council met infrequently, with half its meetings taking place in the first nine months of its existence. The infrequency of its meetings, the limited extent of its contribution to solving problems (in the case of industrial policy at least) and 'general ineffectiveness' have been remarked upon.[27]

Nevertheless, the Hydro-Electric Board was created during this period after initially being raised at a meeting of the Council. Johnston, formerly one of the leading proponents of Home Rule, was in no doubt as to the reason for this particular development:

> For the first time since the Reform Bill of 1832, a major Scots measure has reached the Statute Book without a division, and for that memorable result the all-party Council of State can be largely thanked.[28]
>
> Meanwhile, and emanating from the activities being stirred up under what was the Council of State umbrella, there was a new spirit of independence and hope in our national life. You could sense it everywhere, and not least in the Civil Service. We met England now without any inferiority complex. Our tails were up. We were a nation once again.[29]

The circumstances were propitious for the Scottish Office. Churchill was content to allow domestic policy to be left to others and gave strong backing to Johnston. There were, indeed, major developments in areas such as Hydro electricity, but opportunities were missed. Butler's Education Act of 1944 was effectively copied in a tartanized form the following year when it might have been possible for the Scottish Office to develop a more distinctive and ambitious piece of educational legislation. It seems that despite its wide power, by the time of the Second World War the Scottish Office could only hope to develop a limited number of initatives even in the most favourable times, even with the second Under-Secretary of State which was gained in 1941.

REACTING TO THE ATTLEE GOVERNMENT

The end of the War saw the election of Attlee's Government. The Labour Government created organizations to run the nationalized industries, which were seen by the Conservatives as centralized bureaucracies which would take control out of Scotland. In Scotland, the Tories played the nationalist card to full effect during this period. Scottish Unionists had stressed the case for Scottish boards of the nationalized industries during debates on the Labour Government's legislation. In May and July 1946 the Labour Government decided to resist pressure for a separate Scottish National Electricity authority but the Hydro Board's area was widened and within the extended area the Board was to have responsibility for generation, transmission and distribution. Walter Elliot, characteristically, led attacks on the Area Board structure during the Committee stage of the Bill nationalising electricity by stressing the Scottish dimension.[30] In order to avoid provoking opposition of a similar kind regarding transport, the Labour Government decided to include a Users' Consultative Committee for Scotland in its legislation.[31]

At their annual conference in Glasgow in May 1949, the Scottish Unionists passed a resolution agreeing to hold a special conference within three months to consider ways and means of attaining 'effective Scottish control of Scottish affairs', to appoint a Committee to submit proposals to this conference, and to urge the immediate adoption of the conclusions of the conference as part of the party's policy at the following election. The opponents of this resolution were few. Cdr. T. D. Galbraith MP (Glasgow Pollok) expressed his fear that the party might be on a slippery slope towards the adoption of a policy of legislative devolution. His was a naive view; the Unionists were merely appealing to Scottish national sentiment and not for a moment were they considering establishing any meaningful institutional arrangements likely to promote autonomy.

This was the period when the Scottish Convention was actively campaigning for a Scottish Parliament. A number of Conservatives were associated with or, perhaps more precisely, cynically using the Convention. Galbraith's alternatives proposed and rejected in May 1949 are of note as these were to be the very ideas which the party adopted as its special conference later that year. Galbraith proposed separate Scottish boards for railways and electricity and

> wherever it is practicable and in the interests of Scotland to do so, to introduce similar measures in regard to other industries and services which are incapable of denationalization.[32]

Additionally, he suggested that the administrative machinery should be strengthened by the appointment of more junior Ministers. These very proposals rejected by the conference in May 1949 were, in fact, to be the substance of the Unionist policy document, *Scottish Control of*

Scottish Affairs, published after the special conference in November. Inadvertently, Galbraith had shown the real nature of the Unionists' proposals for Scottish control of Scottish affairs in his opposition to the resolution.

In a private submission, dated July 4, 1949, to the Committee established by the May 1949 conference, Walter Elliot submitted proposals which were to be adopted by the party:

> the first and most practical step to be taken is the creation, not of one or more additional Under-Secretaryships, but of a Deputy Secretary of State for Scotland [who would be] a Minister of Cabinet rank, though not a member of the Cabinet, as is the position of several Ministers today. That is to say, he would be a Privy Councillor, he would receive Cabinet papers as a right, and would, if summoned to the Cabinet, or if deputizing there for the Secretary of State, be present as an equal. To mark the significance of his office he could be designated 'Minister of State for Scotland' on the analogy of the Minister of State for Foreign Affairs.[33]

Elliot also gave support to the proposal, which the General Assembly of the Church of Scotland had put forward, that an enquiry into the financial relationship between Scotland and England should be undertaken. The final suggestion in Elliot's submission, though he accepted that it was 'much more debateable', was for annual meetings of representatives of local authorities presided over by the Minister of State. This would 'cope with the undoubted feeling that no Scottish forum or meeting place exists for the general consideration of specifically Scottish problems' while avoiding the creation of a Scottish Parliament which would 'almost inevitably foster – especially in difficult times – a tendency to separation'.[34]

James Stuart, at the special conference which was held in private in late November 1947 in Glasgow, informed the conference that Churchill had endorsed the proposals which the Committee established by the Annual Conference in May had proposed. The Committee had been chaired by Stuart and consisted of equal numbers of MPs and members of the Central Council Executive of the Scottish Unionist Association.[35] Unanimous acceptance of the proposals was reported following the closed meeting. The ensuing policy document, *Scottish Control of Scottish Affairs* declared,

> Union is strength. So it has proved. So it must prove. That is the policy of the Unionist Party.
>
> But union is not amalgamation. Scotland is a nation.

The document strongly criticized the centralization in London caused by the Labour Government's nationalization programme as a 'new despotism', and outlined four major proposals:

> 1. The establishment of a 'Deputy to the Secretary of State for Scotland with the title and position of Minister for Scotland (paras. 8–9)

2. The appointment of an extra-Parliamentary Under-Secretary of State (para. 11)

3. The appointment of a Royal Commission 'to review the whole situation as between Scotland and England in the light of modern developments, and to make recommendations' (para. 12)

4. The creation of separate executive authorities for Scotland 'for those industries which it will be impossible to denationalize' (paras. 13–18)

Other proposals adopted by the Unionists included giving 'increased status and responsibilities and wider discretion' to the heads of Scottish offices in UK Ministries, reversing the trend towards centralization with regard to central-local relations, and recommending that separate Scottish Bills should be introduced where Scottish law or conditions differed materially from those in England.

At a press conference the day after the conference, Walter Elliot stated that the remit of the proposed Royal Commission should be 'as wide as possible' but would exclude consideration of the creation of a Scottish Parliament.[36] This was quite remarkable, given the background to which the Unionists had convened their special conference and the title adopted for their policy. The Dean of the Faculty of Advocates and prominent supporter of the Scottish Convention, John Cameron – father of Lord Cameron of Lochbroom, Conservative Lord Advocate from 1984 to 1989 – criticized the policy:

> To have gone so far and to have stopped at the logical and, indeed, democratic conclusion seems strange because such a large measure of administrative autonomy – in administration, both governmental and industrial – would seem to demand for coherence that there should also be side by side with administrative autonomy, control of domestic finance exercised through an equally separable and recognizable legislative machine.[37]

The Scottish Convention published a pamphlet written by James Porteous criticizing the Unionist document. Porteous argued that the proposals did not amount to Scottish Control of Scottish Affairs, 'so long as the responsible Government is in London, control of Scottish affairs is bound to be centred there'. His statement that administrative devolution 'without legislative devolution can only apply within a very limited sphere' might be seen as ambiguous.[38] Either administrative devolution was a misnomer or else democratic principles demanded that a Scottish Parliament should be established.

In response to the Unionists' *Scottish Control of Scottish Affairs*, a Ministerial Committee of the Attlee Government met to discuss the possibility of greater autonomy for relevant Scottish bodies in January 1950. Papers were presented by Hector McNeil, Secretary of State for Scotland and Herbert Morrison, Lord President of the Council and

principal architect of the Government's nationalization programme.
The conclusions were described by the official historian of the
nationalization of British industry:

> The Secretary of State favoured a separate Road Passenger Trans-
> port Executive for Scotland and thought it would not be imposs-
> ible to organise the generation of electricity for Scotland
> independently from England and Wales and to transfer Minis-
> terial responsibility for the already existing Scottish Gas Board
> from Fuel and Power to him. The general opinion of Ministers,
> however, was that there was nothing in the pamphlet to need a
> change in Government policy in favour of industries being or-
> ganized on a Great Britain basis under the appropriate Minister
> for the whole country.[39]

Clearly, the Unionist document was taken very seriously by the
Government. But the fact that *Scottish Control of Scottish Affairs*
amounted to fairly minor recommendations meant that the debate
between the Government and Opposition amounted to little more
than shadow boxing.

THIRTEEN YEARS OF CONSERVATIVE RULE

On their return to power in 1951 the Conservatives did not, however,
fully implement *Scottish Control of Scottish Affairs*. James Stuart became
Secretary of State. Elliot's poor personal relations with Churchill
meant that the Conservatives' most able Scottish Member remained
outside Government. The office of Minister of State was established
and Lord Home became the first incumbent. As Home recounted in
his autobiography, Churchill had directed him in the remit of the new
post to 'Go and quell those turbulent Scots, and don't come back until
you've done it'.[40] According to Home, the success in quelling the
Scots had something to do with his attendance in the Lords which he
attended

> once a month on a fairly carefully-staged occasion to get the
> maximum publicity for Scottish affiars. This did the trick.[41]

In reality, the receding Nationalist tide was the result of the failure of
the Scottish Convention to gain support where it mattered, in
Parliament.

Attlee had stated in his response to the Loyal Address in 1951 that
the appointment of an 'amiable peer' as Minister of State was
'window-dressing'. The Scots had asked for bread but 'do not even
get the Stone',[42] observed the leader of the Opposition in a jocular
reference to the Nationalist stunt of Christmas 1950 when the Stone of
Destiny had gone missing from Westminster Abbey. The rhetoric of
the Conservatives' Scottish policy was further challenged during the
debate of the King's speech. On being challenged to explain when the
Minister of State would attend Cabient meetings, Stuart had replied
that it would normally be in his absence which the former Labour

Scottish Secretary Hector McNeil stated would have been the 'normal experience of any Parliamentary Under-Secretary'.[43]

Even with the second largest contingent of Unionist Members elected since the War, Churchill had problems filling the other Scottish Ministerial offices. Stuart objected to the appointment of Lady Tweedsmuir as an Under-Secretary on the grounds that she was 'comparatively inexperienced and [he] disliked the idea of women Ministers', according to his Parliamentary Private Secretary.[44] But it was the Law Officers which provided greatest problems. There was only one Scots lawyer amongst the MPs returned in 1951. James Clyde became Lord Advocate until his elevation to the Lord Presidency of the Court of Session in December 1954. His successor as Lord Advocate was W. R. Milligan, who also succeeded him as Member for Edinburgh North a month later. Milligan had been Solicitor General, outside Parliament, before becoming Lord Advocate and was succeeded in that post by William Grant who entered Parliament in 1955 as Member for Glasgow Woodside.

Stuart admitted that there were no proposals for dealing with the nationalized industries at that time. It was Labour's turn, now in Opposition, to play the Scottish card, though the Conservatives were able to retain the advantage for some years into their thirteen-year-long rule. It was Walter Elliot, from the backbenches, who had explained the Scottish Unionist policy, if not the Conservative Government policy, regarding electricity when he spoke in these debates. Elliot explained that the Unionists did not favour merging the Hydro Board with the two southern Boards but believed that the latter ought to be responsible to the Scottish Secretary.[45] The South of Scotland Electricity Board was set up in 1954, and though the MacKenzie Committee proposed the amalgamation of the Hydro Board with the SSEB in November 1962[46] this was never realized.

The outgoing Labour Government had set up a Committee to enquire into the financial relations between Scotland and England which reported in July 1952.[47] The report set out to challenge the Nationalists' assertions that Scotland was at least a viable economic entity. It was an exercise in political propaganda rather than scientific investigation. On the day of its publication, Churchill announced that the Government accepted Catto's findings – in substance, that Scotland contributed a smaller share to the cost of Imperial Services than its size demanded, and that Scotland was inextricably linked economically with England. The Prime Minister also announced the establishment of a Royal Commission on Scottish Affairs.[48] As shall be shown later, this was as much an example of 'window dressing' as had been the Government's other Scottish policies.

These early years of the 1950s have been described as Churchill's Indian Summer[49] and, for Scotland at least, they must be seen as years of lost opportunity. Stuart was the third son of the Earl of Moray, educated at Eton and had served as Equerry to the Duke of York after the First World War. In 1921, he had introduced the future King George VI to Lady Elizabeth Bowes-Lyon. Stuart's autobiography, written in the mild, even modest tone of this diffident aristocrat, portrays a figure who had reluctantly, and perhaps inadvertently, become an MP and a Cabinet Minister.[50]

Stuart was not part of any inner Cabinet but has been placed inside that broader group of Ministers which had led political columnists to characterize the system under Churchill as 'Government by Crony'.[51] The Secretary of State had a close personal relationship with Churchill, whom he had served as chief whip from 1941 to 1948. His relationship with Churchill was comparable to that enjoyed by Tom Johnston. But Stuart was a very different kind of man. He avoided any major disaster and saw this as quite an achievement in itself.

Yet the circumstances could hardly have been better. Stuart had influence in the Cabinet and was as close to the centre of power as almost any previous incumbent. The Unionists won the largest share of the popular vote in both 1951 and 1955 and, as Labour, had 35 seats in 1951, and then had a net gain of one over Labour in 1955. Rab Butler was Chancellor of the Exchequer until December 1955, following a policy of full employment and accepting the need for state intervention. Stuart did not oppose state intervention, indeed his political philosophy was almost devoid of dogma as much as his style was lacking in imagination and initiative. In effect, Stuart exemplifies the problems of a political structure which had become rationalized and concentrated under a single Cabinet Minister with multiple responsibilities. The wholly undynamic personage filling the office of Secretary of State could negate the most propitious circumstances for social and economic development.

SCOTTISH PUBLIC ACCOUNTS AND THE BALFOUR COMMISSION

Nationalist activities in the late 1940s had led to the establishment of a committee under Lord Catto by the Attlee Government, charged with considering and advising on the

> practicability of making a reliable return of the revenue from, and the Government expenditure in, Scotland and the rest of the United Kingdom and the balance of revenue available for general expenditure, and also to consider and advise on the practicability of making a return of Scotland's share in the imports and exports, visible and invisible, of the UK, and of Scotland's economic balance-sheet.[52]

From around the early 1890s, separate financial returns, giving the revenue contributed from the constituent nations of the United Kingdom and expenditure on their services, had been published most years, until 1921 when the practice was discontinued. The returns had been published in an attempt to demonstrate that Ireland was subsidized and that the Irish Nationalists had a weak economic case. The discontinuation of the practice was a direct result of the Irish settlement. Scottish Nationalist activity in the 1930s had resulted in the publication of White Papers containing similar information in 1932 and 1935 but, as with the earlier information, the gaps in information meant that they were far from definitive. F. C. Thomson, Scottish Unionist whip, had written to Sir John Gilmour in October 1932 urging that 'up to date' information be supplied about financial relations between Scotland and England and called for administrative reforms, including a call for the Scottish Office to be based in Edinburgh.[53]

The 1932 White Paper suggested that Scotland contributed only 5.62 per cent towards the cost of Imperial Services, with the remainder provided by England and Wales, and the return of 1934–35 suggested that Scotland contributed 8.63 per cent. Scots were net beneficiaries on both occasions, at least according to the Treasury. However, there was debate on what constituted a fair comparison of public accounts within Britain. The Goschen Formula, whereby an 11:80 proportion was given to Scotland, was thought to be outdated and arbitrary. A population-based comparison would fail to take into account need, and the net assessment of public accounts was crude and simplistic. The influence of expenditure and benefits accruing from the Empire further complicated the issue.

Similar arguments surrounded the Catto Report. It was published on July 24, 1952. The conclusions were predictable. Roughly one-third of revenue could be attributed directly, though all but 10 per cent could be estimated fairly accurately at least. Around 20 per cent of expenditure could not be attributed to English and Welsh, Scottish or General services. Great problems were discovered in assessing Scotland's share in external trade and Scotland's balance of payments with other countries including the rest of the United Kingdom. The Committee stated that Scotland and England were closely integrated economically and each benefited greatly from unrestricted access to the markets of the other. There was little in Catto which was unexpected, nor could it be described as definitive.

On the day of the publication of the report, Churchill announced that the Government accepted Catto's findings and that it had decided to establish a Royal Commission on Scottish Affairs. This had, of course, been part of *Scottish Control of Scottish Affairs* and was not, in reality, the Government's reponse to the report. No debate was held on the floor of the House of Commons on Catto, and there appears to have been little pressure for a debate. The appointment of the Royal Commission may have deflected attention away from the issues involved. The decline of the Scottish Convention may also have been a factor.

The remit of the Royal Commission on Scottish Affairs was set out in Parliament in July 1952

> to review, with reference to the financial, economic, administrative and other considerations involved, the arrangements for exercising the functions of H.M. Government in relation to Scotland, and to report.[54]

Two years later, on July 4, the Balfour Commission reported, by which time the National Movement had almost disappeared. John MacCormick, leading campaigner of the Scottish Convention, noted later that the Commission was 'not composed of persons likely to make such recommendations as would cause the Government any serious concern'.[55] In this respect it did not differ from most other Royal Commissions. But MacCormick was correct in expecting unexciting recommendations from the Balfour Commission.

The report's recommendations amounted to an exhortation that Scotland's 'needs and points of view should be known and brought into account at all stages in the formation and execution of policy'[56] and the proposal that a few minor responsibilities should be transferred to that 'invaluable asset to Scotland', the Scottish Office. In 1955 and 1956, by various Transfers of Functions Orders, responsibility for Justices of the Peace, Animal Health, Roads, Bridges and Ferries was gained by the Scottish Office. The Conservatives' interpretation of 'Scottish control of Scottish affairs' was merely an unimaginative and unambitious tidying up operation within the administrative apparatus of the Scottish Office.

In November 1954 the Scottish Unionists Members Committee – the backbenchers – set up a committee to study the Balfour report.[57] A month later they issued their response which had little difficulty in being more adventurous. Their proposals related to Parliamentary practices. They recommended that the Scottish Grand Committee should be split into two Standing Committees which would consider Bills, and the added (English) Members, who ensured that the Committee reflected the composition of the Commons, would be dispensed with.[58] However, despite their stated intention of bringing forward these proposals during the Commons debate on the Balfour Report, the Members who put them forward did not even mention them in the Parliamentary debate on February 1, 1955.

ADMINISTERING THE FAILING SCOTTISH ECONOMY

During the depressed thirties Scotland had suffered higher than average levels of unemployment and economic stagnation. Scottish distinctiveness was notable in a catalogue of social and economic indicators. The special measures adopted by Governments in the decade before the War were largely superficial. In Cabinet, various Scottish Secretaries had argued for special measures to be taken to cope with Scotland's problems. A Commissioner for Special Areas with responsibility for Scotland was appointed after Sir Godfrey Collins, Secretary of State had pressed for this office in late 1934. Other measures of limited consequence and of a cosmetic nature were also effected.[59]

The Coalition Government's White Paper on Employment Policy, published in 1944[60], stated that the maintenance of a high and stable level of employment was one of the primary aims and responsibilities of British Governments. However, the Attlee Government's employment policy and those of the Government's in the Butskellite tradition which followed devised employment strategies in a highly centralized manner. Economic and employment policy was not to be 'devolved' to the Scottish Office. Instead, Whitehall encouraged and cajoled industry northwards.

In 1963 Gavin McCrone, then an academic economist, wrote that government policy 'may be summed up as the provision of an environment which encourages growth'.[61] Regional policy somehow fitted into this. One study identified four distinct phases between 1945 and 1974. The first phase covered the period of the Attlee Government, the period of 'active regional policy'. The years 1951–58 represented a 'period of passive regional policy in which both the IDC [Industrial Development Certificate] policy and the government's factory building programmme were largely in abeyance and in which practically no financial inducements were paid to manufacturing firms'. This was followed by a 'transition from passive policy to a period of more active policy' in the years 1959–62, before the 'sustained period of active regional policy'[62]

Regional Policy was not the prerogative of the Scottish Office but must have come before Cabinet. Whether 'Scotland's Ministers' took much interest in debates is uncertain during the second phase, but what is clear is that any involvement in discussions had negligible effect. The unimaginative managerialism of the Scottish Office during the thirteen years of Tory rule did not help Scotland face the need for economic diversification, mitigating the run-down of the old traditional industries, as had been argued as necessary from at least the 1930s by individuals such as Charles Oakley.[63] No distinctly Scottish response emerged from Government. By the time of Macmillan's Local Employment Act of 1960, a meagre step towards an active regional policy, it was evident that considerable problems had emerged. The 'environment of growth' simply had not been provided for in Scotland.

The downward trend in Scotland's share of UK national income since the twenties, especially the relative decline in Scottish wages and salaries compared with the UK was noted in a major study published in 1955.[64] Scottish Gross Deomestic Product fell from 9.3 per cent of total UK GDP in 1951 to 8.7 per cent in 1960.[65] Emigration levels hid the true extent of the problem.

The 1959 General Election had been fought by the Conservatives on the record of the Government. Harold Macmillan stated that he could not remember any period of his lifetime when the economy had been so sound and prosperity so widely spread.[66] However, 'You've never had it so good' was a particularly imprudent slogan in Scotland; unemployment rose to over 100,000 in 1958–59 for the first time in the post-war years.

Regional Policy was effectively a social strategy rather than an economic strategy. It attempted to ensure that areas such as Scotland did not suffer high levels of unemployment and its social consequences, rather than creating a sound, stable and home-grown economic base. The successes of Regional Policy were within thirty years to face the prospect of closure – Ravenscraig (established in 1958), British Motor Corporation at Bathgate (1961), Rootes at Linwood (1963), Wiggin's Teape pulp mill at Fort William (1966) are all monuments to the regional policies of these years, and now classic examples of the failure to develop an integrated and healthy economy for Scotland. Instead of providing a coherent Scottish national plan, regional policy offered uncoordinated industrial development.

The semi-official Scottish Council for Development and Industry sponsored a report on the Scottish economy. John Toothill, managing director of Ferranti's, chaired the investigation, which was assisted by staff seconded from the Scottish Office. The Toothill Report, published in November 1961, included a section dealing with governmental machinery. It proposed that a new department should be set up in the Scottish Office to coordinate industrial and planning functions and including an economic unit to advise on such matters. As a result, the Scottish Development Department was established in June 1962, taking over the Scottish Home Department's duties for industry, development, electricity, roads and local government and the Scottish Department of Health's duties for housing, planning and environmental services. The Scottish Home and Health Department was created and the Department of Agriculture and Fisheries came into being.

In effect, the Governments of the thirteen years of Tory rule from 1951 to 1964 had done little to bring about any real measure of 'Scottish control of Scottish affairs'. Elected in 1951 on a platform which had stressed the Scottish national dimension, the Conservative measures respecting Scotland were superficial. The consensus which had developed from before the end of the war had recognized an extended role for the state. But this was to be the prerogative of centralized bureaucracy based in Whitehall. Scottish economic performance was a cause for concern. In 1956 the Church and Nation Committee highlighted a key problem when it reported to the General Assembly of the Church of Scotland that

it is regrettable that Scotland has had to be so dependent on outsiders; 116 of the factories on Scottish industrial estates have been established by English firms and 325 by American organizations.[67] The declining heavy industries and the failure of indigenous Scottish industry to make much progress only emphasized the importance of regional policy directed from London as a social ameliorative rather than an economically regenerative programme.

Conservative Governments, as much as the Attlee Government, offered Scotland a few minor palliatives; regional aid from London but no Scottish control of Scottish affairs. In April 1959 the Convention of Royal Burghs, which had been instrumental in establishing the Scottish Office in 1885, met in Edinburgh and approved a resolution moved by the Provost of Arbroath, that

at this time of heavy unemployment in Scotland the Convention take the initiative in setting up a single body to represent the collective views of Scottish local authorities on distribution and expansion of industry in Scotland and any ancillary matters pertaining to Scotland's economy, and to agree on the terms of any recommendations which they may wish to make to the Government from time to time on the economic issues with which Scotland is faced.[68]

Representative Scottish opinion at least had some idea of the needs of Scotland.

Unionist Party Opposition To
Scottish Home Rule

In 1881, the Liberal peer Lord Rosebery stated that Home Rule had begun to be 'distinctly and loudly mentioned in Scotland[1].' Rosebery was not advocating the creation of a Scottish Parliament but was proposing that a Secretaryship of State be established in order to prevent an Irish-type situation developing in Scotland. In the late Victorian years Ireland plagued British politics and became entangled in debates on Scottish Home Rule. Conservative opposition to Irish Home Rule was to be the dominant influence on Conservative attitudes to Scottish Home Rule at least until the settlement of December 1921. Similarly, Liberal support for Scottish Home Rule was related to their support for Irish Home Rule.

Nevertheless, genuine Scottish grievances, independent of the Irish question, existed which played a part in stimulating the demand for a Scottish Parliament. These were met with force by Conservative politicians who articulated the technical problems inherent in creating a Scottish Parliament within the United Kingdom as well as voicing fears concerning the possible radical content of a Scottish Parliament's legislative output. The benefits of government from London were weighed against these and felt to be overwhelming. The arguments of the late nineteenth and early twentieth century were the same as those in the lead up to the referendum in 1979. The only differences were those of emphasis and Ireland was no longer the bogey which it had been.

OPPOSITION UNTIL THE IRISH SETTLEMENT OF 1921

British party politics were transformed dramatically in the late nineteenth century as a consequence of the Irish issue. Liberal Unionists broke with their party to join the Conservatives and in Scotland particularly gave a new lease of life to their former opponents. Scottish Liberals had edged towards support for Scottish Home Rule after Gladstone's enunciation of Liberal support for Irish Home Rule in 1886. One reason for the official adoption of Scottish Home Rule had been that it placed Irish Home Rule in a more acceptable framework for effecting constitutional change.[2] The emergence of the idea of Home Rule All Round had its antithesis in the Conservative position of Unionism All Round. Unionists who had left the Liberal Party over Irish Home Rule were not likely to approve of Scottish Home Rule.[3]

The Scottish Conservatives had good reason to stress their opposition to Irish nationalism. Votes were to be won from among the greatly increased electorate following the 1884 extension of the franchise. By stressing their unionism and developing links with the Orange Lodge the Scottish Conservatives, with the Liberal Unionists, were able to tap support which they had feared would not come to them. A member of the Grand Orange Lodge was co-opted onto the executive committee of the Western Division of the party and in 1912 the Scottish Conservatives and Liberal Unionists were incorporated into one party calling themselves the Unionist Party. Though the Conservatives' relations with the Orange Order was strained after the First World War when the Irish Treaty was being negotiated the link was to remain in evidence for at least a further forty years.

At the turn of the century a grouping of Conservatives who supported Scottish Home Rule emerged. The Round Table Movement which had developed out of Lord Milner's 'Kindergarten' – those who had served under Milner when he had been High Commissioner for South Africa, 1897–1905 – came to lend support to the idea of Home Rule All Round. The Movement's principal aim was Indian self-government, but the Irish question had forced them to consider the issue of Home Rule within the United Kingdom. Liberals as well as Conservatives were involved in this Movement and it is probable that the Liberals originally had pressed the issue of Home Rule. The concern for Imperial Unity and the view that federalism was the best means of accommodating national differences without secession was allied with their hope that Home Rule All Round would relieve the congestion in Parliament and separate local from Imperial affairs.[4]

The leading Conservative proponent of federalism in the Round Table movement was F. S. Oliver. Under the pseudonym 'Pacificus' Oliver argued for federalism on the grounds that it would end the 'long and dangerous controversy [Ireland], and also for the sake of bringing the hope of Imperial Union a stage nearer'.[5] Those Conservatives who gave support to federalism before the War were mainly concerned with the 'chance it offered of restricting the scope of Irish Home Rule'.[6] Oliver's views were, however, very much in a minority. The Easter Rising in 1916 brought Ireland back to the fore. A letter in the *Times* in April 1918 signed by nine Conservative MPs urged support for the

> ultimate goal of Federal devolution. Apart altogether from the urgency of Ireland, we are deeply impressed by the need of a far-reaching system of federal devolution for the United Kingdom.[7]

Two days later, the prolific F. S. Oliver had a supporting letter published in the paper, as did L. S. Amery.

At the General Election following the war the *Scotsman* noted that many Unionist candidates referred to devolution in their election addresses.[8] But the Scottish Unionists were far from adopting a policy of legislative devolution for Scotland. In early June 1919, Major Edward Wood – one of Milner's disciples and Conservative Member for Ripon – proposed a resolution in Parliament which was carried by 187 to 34, supporting the creation of subordinate legislatures within the United Kingdom.[9] The resolution also called for a Parliamentary body to consider and report on a measure of federal devolution for England, Scotland and Ireland. Scottish Members voted overwhelmingly for the resolution. Seventeen Liberals and five Labour Members as well as thirteen Scottish Unionists supported it with only one Scots MP, Sir Henry Craik, Unionist Member for the Scottish Universities, opposed. Once more the Irish question dominated proceedings. During the debate, a Liberal Member remarked on the fact that 'some of the strongest speeches in support of the principle of devolution' had been made by Unionists.[10]

The Speaker's Conference which was established following the resolution of June 1919 met from October 1919 to April 1920. The Conference consisted of sixteen Members of both Houses of Parliament and met between October 1919 and April 1920. Two reports were produced. One report, signed by Speaker Lowther, and twelve others proposed that Grand Councils of all elected Westminster MPS together with half as many Members from the Lords, selected by a committee in the Lords, should meet for each of the constituent nations. These Grand Councils would be subordinate to the Imperial Parliament, which would be able to override their decisions. Murray MacDonald with twelve others proposed a federal scheme with elected chambers for the local Parliaments with the possibility of second chambers. The executive would be appointed by the Sovereign answerable to the Home Secretary.

Hanham, in his study of Scottish nationalism, expressed doubts about the sincerity of the Conference in its deliberations and suggested that the new power of the Conservatives after 1918 was a factor in the failure to implement even the weakest of the schemes.[11] More significantly, during the period when the Conference met the Irish Home Rule Bill was introduced. This led the Conference to restrict its inquiry to Britain and explains why its conclusions failed to attract much interest. Scottish Home Rule was only an issue so long as it was seen as facilitating a resolution of the Irish problem.

Five years later, after the Irish settlement, Conservatives were less inclined to look favourably upon the idea of federalism. At the debate on the second reading of the Government of Scotland Bill in May 1924, Tom Johnston reminded the House that thirteen Scottish

Unionists had supported the resolution of June 1919. In response, F. C. Thomson, Unionist Member for South Aberdeen explained that he had supported the resolution in 1919 as it advocated Home Rule All Round which the Bill of 1924 did not.[12] Sir John Baird argued similarly; he supported the principle of devolution but not the form presented in the Bill. The support that had existed from Scottish Home Rule in the Conservative ranks prior to the Irish settlement soon disappeared. This was by no means the last occasion when Conservatives were to withhold support for a proposed piece of legislation while disingenuously claiming to support the principle of devolution.

The Irish settlement did not rid Scottish politics of the Irish issue however. Conservatives continued to see themselves as 'Unionists' after 1922.[14] J. M. McEwen may have been correct about England and Wales, but it was not the case in Scotland that with the Irish settlement 'the term "Unionist" had lost its original meaning, and was heard less and less'.[15] In the 1930s, when Scottish nationalism appeared as a force, however minor, Unionists were not slow to harness religious and national bigotry in an unscrupulous and divisive manner. Sir Robert Horne, for example, maintained that Irish immigrants constituted 25 per cent of the population in the industrial districts of the West of Scotland. According to Horne, what was believed to be Scottish Home Rule would turn out to be a 'form of very insidious Irish domination in our politics'.[16]

The demise of both the importance of Ireland in the minds of politicians and the electorate and the decline of religious affiliation as a determinant of voting behaviour have removed one bogey from the Conservative armoury. Indeed, Nationalists in the 1970s were often keen to point to the example of Eire and the attendant benefits of self-government.

OPPOSITION TO RADICAL POLITICS

The strength of the anti-Conservative parties in Scotland from the time of the Great Reform Act undoubtedly affected the attitude of Conservatives to the idea of Scottish Home Rule. Home Rule, along with extensions of the franchise and curtailment of the powers of the House of Lords, was seen as a 'logical step towards a fourth radical aim, the advance of democracy'.[17] Though Conservatives had strongly supported the creation of the office of Secretary for Scotland, they were not receptive to the idea of legislative devolution. Special concessions for the Scots were one thing, returning power to them was quite another, given the anti-Conservative attitudes north of the border.

One of the leading proponents of Home Rule in the late nineteenth century was R. B. Cunninghame Graham whose advocacy of a Scottish Parliament was linked with his desire to bring about radical

political change, particularly land reform. Speaking to a Home Rule
Motion in Parliament in 1889, Cunninghame Graham made no attempt to hide this:

> It has been said that in the event of the institution of a Scottish
> legislature we should largely be represented by the merchants of
> the country. To that statement I say, God Forbid! I believe I speak
> the feelings of a large section of the Scottish people when I
> emphatically state that, were such a legislature ever created, we
> should find the working classes much more represented than is
> the case here.[18]

Arthur Balfour's interjection that Graham wanted Home Rule because he wanted socialism in Scotland was fervently agreed to by
Cunninghame Graham.[19] Around this time also, the highly emotive
issue of land ownership and land use was being debated. Dissatis-
faction in the crofting community was leading many to conclude that
Home Rule was the only sure way of obtaining their rights.[20] This,
again, was hardly likely to make Home Rule attractive to the
Conservatives.

Home Rule Bills and resolutions in the late nineteenth and early
twentieth century would be introduced with calls for social and
economic reform. Duncan Pirie, leading Liberal Home Ruler of his
day, outlined three social questions – education, land, and temper-
ance reform – that he expected would be dealt with by a Scottish
Parliament when he introduced his Government of Scotland Bill in
1908. After the First World War the Scottish Labour Members argued
for Scottish Home Rule as a means of radically reforming Scottish
society. Whether the Liberal and Labour Members were justified in
placing such faith in a Scottish Parliament, the equation of Scottish
Home Rule with radical reforms was hardly likely to make it attractive
to Conservatives.

The revived Scottish Home Rule Association of 1918 included a few
Conservatives amongst its membership. However, these few drifted
away after the organization's left-wing bias became clear. The Mar-
quis of Graham (who became the Duke of Montrose in 1925), for
example, withdrew his support in 1922 after making the fairly
common error of confusing Willie Gallacher of the Scottish Cooper-
ative Wholesale Society, who was a member of the SHRA, with his
Communist namesake, who was not. The association of Home Rule
with radical politics and the Irish Question led Conservatives to
identify it with 'Communism, Papism or both!'[21]

Even when the Tories were gaining ground electorally in Scotland
they opposed Home Rule. In June 1928, the *Spectator* noted that
Scottish Unionism was 'for the first time in the ascendant'.[22] An article
in the *Daily Express* in late 1929 stated that Walter Elliot 'would make a
good Prime Minister for Scotland's first Parliament '.[23] Yet the Conservatives were not enticed into support for Scottish self-government

by the prospect of ruling the country. This was probably because they recognized that their support was not solid but was a result of the turbulence of electoral politics as Labour replaced the Liberals. The 1929 General Election confirmed that Scottish Unionism was not so dominant as the press had been suggesting. The Unionist vote fell from 40.3 per cent to 35.6 per cent, and the Tories lost 16 seats from their peak of 38 at the 1924 'Red Scare' Election. The Scottish Unionist political secretary, Col. P. J. Blair, identified the reasons for the decline in Tory support in a letter to Sir John Gilmour. The Local Government (Scotland) Act, 1929 had been an unpopular measure and, Blair noted, the lack of a 'definite and attractive future policy which could be grasped by the Electorate' had its costs. Notably, he pointed out that the leaflets produced by the London office were in many cases 'inappropriate and inapplicable for Scotland'.[24] The Scottish Unionists had reached a peak electorally by default rather than because of their programme or appeal in 1924. They had then failed to consolidate their position by stressing any peculiarly Scottish diamension to their platform and had subsequently declined. This was hardly a party which could look forward to campaigning for elections to a Scottish Parliament with relish.

A study of the 1950 General Election campaign in Glasgow noted that some Labour voters 'expressed anxiety lest a Scottish Parliament should not have a Labour majority'.[25] The 1950 General Election results, with Labour winning 46.2 per cent of the vote and 37 seats and the Tories winning 44.8 per cent and 31 seats, did not provide substance for these fears. Nor really did the results of the 1955 and 1959 Elections. In 1955, the Unionists won 36 seats and 50.1 per cent of the vote (the only party this century to win over 50 per cent of the vote cast in Scotland). But six of these seats were held by Liberal Unionists, as were six of the 31 seats won in 1959. The Unionists had succeeded in playing the Scottish card effectively while the Labour Party appeared as an unimaginative and centralist alternative in the early part of the decade. The Conservative acceptance of the welfare state meant that in this respect there was little dividing the parties; indeed Macmillan's house-building programme might even have suggested that the Conservatives were better equipped to develop the welfare state. The lifting of the post-war austerity during the early 1950s must also have been important. In essence, the Labour Party failed to play the Scottish card in 1955 in the way that Opposition political parties almost invariably do and allowed the Scottish Unionists to benefit. However, at the 1959 General Election the Conservatives vote fell to 47.2 per cent while Labour's rose to 46.7 per cent (Labour won 38 seats to the Tories 31). This was to be the last Election when the Tories were to win more votes than Labour in Scotland.

Both during the 1920s and the 1950s, the Conservatives opposed Scottish Home Rule though it might have appeared that they would have been the largest party in the Scottish Parliament. However, the Conservative support in both cases was fickle. It was hardly the bedrock on which a naturally cautious political party would risk a bold move such as establishing a Scottish Parliament. The electoral evidence does not confirm the fears, probably deliberately exaggerated, of Conservatives, who equated Scottish Home Rule with radical social and economic change. At the same time, the anti-Conservative tradition of Scotland – which is not, of course, the same as a socialist or radical tradition – has remained sufficiently in evidence for the Conservatives to fear the consequences of Scottish Home Rule, even at times when they have been in the ascendancy.

CONSTITUTIONAL PROPRIETY AND SCOTTISH HOME RULE

A major theme stressed in Conservative opposition to Scottish Home Rule has been the technical and constitutional problems which would arise. Although Northern Ireland had a Parliament at Stormont between 1922 and 1972, Conservatives have always maintained that it would be impossible to have a Scottish legislature within the framework of the United Kingdom. The arguments used were the same as those in A. V. Dicey's *England's Case Against Home Rule*, a book written in 1885 during the debates on Irish Home Rule. The basic argument of the book was picked up most forcefully by the Labour MP Tam Dalyell and by Conservatives in the debates prior to the referendum of 1979.

The retention of Scottish Members at Westminster after the establishment of a Scottish Parliament raised problems for Cabinet Government. Would Scottish Members of Parliament be allowed to vote on English matters in Westminster while the equivalent Scottish matters were devolved to a Scottish legislature? Would Scots be allowed to vote on English matters but neither they nor English Members be allowed to vote on English matters? How then would Cabinet Government operate? These were questions asked by Conservatives whenever Scottish Home Rule arose in Parliament. Dicey is concerned with Cabinet Government and the sovereignty of Parliament. Scottish Home Rule would alter the nature of the constitution with consequences far beyond the Scottish dimension which concerns Home Rulers. As Arthur Balfour stated in 1908:

> I cannot permit any proposal to destroy the authority of this House, to do one of two things, either to exclude Scottish Members from this House or to leave them in a commanding position with regard to purely English legislation.[26]

Another matter which has often been regarded by Conservatives as causing insurmountable problems is finance. The Government of Scotland Bill of 1908 was attacked by Balfour because he felt that the relationship between the proposed Scottish Parliament and the Treasury was unworkable. The Government of Scotland Bill of 1914 included revenue raising powers. This too provoked opposition amongst the Conservatives. William Watson, Unionist Member for South Lanark, argued that the complications involved in having two taxing authorities was undesirable. Whether a scheme proposed revenue raising powers or not there were problems which the Conservatives focussed upon.

Arguing that there was a *need* for central control in certain areas has been stressed by Conservatives. Walter Elliot's argument in 1920 was typical, even if the wit was not:

> epidemic after epidemic is stamped out with a skill and precision only possible to a central authority – but then, of course, it does not console a cow as it does a Christian to conceive that it died from a respectably national disease.[27]

This was the same argument which was made successfully during the many debates on establishing a Scottish Board of Agriculture before the First World War. When the Board was established in 1912, the responsibility for animal health in Scotland was given to the Department of Agriculture. Scots were somehow not expected to maintain the high standards of their southern neighbours and animal health was only transferred to the Scottish Office in 1954, following a recommendation contained in the Royal Commission on Scottish Affairs.

Conservatism's fear of change and sensitivity to problems and possibilities of what change might bring necessarily led to an exaggeration of the difficulties involved. However, the proponents of Home Rule have not made much effort to formulate answers and responses to the technical and constitutional arguments put forward by opponents. Neither have the supporters been very clear, and certainly not consistent, in their formulation of the constitutional structures they propose. The very obvious implications for the rest of the United Kingdom have tended to be ignored by Home Rulers. This has not necessarily harmed their cause in Scotland, but greatly weakens their case in the House of Commons through which their proposals must pass. In many cases the technical and constitutional arguments seem to have been aimed at English Members, of all parties, rather than the Scottish MPs or the Scottish electorate. Parliament rather than the wider electorate has traditionally been the focus of attention in the Conservative's arguments against Home Rule.

THE CATHCART BREAKAWAY

One of the most intriguing episodes in the history of the Scottish Home Rule Movement was the breakaway from the Scottish Unionist Party of a substantial part of the Glasgow Cathcart Association in 1932. However ephemeral or even quixotic the episode now appears, it was treated seriously by the Unionists at the time. In 1931, the Nationalists had secured a symbolic victory when the novelist Compton Mackenzie was elected Rector of Glasgow University by beating

Sir Robert Horne, one of the most prominent Unionist opponents of Home Rule, amongst others including Tom Johnston and Sir Oswald Mosely. A press war was being waged between Beaverbrook's *Scottish Daily Express* and the *Daily Record*. The Cathcart episode was fully covered by both papers. Both newspapers conducted opinion surveys which, though rather crude and unscientific, showed considerable support for legislative devolution. Whether this background was important is not clear but this along with the establishment of the National Party of Scotland in 1928 seems relevant.

Kevan McDowell, a Glasgow solicitor, had written to a number of individuals seeking their support for Home Rule within the British Empire. His ideas seem to have resembled those of F. S. Oliver and Imperial Unionists before the First World War. Some time around the middle of 1932 McDowell had written to a number of key individuals asking them to support Home Rule and had received favourable replies from the Duke of Montrose, Sir Alexander MacEwan and Andrew Dewar Gibb. The course of events is not clear but what is certain is that McDowell, acting with the authority of the Cathcart Unionist Council, an offshoot of the Cathcart Unionist Association, established a Home Rule front, the 'Imperial Committee of Cathcart Unionist Association', arranged meetings and made public statements which led to his expulsion from the party.

The Cathcart Home Rulers styled themselves the 'Moderates', seeking to distinguish themselves from the National Party's hardline position and also, no doubt, its socialist-inclined ideas. Eventually the Moderates were forced out of the Unionist party and established the Scottish Self Government Party, usually referred to as the Scottish party, which joined with the National Party in April 1934 to form the Scottish National Party.

In a highly provocative article on the front page of the *Daily Record* in September 1932, McDowell criticized the Unionist party's leadership. On the same day the paper reported that Lord Dalziel of Kirkcaldy, who as a Liberal MP from 1892–1921 had introduced the first Home Rule Bill in the Commons, had joined the National Party of Scotland. Not surprisingly, the official Unionist response was swift and unconciliatory. James Paterson, the chairman of Glasgow Unionist Association, replied by letter to the paper stating that McDowell had acted upon the authority of a 'very small meeting of the Council – a purely administrative body with no delegated power to alter the policy of the Association'. He also critized McDowell for conferring with the National Party and failing to consult the Cathcart Association.

On October 25, 1932, the Scottish Unionists met under the chairmanship of Sir Robert Horne MP to consider the Home Rule Movement, and unanimously agreed that no benefit would come to

Scotland by the establishment of a Scottish Parliament which could not be achieved with greater efficiency in other ways, including reforming the administrative apparatus. The meeting agreed that it was impossible to divide Britain into separate Parliamentary units without doing 'grievous injury to industrial, commercial, and cultural interests in Scotland'.[28] Both the *Scotsman* and the *Glasgow Herald* carried editorials on October 27 on the subject; the former lukewarm about a moderate measure and the latter strongly opposed to the idea. Home Rule was certainly an issue, but far from being implemented.

Concern that the issue was being raised led to a further meeting in November in the Merchants House in Glasgow. Some five hundred individuals opposed to Home Rule attended the meeting, which was chaired by Lord Maclay and a platform party which included Sir John Stirling-Maxwell, Sir James Lithgow, Hugh Cree (president of Glasgow Chamber of Commerce), Professor J. Y. Simpson, Sir Herbert Maxwell and Cecil Weir. The meeting issued a statement asserting that

> representative business and public opinion, which has at heart the best interests of our country, recognizes that Scotland and England are interdependent and form one unit for all practical and for all national purposes . . . Exaggerated nationalism is the root of the evil of world distress today and should not be introduced into Scotland.[29]

The rise of political nationalism in Scotland in the early 1930s in demands for a Scottish Parliament forced the established parties to make clear their positions. Through meetings, manifestos and speeches in Parliament, particularly during 1932, the Unionists made clear their opposition. Even the *Times* letters columns was a battleground. The suggestion that Scottish Home Rule would mean 'giving the Irish and friends of Mr de Valera influence in Scotland' was made by an anonymous writer and Lord Selbourne asked the familiar question

> are the Scottish Members of Parliament still to influence by their votes (and very possibly decide) the corresponding purely English concerns?[30]

The inaugural meeting of the Imperial Committee of Cathcart Unionist Association took place on November 25 in the constituency. The meeting was attended by the Duke and Duchess of Montrose and Sir Alexander MacEwen. Five days later, on St Andrews Day, the Scottish Unionists held their annual conference in Glasgow. A resolution submitted by Sir Robert Horne MP was unanimously accepted which stated that the creation of separate Parliaments would be 'gravely injurious both to the economic and to the cultural life of Great Britain as a whole'.[31] Cathcart Central Council submitted a resolution welcoming self-government for Scottish internal and domestic affairs while accepting the political and economic unity of the British

Empire. McDowell perversely insisted that it ought to be treated as complementary, not antagonistic to Horne's resolution but this was rejected. He then backed down and decided to accept Horne's resolution, which was passed unanimously.

The day following the Unionist conference, a meeting of Home Rulers was held in Edinburgh's North British Hotel. This was, effectively, the foundation of the Scottish (Self Government) Party. The Duke of Montrose was elected President, MacEwen was elected Chairman and McDowell, praised by MacEwen for his work, was elected Honorary Secretary and Treasurer. A fairly prestigious executive committee was chosen from the meeting.[32] Four days later, on December 5, at a meeting of the General Committee of the Glasgow Unionist Association McDowell was struck off the register of members by 52 votes to 5. His 'persistent disloyalty to the Unionist party' was noted, as was the Scottish Party's intention of contesting elections.[33]

The dispute dragged on for almost another two months until, at the end of January 1933, the Cathcart Unionist Association disbanded the Imperial Committee after about 40 members of the Association involved in the committee had resigned. The next evening the Cathcart Imperial Unionist Association, whatever its status was by that time, met and decided to affiliate to the Scottish party.[34]

Whether the Cathcart breakaway had been planned from mid or early 1932 is not certain. It may be that McDowell, Montrose, MacEwen and Dewar Gibb hoped to establish a situation on the right of politics similar to that which already existed on the left. The National Party had been established largely consisting of Labour Party members. However, Labour had a Home Rule tradition which the Unionists did not have. Of course, it may well have been the case that McDowell merely intended to create as much publicity in establishing the Scottish party as he possibly could. In this respect he seems to have had much success.

PLAYING THE SCOTTISH CARD

Though Conservatives have fairly consistently opposed Scottish Home Rule, they have, on occasion, made use of the language of Scottish nationalism, especially when Home Rule has been an issue. John Buchan's view that 'every Scotsman should be a Scottish Nationalist'[35] is an example of a Conservative using the language of nationalism at a time of pressure. Conservatives have stressed their support for cultural nationalism, though theirs is a truncated idea of culture. Conservatives have also played the Scottish card as a means of embarrassing their opponents in Government. The most obvious case of this was during the Post-War Attlee Government.

In 1942 the Scottish National Party had split with John MacCormick's faction, breaking off and setting up the Scottish Convention.

In the years following the war, the Convention became the dominant force in the self-government movement and organised a Scottish National Assembly of 600 delegates in Glasgow in 1947. The Convention was recognized by Conservatives as a means of embarrassing the Labour Government. Attacks on British central government by the Convention were not always easily distinguishable from criticisms of the Attlee Labour Government. The nationalization programme with its lack of a Scottish dimension was certainly a genuine grievance of the Home Rulers. As a consequence, the Home Rulers succeeded in boxing themselves into a corner and gaining the antipathy of a sizeable section of the Labour Party for a long period. The association of Scottish Home Rule with the Conservative cause had developed over this period, but proved to be a fruitless relationship when the Churchill Government was returned to power in 1951.

The death of the former Conservative Prime Minister Stanley Baldwin in 1947 was to set in motion a series of events which offered the Conservatives an opportunity of widening their support in Scotland. Baldwin had been made an Earl in 1937 and his death meant that his son Oliver, who was Labour Member for Paisley, was elevated to the House of Lords. John MacCormick had already been adopted as the Liberal candidate for the constituency. The Conservatives decided not to field a candidate of their own but to support MacCormick as a 'National' candidate against Labour. Around this time the Liberals had been negotiating with the Conservatives; the former were worried about their very survival and the latter had hopes of swallowing up the Liberals and their support. The Conservative agreement not to oppose MacCormick was aided by a number of Paisley Unionists involved in the Convention.

A joint meeting of the local Unionist and Liberal executives adopted a programme which included criticism of the 'process of centralizing the economic control of Scotland in Whitehall' and a statement that a 'measure of devolution in the government of Scotland is a matter of urgency'.[36] The pact damaged the Home Rulers. The Labour Party was alienated and MacCormick failed to win the support of his new allies for his ideas. The *Glasgow Herald*, hardly a paper naturally disposed to the Labour candidate, advised its Paisley readers not to support the Home Rule candidate. Two senior Scottish Liberals, Lady Glen Coats and Sir Archibald Sinclair, denounced the pact with the Tories and urged Paisley Liberals to withhold their support from MacCormick. MacCormick was left in the invidious position of being a 'National' candidate but having been ditched by Scottish Liberal leaders, and sharing a platform with Conservative opponents of Home Rule such as Walter Elliot, Peter Thorneycroft, Sir R. Manningham-Butler and Lady Grant (later Tweedsmuir). In the event, Labour held the seat by a substantial majority. MacCormick's gamble had not only failed to pay off but had a very high price. The Tories never had any intention of supporting Home Rule and Labour felt that the Convention, personified by its leading activist, was its opponent. As Christopher Harvie has noted, Labour never forgot it.[37] MacCormick was by no means a man of the right but a determined campaigner for self-government. Had his gamble paid off and had he entered the House of Commons, the Conservatives would certainly have been greatly embarrassed by his speeches. But it did not and the Unionists were the beneficiaries; the episode lent some false credibility to the Tory claim to support Scottish aspirations for self-government.

Further examples of playing the Scottish card are evident in speeches by Conservative politicians during this period. The centralization of power under the Attlee Government was a major theme of Tory speeches north of the border. Anthony Eden's call for the recognition of 'individuality either in men or in nations' in Dalkeith in June 1949 and Churchill's Usher Hall speech a week before the 1950 election are in this mode. Churchill declared that he 'should never adopt the view that Scotland should be forced into the serfdom of socialism as the result of a vote in the House of Commons'.[38] However Churchill not only failed to endorse Home Rule but he, and Attlee, refused to meet representatives of the Scottish Convention after it had launched its Covenant gathering signatures in support of Home Rule.

It was Churchill's Tory adversary, Walter Elliot who was most adept at appealing to Scottish national sentiment. Elliot would attack Labour's 'twenty years of promises and propaganda gone with the wind' with regard to the establishment of a Scottish Parliament, and attacked Attlee's centralization of power and administration. He even attacked the Labour Party for having three MPs in Scottish seats who were born in England. Such attacks went much further than seems imaginable from a Unionist politician. But Elliot's Scottish nationalism was insubstantial, cosmetic and ugly.

Playing the Scottish card certainly paid dividends in support for the Unionist Party in Scotland. Labour's position had been weakened with respect to its image as a Scottish party, thus allowing the Conservatives to portray themselves as more Scottish. It can be surmised that had Labour been in a position to project a sharper Scottish image then the Conservative support might have been less strong. A similar example of playing the Scottish card was evident in Conservative party activities during the Heath years, as shall be shown in the next chapter.

CONCLUSION

Opposition to Scottish Home Rule in the Conservative party was partly a principled response to the perceived break with constitutional tradition and a fairly typical Conservative fear of change. As might be expected, the fears were expressed in exaggerated language. One crucial factor has been the Conservatives' lack of support in

Scotland. Even when they have polled well the Conservatives have not found the prospect of self-government attractive, probably lacking confidence in their ability to sustain their high support as much as due to some ideological opposition.

Tory opponents, as much as socialist proponents, of legislative devolution stressed the possibilities of a Scottish Parliament implementing radical policies. However, it cannot by any means be assumed that both were correct. Though Scotland has not been inclined to support the Tories at the polls, this does not mean that the Scots have an overwhelming radical or socialist tradition, but may merely reflect a negative characteristic, an anti-Conservative bias.

The Irish influence on the debate was especially strong in the late nineteenth century but has all but disappeared. Scottish Home Rule latterly became an issue in its own right. However, Ireland was the reason why some Conservatives did offer their support for Scottish Home Rule. A federal solution was felt to be a more practical means of tackling the Irish problem. Nevertheless, a minority of Conservatives have consistently supported Scottish Home Rule. The Duke of Montrose exemplifies that brand of Scottish aristocrat with a strong sense of Scottish national identity. Perhaps at the other end of the social spectrum another, more populist, version of Scottish Conservative is to be found lending support to Home Role.

The Adoption of Legislative Devolution

The Hamilton by-election of November 1967 marked a watershed in Scottish politics. Winnie Ewing's triumph had been preceded in March that year by a by-election in Glasgow Pollok where the Nationalists, though coming only third, had won 28 per cent of the vote. Local government elections told the same story; the SNP won 18.4 per cent in May 1967, up from 4.4 per cent at the previous year's burgh elections, and 34 per cent in May 1968. The Conservative reaction was dramatic. With their long tradition of hostility to legislative devolution and constitutional reform generally, they might have seemed less likely than the Labour party to lend support to a measure of legislative devolution.

Other factors allied with the Nationalist advance were to change things. Edward Heath had been elected leader of the party the previous year, the first leader to be elected by the Parliamentary Party rather than emerge following 'magic circle' consultations. The party's poor showing in Scotland in the Elections of 1959 and 1964 forced Heath to recognize the need for some means of revival. A commitment to legislative devolution, though in a most modest form, was to be a major part of Heath's attempt to revive his party in Scotland and of ditching the Nationalists. With the relative demise of the SNP at the 1970 General Election, Heath's scheme was held in abeyance and the Tories' brief flirtation with Home Rule soon passed.

TACKLING THE DECLINE IN CONSERVATIVE FORTUNES

The decline in Conservative Party fortunes in Scotland from the 1959 Election forced the party to consider its image, policies, organization and strategy. The grouse moor image associated with Scottish Secretaries such as James Stuart and Michael Noble, the lack of presence in local government and the party's organizational problems were recognized as weaknesses. Sir Patrick Blair, who had been political secretary from 1922 to 1960, had initiated an inquiry into the party's organization just before his retirement. This had had the strong support of two of the Scottish MPs, Sir Fitzroy Maclean and Ian MacArthur. However, attempts to reform the party's organization at the 1960 Scottish conference had failed.

The party in Scotland was not in the best position possible to meet the Nationalist challenge in the late 1960s. At the time of the Hamilton by-election the Conservative Political Centre's publication list included only two specifically Scottish pamphlets – one was written by Ian MacArthur and entitled *The Grandest Thing In The World* and discussed the purposes of education and the role of the politician, while the other was *Scotland for the Tourist* and had been written in 1962.

It was only after the 1964 General Election that organizational changes were instituted. These changes strengthened the central office, created a single national fund to finance all party activities above constituency level, and established five regional councils to replace the Eastern and Western divisional councils. It was also at this time that the Scottish Party officially changed its name from the Scottish Unionist Party to the Scottish Conservative and Unionist party and a decision was taken to encourage party members to contest local elections under the party banner. Though many party members were elected councillors they stood as 'Independents' or 'Progressives' rather than as Unionists or Conservatives.

These changes owed much to the Scottish Party chairmanship of Sir John George. At the party conference in 1965, with candour uncharacteristic for a party chairman, Sir John identified three areas which he found disturbing. Firstly, the conference was poorly attended at a time of critical importance for the party. Secondly, he noted that though those in attendance were loyal and steadfast they were also ageing party members. This no doubt led to his third concern – the lack of 'fire and controversy' in conference proceedings. Sir John argued that the party had to become more enlivened if it was to avoid being blamed by English Conservatives for the return of Labour Governments in the future.

The election of Edward Heath as Conservative Party leader in August 1965 and the recognition of serious problems and implementation of organizational reforms were followed by the launch, in November 1967, of the Thistle Group. The Group was a sign that younger party members were taking note of Sir John George's warnings. Obviously, Nationalist activity was significant. The Thistle Group consisted of about twelve mainly younger party members, a number of whom were Edinburgh University graduates, including Michael Ancram, Alex Pollock, Peter Fraser and Nicholas Asprey, the former three to become MPs. This ginger group was to become associated with the pro-devolution wing.

The Thistle Group's first publication was concerned with party organization. Its second publication was a paper entitled *Devolution: A New Appraisal*. It criticized the lack of Parliamentary scrutiny of the Scottish Office and the powers of the Secretary of State. The authors stated that the Scottish Secretary probably holds greater influence than Dundas, who told the Younger Pitt, 'I hold Scotland in the hollow of my hand'.[2] They rejected the proposal of Liberal MP David Steel who had suggested, as an interim measure, that the Scottish Grand Committee should meet regularly in Edinburgh. In response, the authors of *Devolution: A New Appraisal*, argued that the Grand Committee could sit wherever it likes but this will serve no purpose unless it is radically reconstituted with a much greater sphere of influence.[3] Michael Ancram, future Scottish chairman and Scottish Office Minister, published the document. Peter Fraser, future Solicitor General Group and Group member, over a decade later successfully proposed in Parliament that the Scottish Grand Committee should meet in Edinburgh.

Instead, the Group advocated an 'up-grading' of the Committee with weekly meetings, though not necessarily in Scotland. This would only be a first step towards federalism. The paper did not outline the areas of responsibility of the federal and local assemblies, nor did it explain whether the scheme would apply to other parts of the United Kingdom. But the authors were explicit on questions of finance:

Fiscal independence is vital. The extent to which we may be at odds with England is doubtful, but this may be necessary for Scottish conditions (e.g. the expert proposals to reduce Corporation Tax, and perhaps Income Tax). The Scottish Parliament would raise her own revenue and remit a proportion to the Federal Treasury.

They even suggested that there was 'no bar to a separate monetary policy for Scotland'.[4]

The Group's nationalistic inclinations were apparent in other areas including its comments on higher education. Ancram, Alex Pollock and Nicholas Asprey argued that Scottish Universities ought to

guarantee a certain number of places, if not a majority, to Scottish students with a set of broad qualifications, and so prevent sixth-form education in this country becoming merely a glorified university entrance course, as it has south of the border.[5]

In a resolution submitted for debate at the 1971 Scottish Conservative conference in Aberdeen, Pollock submitted a resolution on behalf of the Group which called on the Government to 'pursue economic policies which will encourage the return of patriots to Scotland'.[6]

Teddy Taylor, then populist MP for Glasgow Cathcart, was equally aware of the need for the party to change its image. In an article in a Liberal publication, he insisted that

the transformation of the Scottish Conservatives to a Scottish People's Party would not be completed until the Party has a clear and precise policy to fight against the evils of London-based centralisation and domination. A firm commitment to set up a

Scottish Assembly to take responsibility for Scottish legislation would be an envigorating and persuasive weapon in the armoury of Conservative candidates.[7]
The reform of the organization and the involvement of more dynamic politician such as Sir John George were hopeful signs for Heath. However welcome these were, the need for some novel policy initiative was particularly felt in light of Nationalist advances. Advocating legislative devolution was to be just that course. The impetus of the Hamilton by-election can hardly be exaggerated. On November 16, two weeks after Hamilton, a secret meeting was held, attended by senior Conservatives, and it was decided that action would have to be taken to meet the Nationalist challenge. As Ramsden states in his study of the making of Conservative Party policy, it was decided that the devolution policy should be left to a policy group of the Scottish Conservatives and 'above all that it should be seen to be done by Scotsmen'.[8] Heath appealed for imaginative and electorally appealing policies. The negative response to Conservative social and economic policies led to the constitutional question being given prominence. However, subsequent erosion of support for the SNP led the Shadow Cabinet to lose its interest in Scottish questions.[9]

THE DECLARATION OF PERTH

Ted Heath's concern with the rise of the SNP was noted by Richard Crossman in his diaries. In an entry following the Hamilton by-election, Crossman noted that Heath had remarked at the Broadcasting Committee meeting that nationalism was the 'biggest single factor in our politics today'.[10] In 1967 a committee under Sir William McEwen Younger had established to review the machinery of government in Scotland in response to a resolution passed by the party's Scottish central council. The committee's first meeting was held on December 14 that year – six weeks after Hamilton.[11]

Considerable controversy was to surround the eventual publication of the committee's proposals, particularly the lack of consultation involved in its proceedings. During the early part of 1968, Sir William and Esmond Wright, the latter having been elected as MP for Glasgow Pollok at the by-election in 1967, met Heath. They proposed the establishment of an Assembly which would be partly directly and partly indirectly elected with powers to initiate and to consider legislation, but leaving Westminster with the final right of veto. Heath's major objection was to the indirectly elected component. His major preoccupation was with entry into the European Economic Community and he feared that a Scottish Assembly with indirectly elected members would serve as a precedent. Heath strongly favoured a significant role for a directly elected Euro-Parliament as a firm foundation for European Union.

At two Shadow Cabinet meetings in May 1968 the interim report of the Younger committee was considered, along with an analysis by Michael Noble. On May 15, two days after the second Shadow Cabinet meeting, Heath presented his colleagues with the proposals he intended to announce at the Scottish Conservative conference three days later on May 18. Heath's speech at the Party's annual Scottish conference in Perth was an instance of party policy making at its least consultative. For many in attendance, the reversal of policy, after a century of opposition to any measures of Home Rule, came as a great surprise. Even supporters of the policy realised that Heath had foisted the policy on the Scottish party, though the extent to which the party members and journalists had become aware of the contents of Heath's speech before it was made is disputed.

In his Perth speech, Heath followed the Balfour report of 1954 in noting the growing trend towards uniformity and centralization and the fear of submergence of Scottish national identity. He proposed the creation of a constitutional committee to consider proposals for change but opposed a Royal Commission as it would be 'too large, slow and cumbersome'. The Conservative Party would recommend the proposals of the Younger committee, of a single chamber taking part in the legislative process 'in conjunction with Parliament', to this constitutional committee. Such matters as the method and timing of elections, detailed powers and procedures, financial responsibilities and means of avoiding conflict with Westminster would be left to the constitutional committee.

Though vague and hardly as radical as the rhetoric in which it was wrapped, this was nonetheless a major reversal in party policy. The grandiosely titled Declaration of Perth upset many within the party but it amounted to little more than an extension of the Westminster committee system. Heath wanted to portray his proposals as a major reform. In doing this he had alienated many within his party whose natural instinct was suspicion of anything which challenged the status quo, but yet who might possibly have accepted the idea if it had been presented in a different manner. Not only did he appear to be proposing a rather radical measure but he presented it as a *fait accompli*. Heath had seen the need to revive the party in Scotland to meet the Nationalist challenge, but he also needed to carry the party with him. Retrospectively, it is clear that Heath overplayed the former while failing to convince his party that the changes were necessary, practical and would not encourage further demands.

Many of Heath's critics, then and later, criticized the leader for 'foisting' devolution on the party. Even amongst his supporters and proponents of legislative devolution, there is a consensus that Heath's speech was badly timed and should have been preceded by more discussion. Helen Millar, herself a strong supporter of devolution in the party, maintained that few members had 'even thought about devolution and appeared shocked' by Heath's speech and 'because the vast mass of the conference-going members had never thought about devolution they were, without doubt, very upset' while only a few individuals were pleased with the leader's address.

Opposition to Heath's speech was made clear to the whips in Parliament by about a third of the Scottish Tory MPs. This was noted by David Wood in the *Times* in July 1968. Wood described the Perth speech as a 'rather pathetic publicist's attempt to catch historic echoes from the Declaration of Arbroath' and suggested that Scottish Tory MPs had not seen the Younger report and that the main points of the report were discovered 'only with difficulty a few hours before the Perth declaration rang out across mountain, loch and glen'. The mainstream view amongst Scottish Conservatives, according to Wood, was that Heath was excessively fearful of the threat posed by the SNP.[12]

Opposition to Heath's Perth Declaration was heard at the Scottish Conservative conference in Leith in 1969. A supporter of a resolution rejecting a directly elected Assembly critized Heath's speech at the previous year's conference as 'unimpressive, pretentious and redolent of gimmickry'. However, a more conciliatory position was adopted, supported by such opponents of legislative devolution as Lord Strathclyde, which was to await the findings of the Home inquiry. No doubt the impending General election was a factor in this appearance of unity.

While Scottish Tory Members such as Betty Harvie Anderson, Lord Strathclyde and Tam Galbraith felt that Heath had foisted the policy on the party, most English Tories seem to have been unaware of the policy, or at least did not take it seriously. During a Parliamentary debate in January 1976, the right-wing Conservative MP for Beaconsfield Ronald Bell argued that though the Scots had been debating devolution for years it was 'new to the people of England'. Heath had interjected to state that there had been 'intensive discussion not only in this House and in the Scottish Members' Committee but in the whole party in Scotland' during his leadership and that there had been 'thorough discussion throughout' in the policy committee of the party consisting of English and Scottish Members. Bell's response typifies the attitude of many Conservative backbenchers; he replied that Heath's failing was to think that

> if something is discussed in the policy committee of the Conservative Party, which is a very small body, it is somehow percolated and permeated through the whole party, and we all know about it.[13]

SCOTLAND'S GOVERNMENT: THE REPORT OF THE
CONSTITUTIONAL COMMITTEE

The Labour Party in Scotland's response to the Nationalist pressure
had initially been to propose, in July 1968, that the Scottish Grand
Committee meet occasionally in Edinburgh during the next Session of
Parliament. This was superseded by the Wilson Government's establishment of the Royal Commision on the Constitution in Autumn
1968. Heath opposed this on the grounds that it would be too cumbersome and that action had to be taken as quickly as possible.
Instead, the Tory leader himself set up a Constitutional Committee in
July 1968 with Sir Alec Douglas Home as its chairman.

A number of distinguished members were appointed to this body,
including Sir David Milne (former Permanent Under-Secretary at the
Scottish Office), Sir Charles Wilson (Principal of Glasgow University),
J. D. B. Mitchell (Law Professor at Edinburgh University), Sir Arthur
Goodhart (former Professor of Jurisprudence at Oxford), and Lord
Avonside (a Court of Session Judge). The last member was, however,
forced to resign the following month because of his judicial position –
though not before it was pointed out that a (dormant) Scottish tra-
dition of active judicial participation in public life existed. The former
Australian Prime Minister, Sir Robert Menzies and Sir Kenneth
Wheare, Rector of Exeter College, Oxford and an authority on federalism were appointed as advisers to the committee.

There was some confusion and controversy over the remit and
status of the committee; it was not clear whether the committee was to
assume that an Assembly was to be created and recommend a particular scheme or whether the committee was to consider whether the
principle of legislative devolution was desirable. This was overcome
when the committee agreed that it was within its remit to reject an
Assembly though their primary task should be to recommend on the
practicalities and details of establishing an Assembly. This compromise allowed the two members most opposed to legislative devolution, Sir Charles Wilson and Professor J. D. B. Mitchell, to serve. The
remit was questioned by Conservative opponents of devolution who
maintained that the party had not yet decided its position. As it
became clear that the committee would report favourably, Tory anti-
devolutionists suggested that the Committee was not, in fact, a Conservative Party committee at all.

After seventeen meetings over eighteen months, the committee
reported on March 16, 1970. In presenting the report, *Scotland's
Government*, Sir Alec Douglas Home stated that the party's policy
would not be decided until after the Scottish conference in May and
suggested that Parliament would probably have to await the report of
the Royal Commission on the Constitution. This reflected the
changed political environment, the impending General Election and

signs of Labour recovery in the UK polls. Opposition to legislative devolution in the Conservative Party was growing and, most notably, the SNP was in decline.

As expected, *Scotland's Government* rejected independence and federalism. The latter was seen as legalistic and requiring a written constitution, and the committee felt that 'having the advantage of an unwritten constitution, it would be reactionary and unwise to disturb and discard it'.[14] A Stormont-style solution was seen as inappropriate as Stormont reflected the peculiar problems and needs of Northern Ireland and the equivalent reduction in the number of Scottish MPs at Westminster was felt to be an unacceptable price to pay. This also suggests that the Conservatives were optimistic of recovery in Scotland. Instead, it was proposed that a 'Scottish Convention' (the term 'Assembly' was avoided to prevent confusion with the Church of Scotland's General Assembly) should be established. This was to be directly elected with around 125 members meeting about forty days each year with its timetable regulated to fit in with Westminster. Elections would be held at the same time as elections to the House of Commons, though no opinion was expressed as to electoral divisions other than that they should take account of both those of the Commons and the new local government structure which was then being considered. The view expressed on proportional representation was that it

> would run counter to the system chosen for Parliamentary elections and would add a complication which we doubt is justifiable.[15]

Given the relative strength of the Conservative and Labour Parties in Scotland it would seem that the Committee's rejection of proportional representation was unusual though, of course, support for electoral reform was relatively weak in the party. The Tories may have expected their fortunes to improve but it is more likely that they feared the precedent might strengthen the case for electoral reform at Westminster.

The powers and functions proposed for the Convention were limited to those performed by the Scottish Grand Committee and Scottish Standing Committees. Legislation declared by the Speaker or by a vote in Parliament to apply only to Scotland would have their Second Reading, Committee and Reports stages taken in the Convention. Legislation would then return to Westminster where it could be amended and given a Third Reading before being sent to the Lords. This would 'preserve the essential principle of the sovereignty of Parliament'.[16] Legislation could not be initiated by the Convention. The amount of Scottish legislation which would be passed on to the Convention was unclear. The report stated that Parliament 'may well prefer' to retain the power to decide on a Government motion whether an issue should be devolved.[17] What seems to have been proposed was an Assembly which could not embarrass a Conservative Government in London and which would, therefore, have to be wholly subservient to Westminster. A number of other assumptions of Parliamentary sovereignty were to be found in the report. Bills would be introduced and piloted through the Convention by Scottish Office Ministers or Law Officers. In presenting the report, Home said that in the case of a Secretary of State being unable to pass legislation through the Convention it would be possible to modify and renew the attempt or even to introduce it in Parliament. J. D. B. Mitchell noted problems following from this in his note of dissent at the end of the report:

a report or the Third Reading stage in the Commons would be used by a Government to 'correct' amendments made which it found inconvenient, or else the measure would be dropped. There is a risk of increasing irritation on the one hand, and, on the other, a danger of increasing delays in carrying through schemes. Such delays are costly.[19]

Home's response to this problem given at the press conference presenting the report is indicative of the extent of devolution intended. He stated that it was likely that the Government would keep the 'very controversial Bills – perhaps two a year – in London'.

Without an executive, with deliberative responsibilities shorn of any powers to challenge or confront Westminster over matters of disagreement, the Scottish Convention was a mere talking shop. John Mackintosh's criticisms of Heath's Declaration of Perth were equally appropriate to the Home Report:

once such an Assembly were denied the right to propose or reject measures, it would be denounced as a farce. If, on the other hand it could introduce, amend or reject bills, there would be the fiercest resentment at any suggestion that these proposals could then be reversed by an English-dominated House of Commons. The fact is that one set of Ministers cannot be held responsible to two different elected chambers whose political composition is most unlikely to be exactly the same.[19]

At the time of the publication of *Scotland's Government*, at least two Scottish Conservative MPs, Michael Clark Hutchison and Jock Bruce Gardyne, stated that the proposals would have a low priority at best. It was generally assumed that the recommendations of the Wheatley Commission on local government reform had to be dealt with first and that the findings of the Royal Commission on the Constitution would need to be studied when published. One of the greatest weaknesses of the Home report was the failure to consider the entire constitutional framework, including both central and local government. Home's remit had been too narrow, as the constitutional lawyer A. W. Bradley noted.[20]

THE HEATH GOVERNMENT

It was political rather than constitutional or legal considerations that explain the failure of the Heath Government, elected in June 1970, to implement the Home Report proposals. At the 1970 conference, two months after publication of *Scotland's Government*, the party gave support to the findings of the report despite the strong opposition of Lord Strathclyde, his son Tam Galbraith MP and Vera Findlay, former President of the party. It was clear that opposition to an Assembly was building up and, with an election approaching, it was to be expected that the party would adopt the Home Report and avoid open conflict.

Devolution played no part at the meeting of senior Conservative politicians at the Selsdon Park Hotel in Surrey in January 1970 to discuss the priorities of a Conservative Government. Entry to the EEC, reform of industrial relations law, immigration controls, the introduction of a pension scheme for those over 80 years old, law and order and the streamlining of the machinery of justice were discussed. Though Sir Alec Douglas Home was in attendance devolution was not on the agenda. The decline in support for the SNP, as witnessed at the South Ayrshire by-election in early 1970 when the Nationalists came last, 2000 votes behind the Tories, the lack of enthusiasm in the Tory ranks and competition from an already ambitious and crowded programme for government resulted in devolution slipping off the Conservative agenda. Strong opposition to devolution among Scottish Conservative MPs including Michael Clark Hutchison, Tam Galbraith, W. H. K. Baker, Sir Fitzroy Maclean, Patrick Wolridge Gordon, Betty Harvie Anderson, and Jock Bruce Gardyne also aided in this.

The commitment to a Convention in the manifesto was lukewarm. In a speech in Glasgow eight days before the Election, the party's Scottish Chairman Sir Menzies Anderson failed to mention the establishment of such. As Chris Baur, the *Scotsman's* political correspondent remarked, Anderson's speech illustrated:

> the way the Scottish Tories have been making use – often indirectly – of the Convention idea as an election prop, without making it clear how far the party are committed to establishing such a body.[21]

Heath's overall majority of 30 was a result of gains in England, though three gains were made in Scotland – Aberdeen South, Ross and Cromarty and Aberdeenshire West – on a 2.85 per cent swing from Labour. In England the Conservatives increased their share of the vote by 5.6 per cent but only by 2.3 per cent in Scotland from their 1966 position. With only 23 Scottish Conservatives, against 44 Scottish Labour MPs, Gordon Campbell, the new Scottish Secretary was well aware of problems likely to arise as a consequence of setting up the

Convention. The opposition shown to the Housing (Financial Pro-
visions) (Scotland) Act, 1972 by Labour local authorities must have
further convinced Scottish Tories that a Convention controlled by the
Labour Party would spell trouble. The Housing Act was being defied
by 25 Scottish local authorities, accounting for half the Scottish population at one stage in 1972, and official inquiries, delay in the payment
of central subsidies, and action in the Court of Session had to be
instituted by the Government. Opposition to the Government's Education Bill in the Scottish Grand Committee and the case of the Upper
Clyde Shipbuilders affected the Conservative Party's attitude on the
Convention. Though the Labour Party in Scotland failed to reach the
same conclusion, the Tories were frightened of the radical nature of
any Scottish legislature. The already lukewarm attitude of the party to
Scottish devolution became colder as the problems of governing
Scotland with minority support became clear.

Two specifically Scottish matters were included in the Queen's
speech at the opening of Parliament in 1970. Firstly, there were
measures to improve the organization of Sheriff Courts and secondly,
proposals were to be

> worked out in full consultation with all concerned for local
> government reform in England, Scotland and Wales associated
> with a general devolution of power from the central government.
> At a later stage plans will be laid before you giving the Scottish
> people a greater say in their own affairs.[22]

Local government reform was to have priority and was seen as a
separate matter rather than complementary to the Convention idea.
However, the two-tier structure of local government, and especially
the creation of Strathclyde Region, strongly suggested that the Tory
commitment to a Convention had been dropped. Almost half of
Scotland's population was contained in Strathclyde, which would
make the relations between the Convention and local government
extremely problematic. The Younger Committee, whose findings had
been the basis of Heath's Perth Declaration, had clearly set out the
priorities for reforming Scottish government:

> We feel most strongly that whilst any proposals for the reform of
> the central government mechanism must be seen in the context
> of a reformed local government structure, they must not be
> subordinated to it. The mechanism of government in Scotland
> must be settled first, and the local government structure must
> then be designed as a coordinated component of that
> mechanism.[23]

Heath's response to criticisms made by John Mackintosh concerning
the ordering of his priorities is noteable:

> We for our part have always held the reform of local government
> is a matter of importance and urgency for the people of Scotland
> and that there should be no avoidable delay in putting in hand

the complex arrangements needed to implement it. The question of devolution, while clearly a related matter, has always seemed to us one which should be pursued separately, and later, in a United Kingdom context.[24]

The need to await the findings of the Royal Commission on the Constitution was to be another excuse for prevarication on the part of the Heath Government. This ran counter to Heath's statement when he set up the Home committee. Then, he had maintained that a quick response was required and that a Royal Commission would take too long. In December 1976, at the Second Reading of the Scotland and Wales Bill, Heath was to state that the chairmen of the Royal Commission (Lord Crowther until his death in 1972 and Lord Kilbrandon subsequently) both asked him to await their findings before proceeding with a scheme of devolution. However, in two important articles in the *Spectator* in February 1977 Geoffrey Smith noted that Kilbrandon did not recall making such a request and that no member of the Royal Commission could recall Crowther informing them of such a request.[25] Moreover, as Vernon Bogdanor has remarked, had Heath required, he could have requested the Commission to issue an Interim Report on which some immediate action could have been taken.[26]

During the Wilson Governments in the 1960s, Scotland had benefited from the extended regional policy which the Conservatives under Macmillan had inaugurated. Labour's interventionist approach, encouraging industry to set up and invest in depressed areas through measures such as Regional Employment Premium commanded little support amongst the Opposition Tories. Opposition to propping up 'lame ducks' had been voiced by the Conservatives. The Heath Government's new approach was initiated with a mini-budget in October 1970 which abolished investment grants thought to discriminate against service industries and replaced these with 'tax incentives'. These tax allowances and reductions were intended to encourage investment on new plant and machinery through a system of depreciation allowances which permitted 100 per cent accelerated depreciation allowance in development areas and 60 per cent elsewhere. Relaxation of the Industrial Development Certificate system and the Office Development Permit controls as well as the intention of abolishing Regional Employment Premium in 1974 were very much in line with the Heath Government's economic philosophy of permitting greater freedom for firms to decide where they should site their plants.

This change in emphasis from direct grants to tax incentives coupled with an emphasis on greater market freedom favoured the South-East. As one commentator remarked:

Unfortunately the recession which afflicted the economy during the early 1970s (unemployment reached the emotive figure of one million during the winter of 1971–72) depressed the motivation to invest throughout the country. It became apparent that the switch to tax incentives had been mistimed and had actually worsened the regional problem; at times of excess idle capacity, our returns and reduced liquidity, central grants were likely to have encouraged investment while tax concessions are, at best, ineffectual.[27]

Opposition to the Government's handling of the economy grew in the regions particularly hit economically. In Scotland unemployment and emigration rose to a peak in 1972. Heath's determination to curb state intervention and not to prop up 'lame ducks' proved difficult to sustain. The work-in at Upper Clyde Shipbuilders and the miners' strike for increased wages in 1972 challenged the Government's strat- gegy at its core. Public investment of £35 million in UCS, announced in February 1972 and the victory of the miners directly contradicted the basis of Heath's approach. These proved only part of a fundamental change in policy. In Spring 1972 the Government re-introduced in- vestment grants and regional development grants.

The economic background was also significant in the revival of the Nationalists. Conferences sponsored by the Scottish Trades Union Congress on unemployment in February 1972 and January 1973 pro- vided an important platform for the Nationalists. The economic situ- ation was harming the Scottish Conservatives and the SNP were able to take advantage. The March 1972 budget, the *Industry and Regional Development* White Paper published by the Department of Trade and Industry, and the consequent Industry Act, 1972 returned Govern- ment to an active regional policy. However it was a case of too little, too late, too reluctantly.

Sir William McEwen Younger, chairman of the Scottish Conserva- tive Party, had made a speech to Leith Chamber of Commerce as early as June 1972 in which he had urged state control of oil and had criticized the Government's handling of the North Sea developments. His call for a Scottish Development Fund had been ignored by the Government. Similar calls had been made by others including the former Tory Secretary of State Michael Noble and the Scottish Council (Development and Industry). By late 1973, the Heath Government was having difficulty in projecting a credible Scottish policy. It had ignored calls from within its own ranks for special measures to ensure that Scotland gained the full benefits of the North Sea developments and it had allowed devolution to slip away. From the beginning of the Middle East war, Heath's major preoccupation was, inevitably, the energy crisis. The rise in oil prices and the miners strike left no time to publish the promised Green Paper on Scottish Government. By the time of the Election in February 1974 the Tories position in Scotland was weak. It was the SNP and not Labour, who lost even more support than Tories, who benefited.

PREVARICATION AND KILBRANDON

The Conservative Government evaded and prevaricated on their devolution policy throughout Heath's period as Prime Minister. Secretary of State Gordon Campbell stated in May 1971 that the Government might publish a Green Paper after the local government reforms had been completed. The Convention would be included amongst the proposals but it would remain to be seen 'whether Parliament will approve of our ideas'.[28] Almost exactly three years after the Perth Declaration and one year after the publication of *Scotland's Government* the Tory commitment to a Convention had been reduced to an uncertain intention to include it in a discussion paper amongst other possibilities at some unspecified future date.

Meanwhile, the party in Scotland was moving away from the commitment too. At the conference in May 1973 a resolution requesting the Government to reaffirm its intention to set up the Scottish Convention was defeated by a large majority. The veteran Nationalist Wendy Wood, who had spent six days the previous December on hunger strike in an attempt to force the Government's hand on devolution, had unsuccessfully attempted to enter the conference hall. If it had been her intention to ensure that the normally placid and banal proceedings of a Scottish Tory conference should be enlivened then her presence proved unnecessary. Geoff Campbell, chairman of the Scottish Conservative Trades Union Advisory Committee and mover of the 'resolution, accused the Scottish Conservative MPs of hiding behind a Parliamentary majority in England and later, Nicholas Fairbairn, in characteristic quotable style, argued that a Scottish Assembly would not be Labour-dominated:

> Those who say so are pacifists and pinks. Who the hell is frightened of the Labour Party anyway?[29]

The answer to Fairbairn's question was implicitly given by Iain Sproat, then becoming one of the leading opponents of legislative devolution. Sproat pointed to the difficulties the Government had been having in its relations with local authorities.

> How much more difficult it is going to be to handle a Labour-dominated assembly? It would provide a splendid platform for irresponsible elements and publicity-seekers, and for extremists like Jimmy Reid.[30]

Notable statements on the issue of the Convention were made in the speeches of Gordon Campbell and Ted Heath. Campbell reiterated the promise of a Green Paper before the end of that Parliament. His cautious, non-committal approach contrasted with Heath's more forceful speech. Campbell was 'much disposed to listen to his senior civil servants and Sir Douglas Haddow, Permanent Secretary at the Scottish Office, was a 'pronounced sceptic' on devolution.[31] Heath was critical of the decision taken by the conference and maintained that the proposals for a Scottish Convention originated from the pressure of the Scottish Party conference in 1967. Referring to the Younger report, Heath said

> I pledged then and I pledge again today to give the people of Scotland genuine participation in the making of decisions that affect them, all within the historic unity of the United Kingdom.[32]

This speech at least provides some evidence that the leader was still committed to legislative devolution.

Events towards the end of the year ensured that Heath was never able to fulfil this pledge, if it had been his intention. The Yom Kippur war in the Middle East led to a quadrupling of the price of oil. This made coal a more valuable asset and placed the miners in a strong bargaining position. Also, the North Sea oil resources gave the SNP a propaganda weapon which they used effectively; this valuable commodity was presented to the electorate to refute the idea that Scotland was too poor to become independent. The publication of the Royal Commission on the Constitution on October 31 served further to bring the issue of Scotland's constitutional status to the fore. Only days after Kilbrandon reported, Margo MacDonald won a by-election in Govan for the SNP. Oil and devolution were then set to be important issues in Scottish politics at the elections in 1974.

While the Conservative Party itself gave no evidence to the Royal Commission, six members of the Bow Group presented their views which had been published as a Bow Publication in February 1971. The paper made little reference to Scotland or to legislative devolution and dealt largely with the structure of English local government, proposing a regional tier.[32]

Other bodies which were normally sympathetic to the party did give evidence, including the Scottish Chamber of Commerce. In written and oral evidence they proposed a Scottish Senate deriving its powers from local government, which bore a resemblance to the Redcliffe-Maud Commission's proposals for provincial councils for England. Questioned in the oral session by Lord Kilbrandon as to how the Senate would supervise the Scottish Office, a representative of the organisation stated that it 'could complain and it could influence by consultation'.[34]

In their written evidence, the Scottish Confederation of British Industry supported devolution though they were far from clear on what they meant by this and were equivocal on an Assembly:

> The CBI Council in Scotland has not succeeded in identifying any advantages which such an Assembly would hold out but on the other hand we cannot see that any disadvantages would be involved. It is felt however that it would add unnecessarily to the complexities and cost of Government . . . In any event, as it seems that this is more a political than an industrial problem, we have indicated our preference not to express a firm opinion.[35]

The CBI thought it wise to recommend that no decision be taken until after public reaction to the reform of local government had been gauged. In their oral evidence, the Scottish CBI were less equivocal. Their spokesman expressed concern that the Assembly would concentrate on social legislation while they wanted tax cuts. When a member of the Royal Commission suggested that it was 'not so much that you are against a separate Parliament, as that you think it unlikely the political complexion of that Parliament would suit your interests', the CBI representative concurred.[36]

Responses to Kilbrandon from Conservatives were by no means uniform. Sir William McEwen Younger was critical of proposals to abolish the post of Scottish Secretary and reduce the number of Westminster MPs, which Kilbrandon had seen as the price of an Assembly. Iain Sproat saw the Commission's rejection of separatism as the only acceptable part of its conclusions. He argued that an Assembly would lead to conflict, create another layer of administration, and diminish Scotland's influence in the British political system. Perhaps his most devastating criticisms related to the original motivation behind establishing the Royal Commission and its appeal at publication. He sensed

something ultimately phoney, something deceiving, in the concept of an Assembly that pretends in some not inconsiderable way to be a national Parliament, and yet in reality possesses only the powers of a glorified local government unit; something faintly ludicrous and disagreeable in somebody strutting about calling himself 'Prime Minister of Scotland', but with functions limited to dealing with roads, coordinating tourism etc.[37]

Lord Crowther-Hunt, one of the Commissioners, had produced a minority report in which he had doubted whether a Conservative Government would implement a scheme of devolution as suggested in the majority proposals. Nevertheless, Heath set up a committee structure, the major element of which was the Constitution Unit of the Privy Council, to consider the Kilbrandon proposals. This was to be inherited by the Labour Government.

Manifesto commitments to set up a Scottish Oil Development Fund to finance additional services in areas affected by North Sea developments, abolition of road bridge tolls, developing new sports facilities – including a new Hampden Park, the renovation and replacement of rundown housing and replacement of obsolete industry were to be, almost incredibly, 'in addition to expenditure to which Scotland as an integral member of the UK is entitled'.[38] But with the Heath Government's record of unfulfilled promises to Scotland, it was hardly surprising that Scots turned away from the Conservatives. This decline in support for the Scottish Conservatives was to be even more marked in the Election eight months later in October. From 38 per cent in 1970, the Scottish Conservative vote had fallen to 32.9 per cent in February 1974 and then to 24.7 per cent in October that year.

Conservatives in Opposition, 1974–79

The Parliament which sat between October 1974 and May 1979 was more concerned with constitutional issues than any other in the post-War period. Parliamentary sovereignty and other hallowed traditions and myths of British constitutionalism were debated to an extent unknown since the days when the Irish Question had dominated proceedings. The referendum on European Community membership, which saw collective Cabinet responsibility being temporarily abandoned, the increasing intensity of the problem of Northern Ireland, and Scotland's constitutional status were by no means the only issues to concern the Labour Government. The Yom Kippur War and quadrupling of oil prices with economically disabling consequences, exceptional inflation levels, rising unemployment and poor labour relations were other factors which made governing the United Kingdom an invidious task. The benefits of North Sea oil were to come later, after the fall of the Callaghan Government.

In Opposition the Conservative Party underwent major changes during the period. In economic policy, the new leadership of Margaret Thatcher returned the Tories to the days of Selsdon Man, Heathite moderation was ignominiously dumped. The devolution policy of the party changed too, but without the same haste which marked the changes in economic policy. In opposition in the late 1960s Heath had viewed the Nationalists as a real threat but his actions as Prime Minister suggest that he had adjusted his view following if not prior to the Election of 1970. The Elections of 1974 forced him to return to his earlier view. Mrs Thatcher seems to have had little interest in or knowledge of Scottish affairs and initially accepted the devolution policy she inherited from Heath, but gradually came to oppose vehemently any measure of legislative devolution. Though the Tories only became explicitly opposed to legislative devolution after the 1979 Election, the 1974–79 Parliament saw them lurch away from their flirtation with Scottish Home Rule.

REASSERTING SUPPORT FOR DEVOLUTION

The Heath Government's failure to act on the Home Report and its other preoccupations left it in a weak position in Scotland in 1974. The

February 1974 Election saw the SNP winning seven seats – four from the Conservatives including Moray and Nairn from the Secretary of State Gordon Campbell. The Conservatives had approached the Election promising to consider the Kilbrandon Commission's proposals.

By October the Conservative Party had been jolted into hardening its position. Alick Buchanan-Smith was appointed Shadow Scottish Secretary in February 1974 and immediately set up a committee to consider the issue. At the Scottish conference in Ayr in May an indirectly elected Assembly made up of local government councillors was accepted. Even opponents such as Iain Sproat accepted this latest reverse of policy. With the minority Labour Government likely to call an election at any time, the Conservatives could not risk open divisions especially if they hoped to prevent further losses to the SNP.

Scottish Tory conferences had vacillated in just three years from supporting a directly elected Assembly to opposing an Assembly and then to support an indirectly elected Assembly. The party's credibility on the issue following the Heath Government's inaction was severely damaged. Support for a directly elected Assembly had been voiced by Michael Ancram, newly elected MP for Berwick and East Lothian, at the 1974 conference. Buchanan-Smith left the matter of membership of the Assembly open when he addressed the conference and Heath presented his 'Charter for a New Scotland' in his address promising a Scottish Development Fund financed from North Sea oil, the removal of the Department of Energy's oil division to Scotland and the establishment of an indirectly elected Assembly with autonomy over spending Scotland's share of UK income. The Charter was more radical than his Perth Declaration, especially with the prospect of an oil fund, but it was perceived much more as a reaction to the SNP than had his 1968 speech. Buchanan-Smith's sincerity and determined efforts to rally the party around these proposals were not enough.

The election in October brought further gains for the SNP. The Nationalists won eleven seats and 30.4 per cent of the vote. The Conservatives won 16 seats with 24.9 per cent of the vote. Devolution was firmly on the agenda. Six days later Buchanan-Smith held a press conference and announced that Conservative MPs would support the Labour Government's scheme for a directly elected Assembly. Alongside the Shadow Scottish Secretary and in agreement with him were George Younger MP, Scottish chairman and the two vice-chairmen, Teddy Taylor and defeated Perth MP Ian MacArthur. There had been little consultation with the other Scottish Tory MPs. Though this was hardly remarked upon at the time, it was to develop as an issue in the internal debate on devolution which later ensued. The other initiative taken by Buchanan-Smith was the appointment of the Rifkind Committee, consisting of MPs and other party members, to investigate in detail the party's proposals for an Assembly.

The post-mortem discussions following the October election indicated that the party was in a fairly depressed mood. R. D. Kernohan, chief executive of the Scottish Central Office between 1967 and 1971, wrote that the policy and philosophy of the party was a 'mass of confusion and inconsistency'. His conclusion was pessimistic:

> in the aftermath of two lost elections they [should] consider making a virtue of necessity and accepting the end of the two party system. If they don't they might find it re-established in Scotland, but without the Tories.[1]

This view was not the exclusive property of Scottish Conservatives during the 1970s. Nevil Johnson, who acted as a constitutional adviser to Mrs Thatcher, argued for proportional representation in a book published in 1977.[2]

At the Scottish conference in May 1975 in Dundee the party voted to consider 'some reform of the electoral system' for elections to the Assembly, with the single transferable vote option preferred. A most interesting dimension to the debate was the assumption that an Assembly was now inevitable and that debate should concentrate on the constitution and powers of the body.

The mood of reform was evident in a booklet produced by Barry Henderson and Ian Lang, two party members who were to become MPs in 1979. They saw the Assembly as providing a catalyst allowing the party in Scotland to 'strike out on its own in the field of policy and to stake out a large share of the new political terrain in Scotland'.[3] They argued for 'complete autonomy' in policy formulation for the Assembly.

Malcolm Rifkind was appointed Devolution Spokesman in Scotland and argued the case for a 'new Unionism'. In an article in Q in November 1975, he echoed the views which Esmond Wright had expressed in the late 1960s by arguing that Scottish Conservatism had to relate to the needs and aspirations of modern Scotland and that devolution was in complete sympathy with basic Conservative philosophy. Scottish devolution, according to Rifkind, must be the first step towards a federal constitutional structure.[4] This was the opposite way he was to view things a decade later when he argued that England would have to have federalism before Scotland could be allowed a Parliament.

Outside Scotland, Lord Hailsham shared Rifkind's vision. The day prior to the publication of Rifkind's piece on the 'new Unionism', Hailsham argued for a constitutional conference under the nominal presidency of the Queen to work out a new constitution, the findings being put to a UK referendum.

THE RIFKIND COMMITTEE

The Rifkind Committee appointed by Buchanan-Smith reported its findings three days before publication of the Labour Government's devolution white paper 'Our Changing Democracy' in November 1975. Simultaneously, two other committees had been meeting – one under Willie Whitelaw and the other under Dundee Conservative John Berridge. The Whitelaw committee fulfilled an advisory role and met infrequently. The Scottish Conservative Policy Group under John Berridge had produced proposals early in 1975 which were published in a 'Devolution Brief'.

Berridge's proposals included an Assembly with certain revenue raising and taxation powers in addition to a block grant. The Assembly would be able to reform local government and would be elected by proportional representation with no reduction in the number of seats at Westminster. Third readings of bills would be taken in London with the executive function vested in the Secretary of State, who would be entitled to sit in the Assembly. The Assembly would scrutinize the work of the executive.

The Rifkind Committee's proposals were the last major pro-devolutionary statement of the Conservative Party. It was essentially concerned with minimizing conflict between an Assembly and London and consequently the proposed Assembly was a very weak institution. The Rifkind Assembly was to have no executive and no direct control over the block grant. A separate Scottish executive was expected to lead to making the Secretary of State a 'political eunuch'. The office of Scottish Secretary was felt to have served Scotland well for many years and it 'should not be forfeited for ephemeral gains'.

Rifkind proposed that the Secretary of State should draw his Minister of State and Parliamentary Under-Secretaries of State from the Assembly's membership. This was a most unusual proposal, as all Government Ministers are appointed by the Prime Minister, including junior Ministers. Rifkind was proposing an end to this constitutional norm and the introduction of the constitutional absurdity of a 'hybrid' executive accountable to both the Assembly and Westminster.

The proposed financial powers were almost non-existent. The Assembly would only be able to advise the Secretary of State on the allocation of a block grant the Minister would negotiate with the Treasury. In presenting the report, Michael Ancram stated that the Assembly would be empowered to use any money left over by the Secretary of State after the Scottish Office had taken what it needed for its own priorities. The proposal was as naive as it was absurd.

Similar to the Home Committee, the Rifkind Committee proposed that Scottish legislation should be considered by the Scottish body. The second, committee and report stages would be taken in the Assembly with the Government in Westminster forced to withdraw or amend legislation rejected at the second reading. This power went beyond Home's proposals, as was the power to initiate legislation, though this was to be limited by Parliament's right to reject Assembly bills, force their amendment or withdrawal. The difference was that Home had proposed Westminster to have powers to veto matters before the Assembly legislated, whereas Rifkind's proposals amounted to powers of veto after the Assembly had legislated. Under the Rifkind scheme, Parliament in London was viewed as fulfilling a similar function as the Lords, as a 'second chamber' amending and improving legislation. The assumption of a considerable degree of consensus seems, retrospectively at least, almost incredible.

The Rifkind proposals succeeded in making the Labour's devolution white paper appear almost radical. The confused and conservative proposals of the Rifkind committee amounted, at best, to strengthening the institution of a Scottish pressure group within government. Rifkind denied that pressure had been applied to the committee and that the conclusions were a moderate statement of the position he would have preferred. Discontent with the devolution policy, however, was being increasingly expressed. A charitable interpretation of the Rifkind proposals is that they were an attempt to find a compromise. In fact, they failed to appease either wing of the party.

OPPOSITION INCREASES

Not all Scottish Conservatives accepted the devolution position, and a Parliamentary debate in early February 1975 offered an opportunity for opposition to be voiced. Tam Galbraith, Betty Harvie Anderson and Michael Clark Hutchison spoke against devolution, demonstrating that Buchanan-Smith had failed to unite the troops behind his devolution policy. For the most part, 1975 was a year when the party gave support to devolution while opposition gradually built.

Amongst English MPs, the issue of devolution had simply not been considered until the SNP advances of 1974. The party's commitment to devolution had never been seen as serious until the Nationalist presence in Parliament. The increasing prospect of devolution led to opponents expressing themselves forcefully. John MacGregor, Scotsborn MP for South Norfolk, warned of creating a feeling of resentment in the English regions and suggested that Scotland was trying to have it all ways and instanced the 'over-representation' of Scotland in Parliament. George Gardiner, who became a highly active backbench opponent of Labour's devolution bills, warned that the Government would make 'English Nationalists of all of us'. Nigel Lawson went so far as to claim that Scottish devolution meant the 'oppression of England'. The voice of English nationalism was being heard and it was coming from those who were subsequently to be very close to Mrs Thatcher.

By late 1975 the Conservatives were deeply divided. In November, Tom James of the *Scotsman* suggested that Thatcher was preparing to lead the party into a major change of policy.[5] Two days before, the

Tory leader had met Scottish and Welsh MPs and left them in little doubt as to the possibility of the party voting against the second reading of the Scotland and Wales bill. Amongst Scottish MPs at that time a three-way split was evident. Five MPs, including parts of the old guard, were firmly opposed to devolution – Michael Clark Hutchison, Betty Harvie Anderson, Tam Galbraith, Ian Sproat and Teddy Taylor. Five were believed to be firmly in favour – Alick Buchanan-Smith, George Younger, Russell Fairgrieve (Scottish Chairman), Hamish Gray, and Malcolm Rifkind. The remaining six, previously seen as pro-devolution, were becoming increasingly sceptical of the benefits of an Assembly, or at least of that Assembly proposed by the Labour Government.

Party divisions were becoming increasingly visible. A remarkable instance of this was to be witnessed in the letters columns of the *Scotsman* in November 1975. Michael Ancram had been defeated in Berwick in October after serving only six months as MP, but gained the prospective Conservative candidature for South Edinburgh where the sitting MP Michael Clark Hutchison intended to retire. In a letter to the paper Ancram had criticized the backlash against devolution as the 'unconsidered reaction of a group of people who have been asleep to the realities of the devolution argument for far too long and who have just woken up.' In reply, Clark Hutchison presumed that Ancram was referring to English MPs, and if so the remarks were 'insulting and unfounded'. The sitting MP then attacked devolution as leading to the break-up of the UK and pointedly concluded his letter, 'Many of us were elected over the years on a 'Unionist ticket' including, Michael Clark Hutchison.'[6]

By the end of 1975 the official line was still to support devolution but the opponents in the party were less reticent about speaking out. Supporters, including Michael Ancram and Russell Fairgrieve, were attempting to explain dissent in the party as being of little consequence and maintained that the leadership was in no doubt about its commitment to an Assembly. However, as Labour unveiled its proposals, as English Tories woke up to the prospect of a Scottish Assembly, and as the Assembly was set in the context of the new economic orthodoxy in the party, opposition intensified.

THE THATCHER LEADERSHIP

One of the most remarkable features of Mrs Thatcher's early years as Tory leader was her apparent ambivalence regarding devolution. The Iron Lady's determination to change the party's economic policy appears to have taken precedence over all else. Her interest in Scottish affairs was negligible as was her knowledge prior to assuming the leadership in February 1975. The issue of devolution had played no part in Mrs Thatcher's election as leader. Though she was reputedly less sympathetic to devolution than her predecessor, among the

Scottish MPs who voted for her the issue would appear to have been irrelevant.

Her limited experience in Government had not included any brief which might have given her an understanding of Scottish affairs. Her period as Secretary of State for Education during the Heath Government left her with virtually no experience of Scotland, the DES remit certainly included Scottish universities but that was a doubtful example of Scottish distinctiveness.

Mrs Thatcher inherited a pro-devolution policy and initially she accepted it. One explanation may be found in the opinion polls which suggested overwhelming support for devolution. This support included considerable support amongst Scottish Tory voters. Even as late as October 1975, an opinion poll in the *Scotsman* showed that 65 per cent of the electorate favoured the Labour Government's plans for an Assembly with only 16 per cent against. Amongst intending Tory voters the proportions were similar – 61 per cent in favour, 21 per cent against, with 18 per cent recorded as 'don't know'.[7]

Any doubts about Mrs Thatcher's views on the issue seemed to be dispelled on a visit to Scotland only ten days after her election. At a rally in Glasgow she announced that the establishment of a Scottish Assembly 'must be a top priority to ensure that more decisions affecting Scotland are taken in Scotland by Scotsmen'.[8] As time went by her support waned; the priority was demoted until the party was officially hostile to devolution.

Mrs Thatcher's views on the economy were incompatible with a measure of legislative devolution or the creation of an Assembly. Though the new Tory leader condemned centralization, it would have proved very difficult for a Government to have an economic strategy strictly controlling public expenditure while simultaneously giving spending powers to a Scottish Assembly and establishing a Scottish Oil Development Fund. Creating a new legislature did not square with 'rolling back the state'.

It is unlikely that Mrs Thatcher did not envisage the difficulties her Government was to have in its relations with local government and recognise the parallel and potentially more explosive problems which might ensue with the establishment of a Scottish Assembly. It was not to be long before Mrs Thatcher's views on devolution crystalized, and her public pronouncements favouring the establishment of an Assembly came to an end.

For a period it seemed as if the Tories might set up an Assembly while simultaneously abolishing the Regional tier of local government. In a speech in Scotland in October 1976, Mrs Thatcher suggested this undoubtedly popular proposal. The newly established regions did appear to be remote and bureaucratic and an Assembly was viewed as appealing by the electorate. However, no details were given – not even as to whether the proposed Assembly would be directly or indirectly elected. That same month saw changes on the front bench of the party which suggested that the policy was changing. Teddy Taylor became Spokesman on Trade and Willie Whitelaw, who had been fairly sympathetic to the idea of an Assembly, was replaced by Francis Pym as Devolution Spokesman. Leon Brittan's appointment as junior spokesman on devolution appeared to confirm a change in policy. Anti-devolutionists including Iain Sproat interpreted Whitelaw's replacement as a small victory. However, Pym's appointment was not entirely pleasing to the diehards in the party. The new spokesman announced at a 1922 Committee executive meeting shortly after his appointment that he intended to lead the party on a 'great crusade' for Scottish devolution. The 1922 executive responded by arguing that there was little support for devolution in the party and that an anti-devolution position was steadily emerging. Whether Pym himself was initially a proponent of devolution is uncertain, but it soon became clear that the crusade was not to be. Pym was to be the main articulator of the ambiguous and procastinatory policy which was to precede the open hostility to devolution of the post-1979 period. Anti-devolutionists such as Taylor and Sproat were concerned, especially at first, that Pym was equivocal and that he was anxious not to completely rule out any prospect of devolution.

RESPONDING TO LABOUR'S PROPOSALS

The publication of the white paper 'Our Changing Democracy' in November 1975 allowed for a degree of unity in the Conservative Party. Buchanan-Smith criticised the 'clumsy procedures' for dealing with disagreements between London and the Assembly while Teddy Taylor, in characteristic style, described the white paper as 'an expensive load of rubbish', leaving Sproat to suggest that any Conservative who supported the proposals as 'insane' because an Assembly would 'condemn Scotland to socialism for ever'.

More erudite comments came from John Berridge, who had been chairing the Scottish Conservative Policy Group on Devolution. Berridge asserted that under Labour's proposals the Secretary of State would have greater powers than any other Government leader. The Secretary of State would be empowered to refuse to send a bill for Royal Assent if it was felt that it did not meet the approval of the Government in London. The Secretary of State would, according to Berridge, become 'like a second Queen – able to apppoint a chief executive from the major parties'.

The different nature of the objections to the proposals emanating from the Conservatives reflected the divisions in the party. Proponents of an Assembly disliked the powers of the Secretary of State and lack of adequate provision for the adjudication in the event of disputes between the Assembly and London. Opponents stressed the powers being proposed for the body, its cost and the difficulties that would be encountered by the Conservatives with a weak electoral base in Scotland. Debate over the Parliamentary tactics to be adopted also provided evidence of divisions. In January 1976 the Government initiated a four-day debate in Parliament. The official Opposition disagreed amongst themselves about the wording of the amendment to the motion. A month before this, Buchanan-Smith was rumoured to be considering resigning as Shadow Scottish Secretary if the amendment made no reference to a commitment to an Assembly while around 50 Tory backbenchers were thought likely to rebel against a pro-devolution amendment. Iain Sproat insisted that the election manifesto had committed the party to an indirectly elected Assembly. Whitelaw attempted to find a compromise. On January 6, a week before the debate, the Shadow Cabinet could not decide the wording of an amendment at a two hour meeting. Buchanan-Smith successfully argued for a postponement of a decision until after a meeting of the Scottish Council of the party that weekend.

During the week leading up to the special meeting of the Scottish Conservative Council in Edinburgh the pro-devolutionists refined their positions in speeches in Scotland. Rifkind presented his more detailed views on the white paper; he criticized a separate executive rivalling the Secretary of State, the failure to make the Assembly a chamber of the UK Parliament, and the failure of the Government to include proportional representation in its proposals. More important speeches were made by Scottish Chairman Russell Fairgrieve. In his West Aberdeenshire constituency, Fairgrieve stated that the real decision was between maximum and minimum devolution and 'I come down solidly for maximum'. Two days later in Dunfermline, Fairgrieve went further in explaining his idea of maximum devolution. It involved less Scottish representation at Westminster, unless England too had regional Assemblies. He stated that he was in broad agreement with the Scottish Young Conservatives who had put forward a fairly radical programme for devolution. Following Fairgrieve's speeches George Younger and Hamish Gray expressed their support for his views.

By the time of the meeting of the Central Council, four identifiable groupings in the Scottish party had emerged – a group of diehard Unionists around Iain Sproat and Betty Harvie Anderson; the Rifkind moderates who wanted a directly elected Assembly with restricted powers and no executive, with Buchanan-Smith and Ancram supporting this position; the new 'maximalist' tendency emerging around Fairgrieve, favouring direct elections to a more powerful Assembly; and, finally, the most radical group which supported what amounted to a quasi-federal, semi-autonomous scheme of devolution, which had support in the Scottish Young Conservatives but had no senior party member backing with the possible exception of Heath whose subsequent statements seemed to fit into this category. It was clear that the devolutionists were a diffuse group.

At the Central Council meeting the party voted by 103 to 60 in favour of a resolution moved by Malcolm Rifkind:

> That this Council affirms its commitment to a directly elected Scottish assembly, but condemns the Government's White Paper as unworkable and likely to lead to the disintegration of the United Kingdom, and calls on Parliament to legislate for a scheme of devolution consistent with the good government and essential unity of the UK.[9]

This fairly innocuous resolution was opposed by Teddy Taylor who urged support for an amendment which explicitly rejected a directly elected Assembly. Opponents of devolution claimed a measure of success as only 12 votes had been cast against devolution at party conference the previous May.

The official Opposition amendment to the motion on the white paper affirmed the need for a Scottish Assembly but omitted the words 'directly elected'. On the second day of the debate Iain Sproat clashed with Buchanan-Smith over this matter. The views from the Conservative benches were varied. On the final day of debate, Heath argued for a settlement similar to that being proposed by Jim Sillars' Scottish Labour Party involving Scottish autonomy within the European Community. The Home proposals, he asserted, were no longer adequate. Sir David Renton, a member of the Kilbrandon Commission, speaking from the front bench, argued for the Home proposals. Sproat argued against any measure of legislative devolution.

Around this time the idea of a referendum developed both within the Conservative and Labour parties; Teddy Taylor and Eric Heffer on opposite wings of the parties, but both anti-devolution, were advocates. In the Lords, Hailsham argued for a referendum to 'sanctify' a new written constitution and rejected Home's proposals as impractical on the grounds that 'too much water had flown under the bridge' since they were published. Home himself argued for a body stronger than his Convention and lent support to a referendum on 'separation'. The details of Home's proposals at this stage – an Assembly with limited revenue-raising powers, control of Scottish Development Agency, power to reform local government, election by proportional representation – were undoubtedly much closer to Heath's views than Thatcher's. At a private meeting at Westminster attended by about fifty Conservative MPS Home maintained that only legislating for an Assembly would prevent the return of a majority of SNP MPS at the following election. Doing nothing was not an option, he argued – a remark subsequently made frequently by Conservative spokesmen.

UNIONISM REASSERTED

The drift away from devolution was becoming clear. Buchanan-Smith had failed to convince the party of the need for a directly elected Assembly despite immense efforts. As 1976 progressed it became obvious that the anti-devolution element were in the ascendant, whatever cobbled together statements were made from the front bench.

The anti-devolutionists led by Iain Sproat were highly active. In early May Sproat announced the creation of an anti-Assembly group called 'Keep Britain United' which intended initially to organise opposition amongst MPs but ultimately to join with others in business, commerce and the trade unions. Sproat intimated his hope that it would be an all-party grouping but Keep Britain United transpired to be an almost exclusively Conservative body in Parliament, especially after leading Labour opponents of devolution, including Tam Dalyell, refused to become involved.

The formal launch of Keep Britain United took place at the Pavilion Theatre in Glasgow on May 9 with a number of senior Scottish Conservatives involved – Lord Strathclyde (former MP), Sandy Mutch (Convener of Grampian Region), Teddy Taylor MP, Willis Roxburgh (former Scottish Conservative Vice-Chairman), Alistair Warren (former editor of the *Glasgow Herald*), James Goold (Deputy Treasurer of the party in Scotland), Mary Pinkerton (Scottish Vice-Chairman), Alan Devereux (Vice-chairman of the Scottish CBI), Iain Lawson (chairman of the West of Scotland Young Conservatives) and Jim Shearer (President of Glasgow University Conservatives). Interestingly, the last three were to become active supporters of Scottish Home Rule in the 1980s. The group's most important work was, however, in Parliament where it had a fifteen strong committee including five Scottish MPs.[10] Sproat claimed support on the Tory front bench and strongly hinted that Mrs Thatcher herself was sympathetic.

The Scottish Conservative conference in May 1976 was a remarkable affair with one of the liveliest and most open debates in the party's recent history. Sir William McEwan Younger spoke strongly in favour of an Assembly and went so far as to warn the party that though the Scots did not want independence 'if complete political opposition to devolution prevails at Westminster – and a substantial proportion of English MPs are not well informed about Scottish affairs – many like myself, who do not want independence, might come in exasperation to vote in a different direction'.[11]

Opponents stressed the electoral problems Conservatives would have if an Assembly was established. Mary Pinkerton argued that by voting for the Assembly 'you are saying goodbye to a Conservative Government ever again in Scotland'. The vote on whether to support a directly elected Assembly ended amidst accusations of vote rigging. The chairman refused to take a ballot on the motion and instead declaring the resolution passed by a margin of 2–1, although Sproat insisted afterwards that the vote had been nearer 6–4. The following day, Mrs Thatcher pledged herself to a directly-elected Assembly, but with little enthusiasm.

During the months between the Scottish and UK Conservative conferences in May and October 1976 lobbying by Sproat and his colleagues intensified. English MPs were voicing concern about the commitment. Ted Heath and Sir Ian Gilmour were two of the exceptions. Speaking in Peterhead in September Heath argued that devolution stood for a Conservative principle, and Gilmour told Oxford Conservatives that diversity and decentralization were Conservative ideals.

The publication of the agenda for the Conservative conference in Brighton in October 1976 provided evidence of the concern which had developed. Of the 37 resolutions which had were submitted on devolution, most were opposed to the idea but none were chosen for debate. Devolution was to be submerged in a debate on 'People, Parliament and the Constitution'. Lord Carrington was to reply and there was no actual resolution on which a vote could be taken. Neither the pro- nor the anti-devolutionists were satisfied. The right wing Selsdon group maintained that Conservative policy was being 'dictated by a minority of the Scottish Tory party' while Jimmy Gordon, pro-devolution chairman of the Tory Reform Group, expressed regret at the lack of a debate specifically on devolution.

Unity through equivocation appeared to be the basis of the Conservative leadership's approach. But fringe meetings demonstrated the lack of unity on the policy. Whitelaw and Fairgrieve both argued for devolution while John Biffen made a significant speech later published by the Conservative Political Centre with the title 'A Nation in Doubt'. He dealt with three 'unrelated considerations' – the challenge of the IRA, the issue of immigration as it affected major English urban centres, and the 'political drama' which had led to the rise of the SNP. The end of Empire, Biffen maintained, had 'consequences on the kingdom that had been its heart' resulting in the decline in the appeal of London. Oil discoveries had been important:

> It was no longer possible to use the crude and dubious argument that the Scots were financial dependents of the United Kingdom and unable to afford the trappings of self-government.[12]

However, Biffen did not favour a measure of devolution, arguing that the question was between full self-government or Union. The actual debate on the floor of conference included strong pro-devolution speeches from Michael Hirst, Conservative candidate in East Dumbartonshire and Alistair Smith. Though the idea of an Assembly was accepted in Carrington's reply, the commitment was weak.

The following month another anti-devolution group was launched with strong Tory backing, and with Iain Sproat closely involved. The 'Scotland is British' campaign was supported financially by company contributions and had an office in Glasgow. Its chairman was Sir John Toothill, author of the 1961 report on the Scottish economy and had the support of Lord Weir, Douglas Hardie (chairman of the Scottish CBI), Mr W. Jack (chairman of the Association of Scottish Chambers of Commerce), and Adam Ferguson of 'Keep Britain United'.

The new organization was determined not to be seen as too closely connected with the Conservative party and included former Labour MP for Motherwell George Lawson amongst its members, as well as Danny Crawford (executive member of the Union of Construction, Allied Trades and Technicians), Archie Birt (a member of the short-lived 'Scrap the Assembly' Labour pressure group) and Sir George Sharp (Labour President of the Convention of Scottish Local Authorities). Despite its efforts, 'Scotland is British' was seen as a Conservative party body. As Keating and Bleiman noted:

> for many of the anti-devolutionists on the left of the [Labour] party, it smacked too much of the Scottish Conservative establishment and, indeed, looked uncomfortably like the pro-EEC umbrella group which had out-campaigned and out-spent them in 1975.[13]

Though the party was returning to its traditional Unionist position, the diehards around Sproat were causing the leadership, particularly Whitelaw, embarrassment. Whitelaw and Chief Whip Humphrey Atkins felt that Sproat and his colleagues were undermining the delicate balance the leadership were attempting to achieve between opposing the Government's proposals and claiming adherence to the principle of devolution.

Any doubts remaining about the drift away from devolution were dispelled with the decision to oppose the second reading of the Scotland and Wales Bill in December 1976. The shadow Cabinet met on December 1, two days after the publication of the Bill, and decided to oppose the bill with a three-line whip at second reading. This was despite the statements early on in the Parliament by Buchanan-Smith that the Tories would support Labour's measure of devolution. The decision had been agreed only narrowly – nine members of the Shadow Cabinet favoured the three line whip opposing the bill and seven were opposed.[14]

The day after the shadow Cabinet meeting Buchanan-Smith, George Younger, Malcolm Rifkind, Hamish Gray, Hector Munro and John Corrie met Mrs Thatcher and Atkins to make known their opposition to the three-line whip and appeal for dispensation from shadow Cabinet collective responsibility for Buchanan-Smith. A week later Buchanan-Smith and Malcolm Rifkind resigned from the front bench. Hector Munro, an Energy spokesman, John Corrie,

Scottish Whip, and Russell Fairgrieve, Scottish Chairman, all offered their resignations, but these were refused by Mrs Thatcher. In Scotland, Conservative devolutionists including Brian Meek and Bill Aitken warned of the consequences for Tory support. Heath and Home both supported the right of devolutionists to abstain on the measure. The appointment of Teddy Taylor as Shadow Scottish Secretary marked a decisive turning point for the party. Whatever pronouncements on devolution were to be made, there could be little doubt that Taylor was a vehement opponent of devolution.

The Scotland and Wales Bill proposing the establishment of Assemblies in both Scotland and Wales could justifiably have been opposed by the Tories on the grounds that they were unequivocally opposed to Welsh devolution. The Bill passed second reading on December 13, 1976 by 292 votes to 247 following the Government concession of a referendum on the issue. Buchanan-Smith, speaking from the backbenches, made an emotional appeal for an Assembly and argued that the Opposition should spell out its alternative if they were to oppose the bill. Heath also spoke in favour of the second reading in terms of his 'record of the last ten years'. However, the Conservative front-bench was unwilling to explain its alternative. Neither Thatcher nor Taylor mentioned Conservative support for an Assembly in their speeches.

Seventy MPs defied the instructions of the whips – five Tories voted with the Government (Alick Buchanan-Smith, Hamish Gray, David Knox, David Mudd, and Malcolm Rifkind) while forty abstained. Ten of the sixteen Scottish Conservatives did not follow the whips but the previous hard-core devolutionists were reduced to three with George Younger and Russell Fairgrieve abstaining rather than voting for the second reading. At second reading it had been the devolutionists who had voted against the Tory whips but in committee the Union Flag Group of Diehard Unionists were to irritate the leadership.

Union Flag had been formed out of the fifteen strong Parliamentary committee of Keep Britain United. The group claimed to consist of forty Conservative MPs with a further twenty supporters and met twice weekly to draft amendments and discuss tactics. At its first meeting three secretaries were chosen – Iain Sproat, Scottish secretary; George Gardiner, as English secretary; Ian Grist, Welsh secretary. Amongst the MPs who became involved was Betty Harvie Anderson who resigned as Deputy Speaker in order to play an active part. The involvement of former Minister Graham Page was important given his acknowledged expertise in drafting amendments as were the organisational skills of Marcus Kimball, who acted as an unofficial whip for the group.

A Committee of the Whole House considered the Bill. A study of this stage highlighted the extent of activity of the Union Flag Group. Out of a total of 1062 amendments tabled, 338 were proposed by the

Union Flag Group and only 45 (4 per cent) by the Conservative Front Bench. Union Flag's amendments were 'more robust and radical than those of the front bench'.[15] Only 10 amendments were moved by Conservative devolutionists. A Conservative whip attended meetings of the group but there was little if any attempt to restrain the Diehards. Mrs Thatcher let it be known that discipline would be slackened, evidently in reaction to the damage following Buchanan-Smith's resignation. But it was the diehards who benefited from this relaxation of discipline.

The slow progress forced the Government to speed things up after only three clauses had been debated by placing a guillotine motion before the House. The vote on the guillotine was taken on February 22 1977 and the Government was defeated by 312 votes to 283. The Scotland and Wales Bill was effectively dead. The Union Flag had obviously been important in frustrating attempts to pass the Bill. On this crucial vote there was little sign of a Tory rebellion. Alick Buchanan-Smith and David Knox abstained and Heath was conveniently abroad. Part of the reason may have been a speech the weekend prior to the vote by Pym in which the Conservative devolution spokesman suggested that a constitutional convention should meet to investigate whether broad agreement could be reached. Pym's suggestion was backed by Malcolm Rifkind and Liberal leader David Steel.

The vote was important not only in killing off the proposed legislation but in dispelling a number of myths. It had been assumed by some commentators and politicians that the demise of the bill would result in a tremendous backlash in Scotland. On December 13 1976, Michael Foot had warned of Northern Ireland-type violence if the devolution proposals were rejected by Parliament. Expectations of marches and demonstrations, if not an uglier form of protest, were not fulfilled and three days after the vote Teddy Taylor remarked, with relish but not without some justification, that the supposed 'turmoil, strife, frustration, rage, indignation, and potential civil insurrection' had simply failed to materialize. Conservative opponents of devolution felt that the depth of feeling on the issue was not such as to require them to maintain the pretence of support any issue.

The Scotland Act and Referendum

After the defeat of the Scotland and Wales Bill, a vote of confidence was secured by the Labour Government by a majority of 24 with the help of the Liberals. Polls suggested that Mrs Thatcher was set to become Britain's first woman Prime Minister but the Lib-Lab pact postponed her arrival in Downing Street. A condition of the pact was a second attempt at legislating for devolution, though it seems inconceivable that Callaghan would not try again, whatever demands were made by the Liberals. The Scotland Bill appeared in November 1977. Only four Conservative Members rebelled against Mrs Thatcher's three-line whip at second reading and only two abstained on a guillotine motion. The devolutionists were either significantly reduced in strength or silenced by the prospect of a convention.

Of the 638 amendments about 500 were not debated. A number of significant victories were scored against the Government. The declaratory first clause referring to the 'unity of the United Kingdom or the supreme authority of Parliament to make laws for the United Kingdom or any part of it' was deleted. The 'Grimond Amendment' and the '40 per cent rule' were, however far more important. The first was moved by Jo Grimond, Liberal Member for Orkney and Shetland and permitted the Northern Isles to opt out of devolution. Though moved by Grimond, it was supported by Tories, who, of course, supported it as a wrecking amendment. Grimond rather naively accepted the passing interest in his constituency without really questioning the motives of those on the Tory benches.

The '40 per cent rule' or 'Cunningham amendment' was crucial in the final demise of Labour's devolution proposals, though it did not appear so important at the time. Once more, Conservative support was important though the amendment was moved by Labour Member George Cunningham. The amendment stated that if it appeared to the Secretary of State that 'less than forty per cent of the persons entitled to vote in the referendum have voted *Yes* . . . he shall lay before Parliament the draft of an Order-in-Council for the repeal of this Act'.

The origins of the 40 per cent rule are uncertain, with anti-devolutionists in both the Labour and Conservative Parties claiming credit for it. The precise role of Union Flag members is unclear. Iain Sproat has claimed that the idea of a minimum vote requirement was initially his, but that he realized that it stood a better chance of success if it was proposed by a Labour Member, especially as Union Flag were perceived as being on the right of the Conservative party. George Cunningham has denied this in one of the very few comments he has been willing to make on the subject:

> Whether or not the 40 per cent rule was discussed by Conservative anti-devolutionists I would not know. Presumably it must have been discussed by them after the amendment had been tabled but I am extremely doubtful whether it would be discussed by them before that. Certainly, so far as I and other Labour Members were concerned, this was an initiative which came from ourselves – basically Robin Cook, Bruce Douglas-Mann and myself – and not from any Conservative.'

Cook corroborates this and insists that he had no contact with Conservative backbenchers but Douglas-Mann maintains that there was 'no doubt, some coordination between some members of the Labour opponents of devolution and the Conservatives'.[2] The fact that Cunningham was seen shaking hands with George Gardiner immediately after the vote certainly fuelled suspicions, and the idea that no cooperation existed seems most unlikely. Cooperation was noted by many sources including journalists and MPs and it is almost inconceivable that such implacable opponents of devolution as Cunningham, Cook, Douglas-Mann, Gardiner and Sproat would not have joined forces.

The Lords proved effective opponents. Amendments in the Upper House were not so controversial as those passed in the Commons but taken as a whole amounted to the emasculation of an already weak measure. Challenging the Lords amendments was not, of course, impossible but it was time-consuming and the Labour Government was contemplating an election in the Autumn of 1978 with the Scotland Act on the statute books. Labour's precarious Parliamentary position gave strength to the Lords where the Conservatives put their in-built majority to effect. This and the probable failure of the Government to gain enough support in the Commons – including from its own backbenches – meant that the Scotland Bill was left largely as it was when it returned from the Lords. Royal Assent was given on July 31, 1978.

PYM AND THE SCOTTISH CONVENTION

The deliberate policy of ambivalence which was pursued shortly after Francis Pym became devolution spokesman was designed principally to retain unity in the party. Pym's proposal of a constitutional convention amounted to a strategy of obfuscation and prevarication. Between February 1975 and Pym's enunciation of support for a Convention in February 1977 the Tories floundered about. Clearly moving away from the commitment to devolution but with an eye on the polls, the party was deeply divided. Opinion polls continued to show substantial support for the measure in Scotland, though not in Britain as a whole. During 1977 the convention idea evolved as the Conservative alternative to the Scotland Bill. The Scottish conference heard demands from devolutionists and diehards for the party to be more explicit about the constitutional option it favoured but on the whole, the membership was content with Pym's articulation of the need for a convention.

Debate continued within the party. Buchanan-Smith wrote two articles published in the *Scotsman* in May 1977 outlining his personal preference for an Assembly with an executive, financed by block grant but with discretionary powers to raise or lower taxes by a certain percentage, and a bill of rights governing the relations between the Assembly and the citizen with similar Assemblies for Wales and Northern Ireland and eventually for England. Essentially, Buchanan-Smith's proposals for Scotland were similar to that offered to Northern Ireland in the 1922 Government of Ireland Act.

In late November he was involved in the creation of a cross-party body (though it excluded the SNP) called the 'Alliance for an Assembly' with Russell Johnston, Donald Dewar and Jimmy Milne of the STUC. Milne, a Communist Party member, saw it as 'providing a platform for Alick' to appeal to Conservative devolutionists.[3]

The October 1977 Conservative conference in Blackpool debated a rather general motion on the constitution but, as at the Scottish conference in May, leading protagonists on either side of the devolution debate were not called. Sixty-four motions had been submitted though not all were directly concerned with devolution. In his reply, Pym once more repeated his call for a constitutional convention 'to thrash out practical ways of bringing about a genuine improvement in the government of our country as it affects Scotland and the whole of the United Kingdom'.

On 6 February 1978 Pym again spoke on the theme of a convention in Edinburgh. Whereas his initial suggestion a year before had envisaged a convention spending six months deliberating on the constitution, Pym now regarded the procedure as likely to take longer, perhaps up to three years. It was important that time be taken and the 'right answer' was found, according to Pym, pursuing an argument which ran directly contrary to the Conservative position of a decade before when Heath had insisted on instant action on an Assembly.

Pym suggested that four basic choices could be envisaged for discussion by the convention; the status quo, an inquisitorial and scrutinizing Assembly, a quasi-federal system, and independence. The status quo, as defined by Pym, included changes within the system such as establishing a Select Committee of Scottish MPs or widening the remit of the Scottish Grand Committee. Pym had least to say about independence, of which he was unsurprisingly highly critical. The major problem of the quasi-federal system was that the English and Welsh did not want it, he maintained.

In June 1978 Pym further outlined his proposals for a convention in the *Scotsman*. He altered the positions to be considered by excluding independence. Three options were now to be available to the convention. The first was to strengthen the committee system in Parliament with the possibility of a Scottish Select Committee 'with its own research staff and with sub-committees in every sphere of Scottish Office responsibility'. The committee could examine proposed legislation, call Ministers, civil servants, heads of nationalized industries and public bodies before it. Additionally, the Scottish Grand Committee might meet weekly. The second option involved an Assembly 'separately elected in Scotland, to take over this scrutinizing role in Scotland' which would otherwise be done by a Select Committee. The third option was that of a 'quasi-federal system whereby the UK Parliament retained full sovereignty while subordinate Assemblies in each of Scotland, Wales, Northern Ireland and England were granted concurrent powers to legislate in certain fields'.

In the second article Pym outlined three conditions which would have to be met before a Scottish Assembly was set up: there would have to be 'an acceptance by the English of the position of Scots MPs or an acceptance by the House of Commons of MPs having different powers', there had to be a clear division of powers, and finally, new procedures to improve government would be necessary.

Pym's identification of the problems associated with Scottish MPs at Westminster after a Scottish Assembly was not new. Labour MP Tam Dalyell had been raising it with typical repetitiveness in debates – so much so that the matter became dubbed the 'West Lothian Question', in reference to his constituency. It was also a matter raised a century before in debates on Irish Home Rule. A. V. Dicey in *England's Case Against Home Rule* raised the issue in 1886. Though Pym referred to the issue he made no attempt to consider a response.

On September 10 1979 Pym laid out his views in the fifth major speech on devolution that year. The 39-page text with appendices of fourteen pages included yet another revision of the options which a constitutional convention might consider. Four possibilities were now available: a change in the procedures of Parliament, an inquisitorial Assembly, a scheme of executive and legislative devolution and a quasi-federal solution. The text implied a preference for the inquisitorial Assembly while seeming to accept that quasi-federalism was necessary given the rise in expectations of the Scottish people. The paper was lengthy and reformist in tone. Even a *Scotsman* editorial the following Monday praised the Tory speech, albeit guardedly.

However, ulterior motives may have lain behind this more reformᴌst speech. The Conservative leadership wanted the SNP to oppose the Queens Speech and thereby help cause an election. A fortnight later in Dumfries, Pym called on the SNP to support the official Opposition in this and went so far as to name March 22 1979 as the date for a referendum in the event of a Conservative victory. The Conservative devolution spokesman also swore that if forty per cent of the electorate voted 'Yes' then the Tory Government 'certainly would recommend to Parliament that the Assembly should go ahead'. It was not at all clear how this fitted in with his proposals for a Convention, but it showed how eager the Tories were for an election.

THE OFFICIAL CONSERVATIVE CAMPAIGN

It is difficult to determine exactly when the referendum campaign began. The major efforts were concentrated into the three or four weeks before the vote on March 1, 1979, but in many ways the campaign had actually begun early during the 1974–79 Parliament. The issue dominated Scottish politics after the 1975 referendum on European Community membership. John Mackintosh had been correct to warn that boredom might kill devolution.[4] From 1975, after the publication of the Government's white paper on devolution, a noticeable polarization by party of voting intentions on devolution became apparent.[5] Opinion polls had consistently shown support for some measure of self-government but this dwindled away by the time of the referendum. While a sharp decline in support occurred in the few weeks of the campaign some of the explanations can be traced further back. Few would doubt that the 'No' side were by far the more successful campaigners and there is a strong possibility that had there been a few more days then a majority 'No' vote might have been recorded.

The Conservatives were the only party to campaign officially against the Assembly. The Scottish conference in May 1978 voted overwhelmingly to 'campaign vigorously' for a 'No' vote in the referendum. Unlike the previous year, the major protagonists contributed to the debate and nineteen speakers were called. The Argyll prospective candidate, John McKay moved the resolution with other speakers including Iain Lawson, Nicholas Fairbairn and Adam Ferguson, employing familiar anti-devolution arguments. Impassioned pleas were made by Buchanan-Smith and Struan Stevenson of Kyle and Carrick District Council to reject the resolution. Buchanan-Smith's reminder that the Tories had once been the proponents of devolution was not warmly received.

Around fifty people attended a fringe meeting at the conference which launched the Scottish Tory Reform Group. Alick Buchanan-Smith was closely associated with the group, though he never actually joined, and addressed its inaugural meeting. Despite its decidedly pro-devolution appearance the group was not explicitly devolutionist and Buchanan-Smith made it clear that he would have no association with it if it became a devolutionist front in the party. This was the only formal grouping of Conservatives which came close to being a pro-devolutionist lobby until the final week of the referendum campaign.

Few Conservative opponents considered that campaigning for a 'No' vote was compatible with supporting devolution. Francis Pym, replying to the debate, urged support for the resolution though, once more, proposing the alternative of a constitutional convention. Though the message from the floor of the conference was that a 'No' vote should be interpreted as a vote against the principle of devolution the message from the platform suggested the opposite.

In late 1978 'Scotland Says No,' a cross-party body, was established. This was a largely Conservative-inspired and dominated body. The death of George Lawson deprived 'ssn' of a valuable Labour figure to give it wider credibility. The joint chairmen of 'ssn' were former Labour Lord Advocate Lord Wilson of Langside (who voted Conservative in 1979 and later joined the Social Democrats) and Rev. Dr Andrew Herron, a former moderator of the Church of Scotland. 'ssn' replaced the 'Scotland is British' campaign and deliberately set out to appear less dominated by the Conservative Party. Just before its launch there was some embarrassment when it became known that the organization had been forced to replace its campaign manager and press officer because of the need to dilute its Tory image. The new manager had been a Conservative agent and the press officer also had connections with the Conservatives. Whoever had initially been intended to fill these posts must have been very much more involved with the party.

The formal launch of the Conservative campaign took place on October 11. In a letter to constituency associations in December Russell Sanderson, Scottish Conservative President, explained the strategy to be adopted as agreed by the party's central council in Motherwell on November 4. There were to be three basic parts to the approach adopted. The party would campaign for a 'No' vote 'on the understanding that some members may wish to vote "Yes", the party would co-operate with "Scotland Says No", and constituency associations would be encouraged to establish "Vote No" committees'. It was made clear that party members could quite properly vote 'Yes' without fear of expulsion or any action being taken against them. Sanderson stressed that the Tories were opposed to the Scotland Act but not to the principle of devolution.[6]

The campaign really lifted off in the new year. On January 8 1979 a group of Young Conservatives launched 'Scottish Young Conservatives Say No' backed by Iain Lawson and the rather old Young Conservative Teddy Taylor. There was a determined effort to woo younger voters to vote 'No' through this organization as well as the

'Student Campaign Against the Devolution Act' formed by Brian Monteith, chairman of the Federation of Conservative Students. It was thought that young people would be more inclined to support the Assembly and it was for this reason that deliberate attempts were made to enlist this section of the population through student and Young Conservative organisations.

A survey of 63 Conservative constituency associations conducted by the *Scotsman* in mid-January sought to determine the level of opposition activity. Fifteen constituencies were reported to have declared that they were refusing to commit their organizations to active participation on either side and were not setting up local 'No' campaigns.[7] These fifteen were:

Caithness and Sutherland	Perth and East Perthshire
Central Fife	North Lanark
Dundee East	Inverness
Glasgow Pollok	East Aberdeenshire
North Angus and Mearns	East Edinburgh
Berwick and East Lothian	Central Dunbartonshire
Edinburgh Pentlands	East Fife
Moray and Nairn	

Various reasons were given for their decisions. In some seats lost to the SNP it was thought likely to be electorally damaging to campaign against devolution. While the prospective candidates in some of these seats announced their intention to vote 'No' they immediately made clear their support for an all-party conference or even an Assembly of some other kind. For some constituencies there was a feeling that resources should not be used in the run-up to a General Election. East Dundee's constituency association contained a number of senior members who were devolutionists. In both North Angus and Mearns and Pentlands the sitting MPs – Buchanan-Smith and Rifkind – were committed to voting 'Yes'. Galloway, Banff and East Aberdeenshire were more intent on winning the seats back from the SNP and were anxious to keep their opposition to an Assembly to a very low key. Glasgow Pollok was one of the few areas in Glasgow in which Conservative pro-devolution literature was distributed and included some active supporters. The fear of causing internal disunity, alienating Conservative voters and using up resources with an election pending played a major part in decisions where it was decided not to embark on the course urged by headquarters.

Speaking to Conservative candidates at Anstruther in Fife on January 13, Francis Pym laid out the Tory intentions in the event of a 'No' vote. He made clear that devolution would be a low priority in a Conservative Government's programme and that it would take three years after the election of a Conservative Government to get a new devolution bill through Parliament. A constitutional conference would take within six months to present its conclusions and the

House of Commons would indicate its preference for a particular scheme. Any settlement would have to be within the context of the United Kingdom. There were obvious strains in the Conservative campaign. Those inclined towards support for legislative devolution preferred to stress the commitment to an all-party conference and the need for a better bill and concentrated their attacks on the defects and specifics of the Scotland Act while diehards argued vehemently against devolution in any form. Teddy Taylor directed the campaign from the centre. His uncompromising approach was not welcomed by the few devolutionists in the party's hierarchy. As the campaign progressed Taylor almost completely ignored the constitutional convention. This made all the more valid Buchanan-Smith's warning that Scotland was being offered the Scotland Act or nothing.

LORD HOME'S INTERVENTION

Buchanan-Smith's task of overcoming Conservative loyalty and convincing Tory devolutionists to vote 'Yes' had a major setback on February 14. Former Conservative Prime Minister and party elder statesman Lord Home addressed a meeting at Edinburgh University urging voters to vote 'No'. Home had been the chairman of the committee which a decade before drew up *Scotland's Government*, and had consistently been viewed as a devolutionist since that time. His speech was seen by some Conservative devolutionists as the single most important event to aid the 'No' campaign. Helen Millar of Glasgow Pollok has described his intervention as having a 'powerful, indeed devastating effect on Scottish Tory voters'.[8]

Home concentrated his attention on James Callaghan's launch of Labour's campaign when the Prime Minister had argued that the referendum offered Scots a last chance for devolution. Home categorically rejected this. In declaring his intention to vote 'No', he made clear that he saw this as the only way to ensure that Parliament would correct the defects in the Scotland Act. He outlined five major faults in the Act. First, he felt that an Assembly should raise a proportion of its own revenue. Second, he was critical of the situation whereby Scottish MPs could vote on English bills while no MPs would have a say in devolved Scottish affairs. Home's third criticism of the proposed Assembly was its size. He felt that one hundred members would probably be more than enough and that the 142 proposed would lead to a serious danger of 'over-government'. Fourth, Home was critical of the lack of any machinery by which a bill could be defined as a purely Scottish measure before it was introduced on the floor of the Assembly. His final criticism concerned the system of elections. He favoured the introduction of a system of proportional representation. These points, with the exception of the size of the Assembly membership, were made by Home during second reading and committee stages of the Scotland Bill in the Lords. He had then felt that the West Lothian Question was 'not one of enormous importance'.[9] He had appeared very concerned about the matter of whether Scottish Assembly bills were *intra* or *extra vires* and had been behind an amendment moved by Viscount Dilhorne in respect of this which was withdrawn. During debates on the Bill he had also been a keen supporter of proportional representation and tax-raising powers for the Assembly. His Parliamentary record seemed to confirm that he was a sincere devolutionist.

In his Edinburgh University speech, Home proposed the creation of a Speaker's Conference to deal with constitutional change and suggested three possible alternatives to the Act. His first suggestion was that Scottish MPS at Westminster could form an Assembly. Another possibility was the Northern Ireland model which, but for the religious strife, he felt 'had a lot of merit'. Home's final suggestion was federalism. This part of his speech annoyed devolutionists most. It was at this point that he called for a 'No' vote in order to get a more powerful Scottish Assembly and he stated that he would hesitate to vote 'No' if he thought that the parties would not keep devolution 'at the top of their priorities'.

His speech was very much in the manner of the elder statesman, including a reference to 'the parties' in an attempt to be seen to be above party politics. However, he had made little attempt to argue the case for federalism within the Conservative party during the late 1970s and has remained publicly silent on the issue of devolution since the referendum. Whether it was party loyalty, a cynical attempt to ditch the issue of devolution or a sincere and naive statement of his views is unclear. Whatever motivation lay behind Home's intervention, there is little doubt that his speech was the most important made by anyone during the referendum campaign.

Subsequently, Home has maintained that the SNP presence in Scotland prevented the correct atmosphere in which the issue of devolution could be raised. This implausible argument ignores the fact that it took SNP pressure to bring the issue to the fore. It also ignores the fact that during the years of Conservative Government in the early 1980s the SNP languished at the bottom of the polls and suffered internal divisions which offered the kind of opportunity which Home felt was necessary for considering and implementing devolution. The early 1980s were not at all dissimilar to the years of the Heath Government – years when Home was a senior Government Minister – which had failed to implement his proposals set out in 1969.

A direct consequence of Home's speech was the establishment of the 'Consevative Yes Campaign'. Two Glasgow Conservatives were behind the organisation – Helen Millar of Pollok and Ron Aitken, a former secretary of the Young Conservatives in Cathcart. CYC was a desperate attempt to mitigate the damage done by Home's speech and to convince Conservative voters that it was not disloyal to vote 'Yes'. It was a very small organization financed by personal donations and with little time to organize its campaign.

On February 27, ten Scottish Conservatives stood up to be counted as 'Yes' voters in a further attempt to stop the drift of Conservative support to the 'No' position evident in opinion polls. Alick Buchanan-Smith was joined at a press conference by Malcolm Rifkind, Ron Aitken, Helen Millar, Geoff Campbell (Chairman of the Scottish Conservative Trade Unionists) as well as five Tory councillors – Brian Meek, John Mair, Christine Campbell, Struan Stevenson and James Gilchrist. Buchanan-Smith gave six reasons why Conservatives should vote 'Yes' – a belief in decentralization, the diffusion and dispersal of power; belief in democratic control and the accountability of Ministers and scrutiny of civil servants; belief that the constitution was a living organism; belief that 'change is our ally, it is not to be ignored or blocked or frustrated, but turned to the cause of better government of the people'; belief in the need for a lively political awareness of the needs and aspirations of ordinary people; and a belief in One Nation, that the 'major strength of the United Kingdom is the variety of the different parts within it, and that each part should be allowed to make its own particular contribution to the strength of the whole'. Buchanan-Smith's views were clearly Disraelian and re-formist, reflecting the devolutionist wing within the Conservative Party.

In contrast, the anti-devolution campaign of the Conservatives was slick, professional, well-financed and presented sharp messages. With simple, highly effective slogans the Conservatives claimed that an Assembly would mean 'More Taxes', 'More Bureaucracy', 'Another Tier of Government' and would place Scotland on the 'slippery slope to separatism'. Teddy Taylor argued that rates would soar because, other than the block grant, the only source of revenue for the Assembly would be its control over the Rate Support Grant. This, he maintained, would be reduced thus forcing local authorities to put rates up in order to maintain services. Iain Sproat often used the argument that the Assembly would be dominated by the Glasgow conurbation and the hard left. This conflation of the numerical domi-nance of Greater Glasgow and the 'Red Clydeside' myth was, effec-tively, used to frighten voters.

Young Conservatives produced some imaginative and amusing stickers and leaflets which were mainly distributed in student quar-ters. The Federation of Conservative Students was then almost the only branch of Scottish Conservatism to adopt New Right thinking. Its slogans were typical of undergraduate humour – trivial but with a trace of wit. 'Rock Against Devolution' was a parody of the left-wing Anti-Nazi League's campaigns. 'Devolution is boring' and 'Nice girls say NO' spoke for themselves. One strange leaflet produced by a

Gloucester firm for the FCS displayed a map of Britain and Ireland, though excluding the Western and Northern Isles, surrounded by the words, 'Compassion – Democracy – Freedom – Leadership – Opportunity' with the words 'One Nation' running across the map; this will have surprised the citizens of Eire if nobody else.

On the eve of the referendum Margaret Thatcher had stated categorically that a 'No' vote would not mean that the devolution question would be buried. Francis Pym had spent much energy arguing that a Conservative Government would set up a constitutional convention to consider various options. The Conservative message was clear; A 'No' vote would not be interpreted as opposition to devolution.

THE INCONCLUSIVE RESULT

The only conclusion which can be drawn from the referendum result is that it was inconclusive. On a 63.8 per cent turnout, 51.6 per cent voted Yes. The 40 per cent rule caused immense confusion. Devolutionists had argued that abstentions would be counted as 'No' votes and their opponents maintained that this claim had deflated their potential vote. The unpopularity of the Labour Government, the 1978–79 Winter of discontent, Home's intervention, the 40 per cent rule all served to confuse the issue. Bochel, Denver and Macartney in *The Referendum Experience* see the exercise as a success as evidenced by the turnout, the intensity of public debate, the smooth working of the polling and counting arrangements, and that the question was decided 'on its merits'.[10] This entirely misses the point. As an exercise in public consultation the referendum was a failure, given that nothing conclusive can be interpreted from the result about the views of the Scottish people at that time on the subject under discussion.

It is difficult to assess the importance of the Conservative Party in the achievement of a large 'No' vote but as they were alone amongst the major parties to oppose devolution they must be credited with much of the success. This was probably because of their opposition to devolution rather than the obverse being true, i.e., that high levels of support for the Tories led to substantial support for the 'No' side. Conservatives were doing well in the opinion polls at the time. An ORC poll published on Monday, February 19 showed Tory support in Scotland at 38 per cent – level with Labour – and the SNP a poor third with half the support of the others and the Liberals struggling with 5 per cent. *The Scotsman* noted the importance of the poll in their headline – 'Tories hold the key to March 1st vote'.[11] The electorate viewed strikes and industrial relations as the most important issues (50 per cent) followed by unemployment (32 per cent) with devolution seen as a priority by only 5 per cent of Scots.

The referendum result left the Callaghan Government in a difficult predicament. As the 'Yes' side failed to receive the support of over 40 per cent of the electorate, the Secretary of State was obliged to move

The Referendum Result, March 1, 1989

	% of votes cast	% of official electorate
YES	51.6	32.8
NO	48.4	30.8
ABSTENTION		36.4
TURNOUT		63.6

Referendum Voting Intention by Party

	Jan. 8–20 per cent Yes	Jan. 29–Feb. 6 per cent Yes	Feb. 23–25 per cent Yes
Conservatives	46	32	21
Labour	68	58	66
SNP	95	91	91

Source: System Three opinion polls

the repeal order on the Act. The substantial opposition to the Scotland Act within the Parliamentary Labour Party meant that the whips could not ensure that Labour MPs would vote against repeal. George Cunningham maintained that there were at least a hundred Labour backbenchers prepared to disobey the whips and support repeal. Callaghan himself has accepted that it was his own party which caused the greatest difficulties; Labour's rebellious ranks, rather than the SNP, ensured the defeat of the Callaghan Government.[12] The SNP attempted to put pressure on the Government to move the repeal order knowing that there was no prospect of a Conservative Government supporting a measure of devolution. The Nationalists threatened a motion of no confidence if the Labour Government failed to move the repeal order.

Callaghan refused to move the repeal and called the bluff of the Nationalists, no doubt assuming that the SNP would not bring down the Government and force an Election at which they would suffer heavy losses. The outcome was a no confidence motion which was passed by 311 votes to 310 on March 28. The resulting General Election saw the election of Margaret Thatcher and the loss of nine of the eleven SNP seats. Devolution had not featured greatly in the Election. The SNP accused the Labour Party of failing to fulfil its 1974 manifesto commitment and refusing to move the repeal order. Labour accused the SNP of bringing down the Labour Government and letting Mrs Thatcher into Downing Street.

In retrospect it seems to have been a major error on the part of the 'Yes' side to base their assumptions on opinion polls which suggested overwhelming support for legislative devolution. The Conservative campaigners were correct in their assumption that the 'Yes' vote would certainly fall as the referendum approached. Once the

campaign intensified during the final month leading up to the referendum the 'No' side were convinced that slippage would occur in
support for devolution. This, it was felt, would be pyschologically
advantageous. The belief that a fairly large early dent could be made
in the pro-devolutionist support was based on the belief that devolution supporters were a fairly diverse set of people seeking many
different things, that support for an Assembly was relatively 'soft'
and largely ignorant of the details of the Act which, once explained,
would lead many supporters to change their allegiance.

Additionally, from the Conservatives point of view, it was felt that
there would be a substantial 'No' vote, though perhaps not a majority
against the Act, which would certainly be greater than their share of
the vote at the previous election. In a party system in which the
Conservatives were competing with three other parties for votes, it
was recognised that as the only party officially campaigning for a 'No'
vote they would be able to cream off many 'No' voters come the
Election which had to take place within seven months of the referendum. The pro-devolution Conservatives had always argued within
the party that to campaign against devolution would be electorally
suicidal. However, opponents countered this by maintaining that no
additional support would come the way of the Conservatives if they
joined the other parties in supporting devolution but much would be
gained by campaigning against devolution. Confirmation of the Conservative anti-devolutionists' assumptions appeared evident in an
opinion poll on February 19 showing support for the party lying at 38
per cent – higher than any previous, or subsequent polls.

The Thatcher Years

The election of Margaret Thatcher in May 1979 saw an increase in the Conservatives' support in Scotland from 24.7 per cent to 31.4 per cent and brought with it a net gain of six seats. Seven seats lost to the SNP in 1974 were regained but Teddy Taylor, Shadow Scottish Secretary, lost his Glasgow Cathcart seat to Labour. As the results came in it soon became clear that while Mrs Thatcher would have a healthy majority, it was Labour's night in Scotland. A situation very similar to that of 1970 emerged, with Labour remaining the largest party in Scotland with 41.5 per cent of the vote and 44 MPs.

Margaret Thatcher had been elected on a platform resembling Ted Heath's Selsdon Manifesto. Scotland had played a major part in forcing Heath into a U-turn. But Margaret Thatcher was determined that she would not be brought down by the unions or submit to pressure from recalcitrant local authorities. Mrs Thatcher saw only one lesson in the Heath years. The failure to stick to his policies had been the reason, in her mind, for Heath's downfall. However, the 'Thatcherite' or 'New Right' ideology associated with this interpretation of the earlier Conservative Government did not dominate her first Cabinet.

There may be disagreement on the aims and motives of Thatcherism and just how radical the changes have really been, but after ten years certain features are discernible. Change in the Thatcher years has been evolutionary; there was never an intention to enter on a frenetic 'first hundred days' of radical changes. It would not have been possible – her Cabinet, the civil service and, arguably, the party would not have permitted this. The gradual consolidation of her base in the Cabinet, the party, the higher echelons of the civil service and beyond has been a feature of Thatcherism. Policies have developed in a similar manner. A self-generating momentum has marked the Thatcher years. Scotland could not hope to avoid being affected by these changes even though its voting patterns indicated that it wanted no part in them.

Policy regarding public expenditure and attempting to shift the focus to the private sector differed only in intensity from the years of the Labour Government. Peter Riddell has written that if there was a

Thatcher experiment 'it was launched by Denis Healey'.[1] On the other hand, Geoffrey Maynard has maintained that though elements of Thatcherism were apparent under the Labour Government there was

> a significant change of philosophy which might be summarized as the substitution of an attitude of 'non-accommodation' of wage and other price-raising pressures for an attitude of 'accommodation' to them.[2]

But it is doubtful whether the more confrontational approach can justifiably be described as a philosophical change. In theory at least, there was rejection of Keynesian demand management and a return to classical economics. In practice, economic policy may have been tinged with a particular theoretical bias but more often it was pragmatic, particularly from the March 1982 budget.[3] But it was a pragmatism bounded by assumptions. Trade unions were blamed for poor industrial relations and wage inflation. Excessive public expenditure was thought to 'crowd out' private iniiative. An orientation towards market solutions and a weakening of faith in state prescriptions were assumed.

The overall levels of public expenditure rose – accounted for by the high levels of unemployment – while it was crudely asserted by both supporters and opponents that public expenditure was being cut. Anything which involved changes in regulations was described as 'deregulation' and anything involving a change in the extent or nature of state involvement was characterised as 'privatization'. Changes undoubtedly took place, often substantial, but there does not appear as much coherence as many supporters or opponents of the Government suggest.

THE SCOTTISH OFFICE: APPOINTMENTS AND STYLES

The first matter to be resolved as far as Scotland was concerned was who would become Secretary of State for Scotland. Despite the increase in MPs Mrs Thatcher did not have a great pool to choose from. The obvious choice would have been Alick Buchanan-Smith, but he was ruled out because of his strong and continuing support for legislative devolution. Others were too junior, inexperienced or simply not up to scratch. George Younger became Scottish Secretary because of the lack of an alternative as much as for any qualities he himself had. His temperament and his politics differed markedly from Teddy Taylor's. In the style of a grandee, and with the manners to match, he presided over Scotland rather than led it along any innovative path.

Younger succeeded in being at once part of Mrs Thatcher's Cabinet and simultaneously apart from it, in a manner that only Mrs Thatcher herself could match. In his Scottish fiefdom, he made no pretences to Thatcherite rigour and portrayed himself as a supporter of interventionist old-style Keynesianism, much as Peter Walker was to do in Wales after 1987, as if the Scottish Office was not part of British central government. Younger boasted to the Scottish media of his successes as Willie Ross had done in the 1960s and 1970s. He even emulated Ross in his semi-public threat of resignation when Ravenscraig steel plant was threatened with closure. The position of George Younger in economic debates in Cabinet is unclear. A right-wing critic in the *Daily Telegraph* in March 1984 maintained that many 'lame ducks' owed their survival to Younger and quoted an unnamed Cabinet colleague who described the Scottish Secretary's approach. Younger would present Scotland 'as an industrial graveyard down to its last national assets, and then intimidate us with the bogey of separatism'.[4] But there is no evidence that he played a major part in macro-economic debates, and he seems to have been one of those Cabinet Ministers referred to by Jim Prior as having 'contracted out of the argument'.[5] All in all, Younger's tenure at the Scottish Office was similar to so many of his predecessors since 1885; he attempted to portray himself as 'Scotland's Guardian' in the Cabinet but otherwise kept his head down and failed to take the lead on new policies. And like previous Secretaries of State Younger, and Rifkind later, was not a senior member of the Cabinet and sat on few major Cabinet committees.

A major claim of the Conservatives was the relative freedom offered to the Scottish Office in determining its expenditure priorities. In 1982, George Younger boasted to the Scottish Affairs Select Committee about his new powers of *virement*, and claimed that compared with the changes his Cabinet colleagues made to their programmes he had 'allocated rather less to transport and housing and rather more to education and law and order than they did.'[6] But this power was severely limited as so much expenditure would already be tied up in ongoing programmes, and the total amount is largely determined outwith the powers of the Scottish Office. The changed political context, particularly with the decline of the SNP, meant that Scotland and the Scottish Office had less influence. The constraints on public expenditure meant that this additional power was almost worthless, if indeed it was a new power at all.

Youngster's ambition to move on to a more senior Cabinet post was finally realised after the Westland Affair, which brought about the resignations of Michael Heseltine and Leon Brittan. As a former Argyll and Sutherland Highlanders officer, Younger had hankered after the Defence Ministry and was no doubt relieved to leave the Scottish Office at a time when the Tories were under considerable pressure on issues such as a cold climate allowance, rates revaluation, teachers' pay and Scottish steel. He had served for longer than any other Scottish Secretary, with the exception of Lord Balfour of Burleigh (1895–1903), and longer than any Secretary of State.

The new Secretary of State was Malcolm Rifkind, who had resigned as a junior Scottish Affairs spokesman in 1977 because of his support for legislative devolution. Rifkind had been Younger's most able junior Minister and proved to be a highly respected Foreign Office Minister of State before entering the Cabinet as Secretary of State for Scotland in 1986. He had no honeymoon period at the Scottish Office, and his skills as a communicator were tested to the full from the start. He inherited considerable problems and approached these in a manner very different from his predecessor.

Rifkind's style was high-profile; his view was that the best form of defence was attack. Initially, in the manner of Younger and each of his predecessors over the century, he attempted to portray himself as the protector of Scotland. His claim in September 1986 that the Greater Glasgow Health Board was the 'best-funded health authority any-where in the United Kingdom' was typical of this approach.[7] A change in approach was notable after the 1987 Election. Rifkind became familiar with the language of Thatcherism. His emphasis became the economic climate created by the Government which helped the Scottish economy rather than the amount of public expen-diture devoted to it. It was as if talking about how much Scotland received in public expenditure was accepting the Opposition's agenda.

As the pool of Parliamentary talent decreased, the problems in-creased. The practice of appointing defeated MPs to the Scottish front bench became a feature of the Thatcher years. In 1959, at the start of the Scottish Tories' electoral decline, J. Browne had been defeated, but was retained as a Scottish Office Minister in his new incarnation as Lord Craigton. Twenty-four years later, Hamish Gray found himself in the Scottish Office as Lord Gray of Contin following his defeat as MP in 1983. In 1987, Peter Fraser lost his seat to the SNP but continued as Solicitor-General.

The greatest difficulty in appointing Ministers to the Scotish Office came after the 1987 Election. With Rifkind and Ian Lang remaining at the Scottish Office and George Younger at Defence, there were only seven Scottish MPs left. Alick Buchanan-Smith refused to serve as Minister of State. Buchanan-Smith was the most able Scottish Tory MP elected in 1987 and, given the opportunity, probably the most likely to lead it to recovery, but his solution would have included legislative devolution. Allan Stewart had been sacked from the Scottish Office in September 1986 and could not be recalled only eight months later without considerable embarrassment. Nicholas Fairbairn had been forced to resign in January 1982 as Solicitor-General, ostensibly for mishandling a rape case. Had this been the real reason for his resigna-tion it would have been a very rare occasion, possibly the only one since 1954 when the doctrine of Ministerial responsibility, (that Minis-ters are responsible for the actions of their civil servants), resulted in

Sir Thomas Dugdale's resignation. Fairbairn's flamboyant and eccentric lifestyle had attracted media attention. This had greatly irritated the Prime Minister and the Glasgow rape case was the opportunity for getting rid of him. She would not contemplate his return to Governmental office in 1987.

This left the rumbustious populist Bill Walker, the smart dogmatist Michael Forsyth and the diffident aristocrat Lord James Douglas Hamilton. Walker could only be considered for Ministerial office in extreme circumstances and not even 1987 was that extreme. Forsyth and Lord James were appointed junior Ministers, the former at least offering a sharp intellect and a controversial reputation to the Scottish Office. In the Upper House, Lord Glenarthur – an obscure aristocrat with an Etonian, 10th Royal Hussars, Cavalry and Guards clubs background – had been appointed to the Scottish Office in September 1986 but was moved to the Foreign Office in 1987, a Department for which his background and tastes were more suited. Lord Sanderson of Bowden replaced him. As Russell Sanderson, he had proved a skilful and successful President of the Scottish Tories in the late 1970s and was a shrewd choice.

In 1967 George Younger had written that the Scottish Office was 'controlled absolutely by Scottish Ministers who are Scots MPs backed by the 71 Scottish Members of Parliament'.[8] The plain fact was that in each Conservative Government since then the Scottish Office consisted of Scots MPs who were opposed by a large majority of Scottish MPs. The notion that the Conservatives had 'no Scottish mandate' could be based on Younger's own words. The perception that the Conservatives had no mandate – whether in a legal or moral sense – made it all the more difficult for them to pursue radical policies without appearing 'anti-Scottish'. Younger's words of over twenty years ago have come back to haunt him and his party:

> Irrespective of party allegiance, no government and no Prime Minister could go against the wishes of the united opposition of these Scottish MPs, and if it were the case they did not act in the best interests of Scotland, the Scottish people would not vote for them.[9]

The Scottish Office has never been anything other than a branch of British government but the perception of it representing Whitehall interests in Scotland, as opposed to Scottish interests in Whitehall, has never been so obviously accepted or forecefully criticised as during the Thatcher years. Neal Ascherson's description of the distinct administrative apparatus without a distinct legislature as a 'political atrocity'[10] might in previous decades have been seen as political hyperbole, but appeared to match the mood of Scotland in the 1980s.

MANAGING THE ECONOMY

Throughout the Thatcher years unemployment has been a major source of discontent in Scotland. Though the Scottish Office had little direct responsibility, the Secretary of State, as 'Scotland's Minister', could not avoid the issue. The Thatcherite prescription for Scotland and other areas with high unemployment had been set out by Sir Keith Joseph in 1975. The unemployed should be persuaded to retrain or 'move if they are to have a steady job'.[11] This was expressed with the subtlety of the Tory populist by Norman Tebbit at the Conservative Party conference in October 1981. The unemployed should 'get on their bikes' and look for work, as his father had done fifty years before. But the number of unemployed far outweighed the number of jobs available, and this view ignored the importance of roots, personal ties, habitual preferences and familial loyalties.

The territorial disparity in the levels of unemployment throughout the United Kingdom has been a persistent feature of the Thatcher years. As the Bank of England stated in 1988:

> The consistency with which the same regions have unemployment rates which are above the national average over time may be taken as evidence that the migration of employees or firms has been insufficient to reduce these disparities.[12]

Employees had failed to move because of the 'paradox of labour'. Firms had failed to move, according to the Government, because of the 'low inter-regional variation in earnings', i.e., the wage rates for workers in areas of high unemployment were not low enough to make it economically attractive for businesses to set up in these areas. Free market doctrine would endorse lower wages being paid in areas of high unemployment. This was encouraged by the Government, particularly in statements from Nigel Lawson and Norman Tebbit. It meant that Scots should accept lower wages in exchange for lower unemployment. This was hardly likely to be a vote winner.

But unemployment was rising in other parts of Britain. The sharpest rise in unemployment in the early 1980s was in the West Midlands, previously a prosperous area. As unemployment affected such areas, the justification for giving special aid to areas such as Scotland diminished in the eyes of the Government. Moreover, the Midlands had done far more to supply the Government with its majority. Additionally, the ideology of withdrawing state support and relying on the 'hidden hand' was pressed by Sir Keith Joseph, Mrs Thatcher's guru and Secretary of State for Industry from 1979 to September 1981. On assuming office, Sir Keith had presented his senior civil servants in the Department of Industry with a reading list which included his own writings, those of Adam Smith, and publications of the Centre for Policy Studies – the right-wing think-tank he had established in August 1974 to learn lessons from the Heath years.[13]

It seemed that the market was to be paramount in Thatcher's Britain, but there were some notable exceptions to this ideology which Sir Keith himself was prepared to make. In January 1981, it was decided to invest £990 million over two years in British Leyland. As Peter Walker later remarked:

> Under any sort of free market doctrine British Leyland would have been allowed to disappear . . . But she [Mrs Thatcher] and the Cabinet were in total agreement that the disastrous effect of that on the economics of the Midlands, on unemployment, on the balance of trade, was such that you had to go and pour vast sums of public expenditure in to see that it was rescued and saved.[14]

From August 1982 major changes in regional policy resulted in a reduction in the number of Assisted Areas. Regional policy had been declining in importance since the mid-1970s and other related policies and considerations were gaining importance including 'inner city' policies, public-private partnerships and the European Community regional funds.[15] Though Scotland undoubtedly benefited from European Community regional grants, the other shifts in policy were less advantageous to Scotland. Once more, the Thatcher Government intensified rather than radically altered policies or developments evident during the period of the Labour Government.

A distinct change of emphasis occurred in 1979 with a downgrading of regional policy, though much continuity was evident;[16] the 'political milieu of the regional problem had changed, as had its intellectual or academic setting', according to Parsons. The decline of nationalism in Scotland and Wales, the recognition of 'inner city' problems, especially after the riots in 1981 and the more widespread nature of unemployment throughout the United Kingdom combined to ensure the relegation of regional policy.[17] Effectively, all that was left, as Norman Tebbit stated in the Commons in 1983, was regional policy seen 'primarily as a social policy'.[18]

In January 1988, the Department of Trade and Industry published a white paper, DTI – the Department for Enterprise which stated that the keynote of future policies would be enterprise and 'its two foundations are open markets and individuals'.[19] It ended the principle of automatic assistance to scheduled areas and the introduction of a more selective system purportedly designed to help small and medium-sized businesses. Regional policy became residualized; it became a social ameliorative with a more restricted territorial coverage.

A sad testimony to regional policy during the Thatcher years was the number of major employers which closed that had once been seen as regional policy successes. A list of closures included Singers in Clydebank, Goodyear nearby in Glasgow, Monsanto in Ayrshire, Massey Ferguson in Kilmarnock, BSR in East Kilbride, Wiggins Teape pulp mill in Fort Wiliam, Talbot's Linwood car plant, the Invergordon aluminium smelter, Caterpillar in Uddingston, Burroughs in Cumbernauld, Plessey in Bathgate, Rowntree Mackintosh in Edinburgh, Gartcosh steel mill. Other major job losses were in old established heavy industries. British Shipbuilders Dundee operations were closed in 1981 with 1,000 job losses. Coal mining declined with around 10,000 jobs lost in the industry during the 1980s. One of the most potent symbols of the industrial policy of the Thatcher years was the steel industry. Employment in the industry had fallen from 25,750 in September 1974 to under 11,500 in Autumn 1982. An attempt to close Ravenscraig in late 1982 was met with overwhelming opposition from within Scotland. Conservative politicians backed the retention of Ravenscraig after the closing down of one of the three blast furnaces and against the wishes of Ian Mac-Gregor, the British Steel Corporation's chairman. Michael Ancram, then Scottish party chairman argued that to 'depart from having a steel-making capacity in Scotland the chances of attracting any industry of merit to Scotland would indeed be slight.'[20] George Younger made it clear that he would resign if a decision was taken to close Ravenscraig.[21] James Goold, chairman of the Scottish CBI, yet to become Scottish Tory chairman, stated that Ravenscraig's closure would have 'far-reaching and disastrous' consequences for the Scottish economy, though he intimated that the Scottish CBI would not be involved in a campaign to save the plant.[22] The campaign was successful. Patrick Jenkin, Secretary of State for Industry, who had argued in Cabinet for closure, announced that Ravenscraig would be retained for at least a further three years.

The battle had been won but three years later the issue of Scotland's steel-making capacity was again in doubt. In August 1985, a British Steel Corporation stragegy document, *BSC: The Future* proposed that Gartcosh cold mill should be closed. Gartcosh was built in 1961 and was Ravenscraig's largest single customer. Opposition on this occasion was less comprehensive. Though the Select Committee on Scottish Affairs strongly backed the plant,[23] as did the opposition parties, there were few voices within the Conservative Party arguing in defence of Gartcosh. The outstanding Tory voice to be raised against its closure was Iain Lawson's. Lawson had gained his reputation as a tough campaigner in the 1978 Glasgow Garscadden by-election when he had successfully undermind SNP credibility and allowed Labour to retain the seat.

Lawson vigorously backed the Gartcosh steel mill and accompanied a deputation of workers on a march to Westminster. During this period he joined the Campaign for a Scottish Assembly and became increasingly critical of Government policy. With considerable skill, he caused his party a headache as he moved increasingly towards the Scottish National Party, and eventually joined it on the day Gartcosh officially closed. The Gartcosh campaign had effect throughout Scotland. One of the few other Tories to back Gartcosh was the Prospective Parliamentary candidate for Gordon in North-East Scotland, which was unlikely to be directly affected by the closure. The campaign was also of enormous importance in the development of a perception that Mrs Thatcher and her party were at best not interested in Scotland and at worst were anti-Scottish. Though the number of jobs lost at Gartcosh was less than at many other Scottish plants, it had symbolic importance.

Inward investment policy continued to operate through 'Locate in Scotland'. Additional offices were established in the United States in 1982 but these came under threat in 1984 with a review of industrial promotions policy by the Department of Trade and Industry. Norman Tebbit, then Trade and Industry Secretary, was behind moves to amalgamate the Scottish offices with those of 'Invest in Britain'. Scottish Tory MPs publicly, and George Younger privately, opposed this move along with strong support from the Scottish political community. The battle was won, but Scotland was still unable to attract foreign investment to the extent of other parts of the UK. In 1987 Wales replaced the West Midlands as the primary British location for inward investment. Given Scotland's peripheral position there was a reasonable degree of success in attracting investment. But Scotland could not expect to depend on inward investment to the extent of other parts of Britain, and had to rely more heavily on its own devices.[24]

The recession which bit deep into the British economy had particularly harsh consequences for Scotland. Peter Balfour, chairman of the Scottish Council (Development and Industry) predicted in October 1980 that Scotland was more vulnerable than England, and that Scottish industry would decline 'much more quickly than English industry'.[25] Taking the 'props away' was bound to lead to Scotland suffering disproportionately. Even the oil industry could make little impact against the recession though the trickle of oil coming ashore at St Fergus in Aberdeenshire became a gushing torrent during the early 1980s. By 1980 the UK was self-sufficient in oil and the following year it had become a net exporter.[26] The timing was propitious. The real price of oil more than doubled in 1979–80.

The major beneficiary was the Treasury. The predicted devastation at the expense of the local community graphically portrayed in John McGrath's 1973 play, *The Cheviot, the Stag and the Black, Black Oil* became a reality. Indeed, almost half of the net increase in real income accruing from oil was invested in overseas assets, facilitated by the abolition of exchange control, one of the first actions of the Government in 1979. The oil played a part, along with the Government's monetary and fiscal policies, in the appreciation of the exchange rate which had a devastating effect on manufacturing industry.[27] From a

Scottish perspective, the discovery of North Sea Oil had as many costs as benefits.

In retrospect, it is clear that the 1979 election marked an important watershed in British history. Just as the Labour Goverment was forced to face economic consequences outwith its control after the Yom Kippur War, so the Thatcher Government reaped economic benefits which it played no part in creating. The quadrupling of oil prices in 1973–74 and the doubling of oil prices in 1979–80 had considerable domestic repercussions. Whoever had won the 1979 election would be in a very fortunate position. With the flow of oil continuing into the next century, the winner in 1979 had an advantage unknown to any Government this century. What had been described by the Nationalists as 'Scotland's oil' became Thatcher's saviour; oil along with the proceeds from privatization cushioned the effects of the recession and government economic policy.

SCOTLAND'S CONSTITUTIONAL STATUS

Throughout the period leading up to the 1979 election, Conservative spokesmen had insisted that the constitutional status quo was not an option. On the eve of the referendum Mrs Thatcher stated categorically that a 'No' vote would not mean that the devolution question would be buried. The 1979 Scottish Conservative manifesto maintained that 'there should be an all-party conference or committee to see if we can reach agreement on improvements in our system of government'.[28] The all-party conference turned out to be fairly meaningless talks which led to minor changes in Parliamentary procedure. The remit prevented discussion of options which had been mentioned in the Tory manifesto and in speeches by Francis Pym; the talks merely considered whether 'the present system of government in Scotland could be improved by changes in the procedure, powers and operational arrangements for dealing with Scottish Parliamentary business.'[29]

Four recommendations were made: that there would be a minimum of six estimates debates in the Scottish Grand Committee each session; the Committee could devote up to six meetings to Matter Day debates, i.e., debates on topics of general or specific relevance to government policy, with the Opposition able to insist on a minimum of four; the abandonment of the practice of having Added Members on the Committee – English MPs added to reflect the party balance in the Commons as a whole; consequent on the abolition of Added Members, it was recommended that the quorum of the Committee should be reduced from seventeen to ten. These recommendations were eventually accepted by the Commons. The abolition of additional Members was inevitable – even with the maximum of 15 added Members the Tories would have had less MPs on the Committee than Labour. By 1987, 54 Conservative Members from outside

Scotland would have been required in order to achieve only a bare overall majority. The possibility of the Scottish Grand Committee meeting in Edinburgh and permitting MPs, other than those representing Scottish constituencies, to speak at meetings was considered but no recommendations were made. The idea of taking the Report stage of Scottish Bills and Adjournment Debates in the Scottish Grand Committee was rejected.

The first meeting to discuss the inter-party talks took place in July 1979 and meetings were arranged in April and May 1980. The Parliamentary debate on the recommendations was eventually held in June 1981. Peter Fraser, elected Member for Angus South in 1979, proposed an amendment expressing a desire that 'the Scottish Grand Committee should for an experimental period be enabled to hold sittings in Edinburgh from time to time'.[30] The proposal was not new. As a Tory alternative to Home Rule it had a long pedigree. During the debate on the Second Reading of the Government of Scotland Bill in 1914, Halford Mackinder had suggested that the Scottish Standing Committee should meet in Edinburgh to deal with matters affecting Scotland. During the last war, when Tom Johnston had been Secretary of State, an experiment in holding meetings of the Committee in Edinburgh had proved a failure when few MPs had bothered to attend. These meetings simply had no appeal as they were powerless.

Fraser's idea was accepted and the first meeting of the Scottish Grand Committee was held on 15 February, 1982 in the Royal High School, the proposed site of the Scottish Assembly. There were seventeen meetings in Edinburgh up to Summer 1988. Only one was held in the year following the 1987 General Election. Once more, the impotence of the Scottish Grand Committee made the Edinburgh meetings lacklustre affairs. The view of Anna McCurley, former Tory MP for Renfrew West and Inverclyde that the sittings in Edinburgh were expensive, a 'sop to the Nationalists' and 'sheer tokenism' seems to have had some support in Government circles.[31]

A Scottish Affairs Select Committee was established along with other Departmental Select Committees under reforms instituted in 1979. A Scottish Select Committee was not envisaged under the original proposals of Norman St John Stevas, Leader of the House. But there was never any prospect that Scottish Affairs would fail to be the subject of a Select Committee in 1979. In adding Scottish Affairs to the list, the Government could maintain that this was a positive response to the all-party discussions which it was conducting. The Scottish Committee was the largest with 13 members and was nominated in late November 1979. Both the size and chairmanship of the Committee were contentious matters. It proved rather cumbersome, and attempts to constitute sub-committees were resisted by those in power. Scottish Conservative backbenchers complained when it was decided that the Labour Party would choose the chairman, as was the case with other Select Committees, and the Tories on the Committee decided to appoint a 'majority group leader', Iain Sproat, in a departure from the procedure of other Select Committees. During its existence, Labour politicians more than Tories sang the praises of the Committee. Donald Dewar, its first chairman, argued the case for a 'growing emphasis on properly investigating and scrutinizing the system, and that information will be gathered, assumptions tested and Ministers pushed to account for their actions in a way that just does not happen on the floor of the House of Commons.'[32] Younger commented favourably in 1982 stating that the Select Committee

sheds greater light on what the Scottish Office does, keeps Ministers and their advisers on their toes and provides evidence, if evidence were needed, that Scottish affairs play a significant part in the Parliament of the United Kingdom.[33]

The Committee investigated a number of matters including white fish authority levies, college of education closures, rural transport, inward investment policy, BBC cuts, civil service jobs dispersal, Prestwick Airport, housing finance, rural transport and the steel industry. The Committee tended to divide on party lines and the investigations into and scrutinizing of the Scottish Office, 'showed the Committee at its weakest and the Scottish Office at its most imperious.'[34] But few imagined that its life would be so short. Writing in 1985, Drucker and Kellas felt that the Committee had an 'assured place in Scottish politics' largely because it could, occasionally, transcend party divides and had sufficient common interests with the Scottish Office.[35]

The 1987 Election altered things completely. With five of the ten Scottish Tory MPs holding Ministerial office, and very little support for the continued existence of the Committee amongst the remainder, the Government had the choice of appointing non-Scots or abolishing the Committee. Allan Stewart, who had served on the Committee between 1979 and 1981, denounced it as a 'complete irrelevance' and made it clear that he had no intention of becoming a member again.[36] Bill Walker wrote to the Committee of Selection informing them that he would not serve on the Committee.[37] For a year the Government wrestled with the problem while the Clerk to the Scottish Affairs Committee wandered around aimlessly not knowing whether he was going to have a committee to serve. Eventually, the Commons Committee of Selection reported to the House that it was uanble to constitute the Scottish Affairs Select Committee. It was obviously felt that abolition was the least provocative course. The Opposition parties together established an alternative Select Committee, but it could neither expect to call civil service witnesses nor be financed through the public purse.

The issue of devolution refused to go away. The perception of the Tories as an alien minority imposing their policies on an unwilling

Scotland encouraged support for legislative devolution. Immediately after the referendum, anti-devolutionist sentiment seemed to be in the ascendant, despite the slender majority which voted 'Yes'. High expectations, even presumptions, of the certain establishment of a Scottish Assembly in the late 1970s were so shaken that pro-devolutionists failed to make much of the fact that they had in fact won more support than their opponents in the referendum. The issue returned slowly onto the Scottish political agenda and by 1987 had forced its place on the British political agenda following the Election that year. A 'post-mortem' on the 1987 Scottish results by the Tories concluded that devolution could no longer be ignored and that the party had to debate the issue.[38]

Scottish Constitutional Preferences, 1979–87

	March '79	March '83	March '87
A completely independent Scottish Assembly separate from England	14	23	33
A Scottish Assembly as part of Britain but with substantial powers	42	48	47
No change from the present system	35	26	14
Don't Know	9	2	6

Source: *Scotsman* MORI and *Glasgow Herald* Systems Three opinion polls

The Conservative position between 1979 and 1987 was simply to deny that legislative devolution was an issue. No debate took place at party conference for over a decade and the Tory devolutionists kept quiet feeling that there was nothing to be gained by rocking the boat. In 1979, Alick Buchanan-Smith accepted a post in Thatcher's Government as Minister of State for Agriculture, Fisheries and Food – though, significantly, not in the Scottish Office. Malcolm Rifkind, who had resigned from the front bench with Buchanan-Smith over devolution, was appointed to a junior post in the Scottish Office. The feeling in the party at the time of their resignations as Opposition front-benchers in 1976 was confirmed. Buchanan-Smith had supported legislative devolution as a matter of principle and thereafter would never compromise on that issue by accepting a post at the Scottish Office. Rifkind was seen as motivated by opportunism; conforming with the consensus, he had expected that an Assembly was almost inevitable and saw dangers both for the party, and himself, in opposing the inevitable. When the inevitable did not occur his pragmatic conservatism permitted him to accept a Scottish Office post and eventually the Secretaryship of State. However, his response that devolution was not an issue could not be sustained after the 1987 Election.

A small hard core of devolutionists persisted but none of these, Buchanan-Smith apart, was in Parliament. Incorrigible devolutionists included leading local government councillors Struan Stevenson and Brian Meek, though they were far from forceful in expressing their views during the 1980s. George Younger, Michael Ancram, Malcolm Rifkind, Douglas Hurd and Ian Lang had all been determined advocates of legislative devolution in the 1970s. Holding office under Mrs Thatcher, or the hope of doing so again, was an adequate corrective for these Tories.

In the post-1987 debate, Struan Stevenson argued for a 140-seat Scottish Senate funded by a direct grant, elected by proportional representation and with a reduction of up to 25 Scottish MPs at Westminster. According to Stevenson, the Tories could be reduced further to a 'decimated rump acting solely as a conduit for Westminster legislation' if they failed to act on devolution.[39] Brian Meek stated that devolution was inevitable whether it took 'ten or fifteen years' and criticized the situation whereby the Scottish civil service is 'one of the most ungoverned bodies in the world, since Ministers leave Scotland on a Monday and don't come back until Thursday or Friday.'[40]

Both Stevenson and Meek were involved in a new internal Conservative body, the Conservative Constitutional Forum, which warned that the Government would face a 'disaster on a grand scale' if they failed to seize the devolution initiative. Along with Michael Fry and former Scottish Tory press officer, Quintin Jardine they were involved in the production of a paper advocating an Assembly which would control a range of taxes raised in Scotland, would have 114 members elected by proportional representation and a reduction in the number of Scottish MPs at Westminster to 57. The paper envisaged the continued existence of the Secretary of State who would have no power over the Assembly. They also proposed the abolition of one tier of local government.

Former Tory MP Sir Russell Fairgrieve, who had retired from Parliament in 1983, and John Corrie, defeated in 1987, supported the federalist position. Fairgrieve had been associated with the maximalist view on devolution during the late 1970s and he had served as a junior Scottish Office Minister from the 1979 Election until September 1981 and no doubt felt uninhibited being both out of the Government and Parliament. Ross Leckie, the defeated Tory candidate in Gordon, expressed his views in a forthright manner after the 1987 Election result was announced. Leckie fell foul of the party leadership for his attacks on the anti-devolutionist position of the party and on the poll tax.

Ross Harper, who had sided with the devolutionists when an

Assembly seemed certain in the 1970s, produced a paper arguing against devolution in May 1988. It was a flimsy document which contributed more to Mr Harper's rise within the Conservative Party than to intelligent debate.[41] A more intelligent contribution came from Michael Ancram. Ancram concentrated on the Labour Party's proposals for a tax-raising Assembly. On the reasonable assumption that taxes would be higher in Scotland under Labour's proposals Ancram argued, less reasonably, that the consequences could amount to 100,000 job losses, potential inward investment being discouraged, footloose industry currently in Scotland moving out and business expansion constrained.[42]

Institutions which traditionally supported the party also entered the debate. The Scottish division of the Institute of Directors declared their opposition to devolution in November 1987. The Institute had asked their 1,300 members for their views and found that 140 were opposed (about 10 per cent of its members) and 39 favoured legislative devolution.[43] The Confederation of British Industry in Scotland continued to oppose devolution. John Davidson made it clear that neither the cost of running an Assembly nor its civil service was a concern of the CBI, but the additional taxation which would follow forced the organization to oppose devolution.[44]

The outcome of the debate on devolution at the 1988 Scottish Tory conference was a foregone conclusion. The previous day Malcolm Rifkind had admitted that if there had been any prospect of a revolt then there would not have been a debate.[45] By a margin of 50–1, the conference voted against any measure of legislative devolution. Brian Meek pleaded with his party to 'put some trust in the people of Scotland', Michael Fry maintained that a party with 'no commitment to the traditions of its country is in the end not a Conservative Party' and Ross Leckie merely antagonized the conference by suggesting that ignoring the wishes of the electorate 'in what is more than a mere constituency, this nation and country has more to do with fascism than Conservatism'.[46] The conference rejected these views and supported the advice of the Lord Chancellor and former Scottish Lord Advocate, Lord Mackay who pointed to the constitutional confusion which would result when Scottish MPs would be able to vote on all English matters while the reverse could not happen as far as devolved matters was concerned.

One dimension of Unionism which had not been heard in Tory debates a decade before, nor in any previous debates was the ultra-Unionist position. A senior Edinburgh district councillor, Kenneth Ferguson called for 'total Unionism' by which was meant a bizarre proposition – to move the 'incompetent lot of officials in St Andrews House' to London and 'slowly integrate it into United Kingdom Ministries'.[47] A similar view had been expressed by Bill Walker, MP for North Tayside, three months previously. Walker had questioned the

need for a Secretary of State for Scotland and supported greater
harmonization between Scotland and England and the removal of
differences in the education and health systems of the two nations.[48]
This integrationist view was in a minority, but probably no more so
than was the devolutionist view in the party.

Both sides of the debate expressed surprise at the margin of the
victory. Advocates of devolution had hoped for 20 per cent of conference votes while opponents had expected to win 90 per cent. Part of
the reason for the margin may have been the extreme language used
by Ross Leckie, who was widely seen as a troublemaker and was
tainted in Tory eyes by his association with Iain Lawson, who had
joined the SNP. Another reason may have been the failure of the chair
to call an amendment from Sir Russell Fairgrieve or John Corrie which
might have won more support. On the other hand it is unlikely that
the behaviour of a substantial group of Young Conservatives in-
cessantly heckling devolutionists aided their side.

*Scottish Constitutional Preference by General Election Voting
Intention March 1987*

	% Con	% Lab	% Lib/SDP	% SNP	% All
A completely independent Scottish Assembly separate from England	11	37	22	57	32
A Scottish Assembly as part of Britain but with substantial powers	52	47	66	40	50
No change from the powers system	32	13	11	2	15
Don't Know	5	3	1	1	3

Source: *Scotsman* MORI poll, March 14, 1987

Polls provided evidence of overwhelming support for Home Rule and
independence had more than twice as much support as the status
quo. The delegates would no doubt appreciate that part of the Prime
Minister's address the following day when she stated that her principles were 'not at the mercy of opinion polls. Neither, I am sure, are
yours'.[49] In the political market place, it had seemed sensible in 1979
for the Tories to exploit that corner of the market which opposed
devolution while all the other parties fought for pro-devolution votes.
By 1989, what had seemed an astute move electorally proved only to
highlight the Tories' isolation from majority opinion, and to increase
the demand for self-government.

REDUCING THE ROLE OF THE STATE

Since the 1987 Election, Malcolm Rifkind has set out his vision of a vibrant New Unionism in a series of speeches. It is interesting that he should refer to a 'New Unionism', given that this was the very heading under which he had advocated Scottish Home Rule in the late 1970s.[50] His frenetic list of public engagements following the 1987 Election allowed him to spell out explicitly the Thatcher Government's programme for Scotland for the first time in anything approaching a coherent form. The Election results may have provoked this activity from this most ebullient of Secretaries of State, but the origins of his New Unionism are to be found before this date.

For the Prime Minister, the most appealing explanation for the Scottish Conservative decline was the argument that Scots had not had enough of her free-market medicine. There had been a surfeit of state intervention and insufficient Thatcherism. What was required, in her view, was a measure which both recognized Scottish distinctiveness and could be portrayed as distinctively Thatcherite. In the mildly offensive terminology of the law officers who draft Scottish amendments to English legislation, there was a need to 'put a kilt on Thatcherism'. This was the message which a trail of Government Ministers brought to Scotland in the months after the General Election.

Nigel Lawson's characteristically forthright speech in Glasgow in November 1987 was an example. The Chancellor of the Exchequer argued that Scotland had not benefited from the 'enterprise culture' of the south because large areas of Scottish life were 'sheltered from market forces and exhibit a culture of dependence rather than that of enterprise'. There was a 'barrier along Scotland's road to prosperity. That barrier is the pervasive presence of a hostile attitude to enterprise and wealth creation, to the enterprise culture on which economic success in a free society depends.'[51] The Scottish edition of the *Sun* summed up Lawson's message, 'Will ye stop your snivelling Jock?'[52]

A group of English Conservative backbenchers, unprompted by the Whips, took to attending Scottish debates in Parliament – a remarkable reversal of past practice, when English Tory backbenchers had to be dragooned onto Scottish Committees. The interventions of these MPs have focused on Scotland's share of identifiable public expenditure, which suggests that Scotland is treated favourably. During debates on public expenditure in December 1987, the Scottish Office budget was attacked as a 'slush fund' and it was suggested that Scots were being 'force-fed with public funds'.[53] Of course, identifiable public expenditure represents only 80 per cent of total public expenditure and ignores defence, which largely benefits the South-East, and Mortgage Tax Relief, which overwhelmingly benefits the

South-East.[54] The fact that Scotland has higher levels of unemployment and disproportionate levels of poverty also go towards explaining Scotland's apparently favourable position.

Criticisms expressed by Lawson and these English Tory backbenchers only served to encourage the view that Conservatism, particularly in its Thatcherite form, is anti-Scottish. The message which Conservatives gave to Scotland in the months following the 1987 Election was hardly likely to endear them to the Scottish electorate. A change of tack became evident during the course of 1988, at least in the articulation of the dependency argument, if not in the message itself. The obverse of the dependency argument was put, especially following the adverse publicity given to Nigel Lawson's speech. This has involved arguing that Scotland has huge potential to develop an enterprise culture. Scotland, it is frequently pointed out, was the birthplace of Adam Smith and the Scottish Enlightenment. In essence the argument remains the same, the difference being one of presentation.

The recent history of the Confederation of British Industry in Scotland would not suggest that the origins of a radical scheme would emerge from that rather conventional body. But, it was the CBI's publicity-conscious Scottish chairman, Bill Hughes who came up with an idea which attracted Mrs Thatcher's support. Hughes became chairman of the Scottish CBI in 1987 and has been described as 'Mrs Thatcher's Scottish Lord Young' because he brings forward answers rather than problems.[55] He has been chief executive and chairman of Grampian Holdings since 1976, a conglomerate based in Glasgow with a variety of interests. He also chaired his local 'Think Falkirk' group, established to encourage the economic development of that town. He became a member of the Scottish Conservative Business Group, set up after the last Election to advise the Tory Party on business matters, though he had no previous involvement with the party, and in 1989 became vice-chairman of the party in Scotland. In true Thatcherite style, he is a self-made man (who, according to critics, worships his creator).

In June 1988, Hughes floated the idea of creating a new agency, 'Enterprise Scotland', which would be formed by merging the Scottish Development Agency, the Training Commission (formerly the Manpower Services Commission), local enterprise trusts, area initiatives, local authority industrial development units and possibly the Highlands and Islands Development Board. His idea would mean a pooling of resources centrally – creating a fund of around £500m annually – and simultaneously decentralizing functions to local enterprise boards run by 'business evangelists'. Enterprise Scotland was to provide 'practical devolution', to create a network of boards backed by public money but run by 'competent and committed' business people. Though the final proposals differed from Hughes' original scheme the general thrust of the policy – a profit-driven, business-oriented body – remained.

The pursuit of an 'enterprise culture' was evident elsewhere. The Government's housing proposals set out in a White Paper in November 1987 and in the Housing (Scotland) Act, 1988 were the culmination of a process of reducing the role of local authorities in the provision of housing. Historically, Scotland has had a larger public housing sector than England (or, indeed, than any other West European, and some East European countries). The incentives for Scots to move to the private sector, taking their council house with them through the 'right to buy' or by buying a privately built house were increased. By preventing local authorities from subsidizing council house rents from rates and cutting back Housing Support Grant, rents rose and the public housing stock deteriorated.

The progressively attractive discounts for those buying their council house, allied with Mortgage Tax Relief, ensured that over 100,000 council houses were sold between April 1979 and the publication of *Housing: The Government's Proposals for Scotland*.[56] A further 50,000 were sold by April 1989. The Kirk's report on housing, a copy of which was presented to Mrs Thatcher, noted that fiscal policies promoting home ownership have had some success but have

> not so much stimulated investment in new housing as encouraged dissipation of money in increased asset values of the present stock. At the same time, restrictions placed on local authorities' capital expenditure have depressed provision and upgrading of social housing below what people need and are willing to pay for.[57]

The encouragement of private investment has been the hallmark of Labour-controlled local authorities including Glasgow District, the largest landlord in Western Europe. Where the local authorities' strategy differs from the Government's is in its emphasis and purpose. Willingness to accept and even seek private investment is, however, very different from pursuing policies which lead to the decline of public sector housing and the development of an extended private rented sector in which many tenants' rights are removed. Considerable agreement exists that the massive, poorly planned housing schemes in Scottish towns and cities have been socially and economically disastrous. The consequences of this were commented upon in another Church of Scotland report, *Just Sharing*, also presented to Mrs Thatcher in 1988. The Rev. Russell Barr wrote that the one word which summed up life in his parish in Easterhouse was despair.

> The despair is tangible. It can be tasted. A little differently, one of our elders speaks of the appalling 'greyness' of the people. Much of the joy and colour of life has been knocked out of them.[58]

Keating, in his study of urban regeneration in Glasgow, also

commented upon the 'frustration which easily gives way to demor-
alization' and the sullenness and resignation of youth in such areas as
Easterhouse.[59] The agreement between those who subscribe to the notion of a
dependency culture and those who would accept Keating's view of
the despair and lack of vitality is tangential. Considerable problems
exist, and the errors made by both central and local government are
noted by both views. However, whereas those who maintain that the
dependency culture ineluctably follows from state involvement,
Keating notes the need for state involvement to solve the problems.
The creation of an enterprise culture, if it simply means replacing
state support with the free market, will not work, according to Keating. The Government's proposals for regenerating four designated
schemes – Castlemilk in Glasgow, Ferguslie Park in Paisley, Wester
Hailes in Edinburgh and Whitfield in Dundee – contained in *New Life
for Urban Scotland* emphasize the role of the private sector, which
seems unlikely to invest heavily in such areas without initial substantial public investment.

Local government has been the particular focus of attention for
Conservative policy initiatives in Scotland designed to tackle dependency. Central to this has been local expenditure. Local government
expenditure was a relatively easy target in the totality of public
expenditure; hard decisions could be left to local authorities which,
increasingly, were Labour-controlled. A significant aspect of the onslaught against the 'runaway train' of local authority spending, as
Younger described it,[60] was the leading role played by the Scottish
Office. As the *Financial Times* stated in November 1981, Scotland had
become 'a test bed for the Government's offensive against local authority spending'.[61] Changes in the approach of central control were
noted by the Convention of Scottish Local Authorities in February
1982:

> There have been rapid moves towards greater central control
> over local expenditure and hence policies. Prior to the passing of
> the 1981 Act, central government had been content to use
> measures aimed at influencing the aggregate level of local expen-
> diture. The 1981 Act enabled central government to control the
> total level of expenditure of individual authorities. The new Bill
> now gives central government powers to control the detailed
> expenditure of individual authorities.[62]

The most significant break with consensus and most controversial
policy in this field has been the poll tax. The rates revaluation in
Scotland of 1985 precipitated a strong reaction amongst the Conservative's middle class support, which was vociferously articulated at the
party's Scottish conference in Perth that year. Revaluations had taken
place in Scotland in 1971, 1978 and 1985 while the last revaluation to
take place in England and Wales was in 1973, resulting in Scotland

having rateable values set a great deal higher than that for comparable property south of the border. In response, George Younger told the conference that rates would be abolished and replaced by a 'community charge'. Around this time Michael Forsyth, Tory MP for Stirling, produced a paper arguing the case for a poll tax as did Douglas Mason of the Adam Smith Institute.[63] In January 1986, the Government issued a Green Paper, *Paying for Local Government*.[64] The prosaically entitled 'Abolition of Domestic Rates Etc. (Scotland) Act 1987' introduced the euphemistically entitled 'community charge'.

The rates were to be replaced by the community charge which was described in the Green Paper:

> a new flat-rate charge – a community charge – for local services, payable at the same rate by all the adult residents of a local authority. Each local authority would determine the level of its own community charge. All adult residents would be liable to pay, not just householders. If each local authority is to be accountable to those who have to pay for its expenditure, clear and comprehensive price signals must be given to all local taxpayers. A community charge will achieve this for all local adult residents will face similar bills.[65]

The importance of local accountability and the flat rate were crucial in the Government's estimation. According to the Government, spendthrift local authorities would be held accountable to a wider section of the community with the least well-off, who gained most from the services provided, no longer able to pass the cost onto the ratepayer, though provision was made in the Act for the Secretary of State to introduce rebates.[66] This was seen as challenging Scots dependence on high levels of services. The less well off would lose, as the Government recognized in a technical appendix to the Green Paper.[67]

The Green Paper was a 'crude version of public choice theory' which postulated that the voter would attempt to maximise his or her utility by voting for the package most likely to be most individually beneficial. Under this theory it is assumed that the level of poll tax will be kept down because of the flat rate, and because far more voters will be paying for local services directly.[68] As Midwinter and Mair demonstrated, the assumptions involved in public choice theory have fundamental theoretical and empirical flaws in relation to the poll tax in terms of democratic theory, fiscal psychology, electoral behaviour and policy analysis.[69]

Within no time the community charge had become publicly known as the poll tax. In a celebrated slip, the Prime Minister referred to it as a 'poll tax' in May 1987.[70] By the time of the 1987 General Election an Act had been passed to introduce the poll tax in Scotland but not in England. If the Tories had wanted to portray themselves as 'putting Scotland first' by introducing the poll tax in Scotland then their plan backfired spectacularly. The unpopularity of the poll tax and the perception that Scotland was a guinea-pig fed Scottish antipathy to the Conservatives in an election in which the poll tax was a prominent issue.

The poll tax was not only intensely disliked but was feared by sections of the Scottish population. Attempts to avoid registering for the poll tax became evident even before the process of registration began. In October 1987 there was evidence, particularly in deprived areas, of a marked decrease in the electoral register.[71] The expected simplicity of introducing the poll tax was not only complicated by deliberate attempts to avoid registration or the campaigns of non-payment but also by administrative problems which appear not to have been foreseen by the Government. The Act was essentially an enabling piece of legislation which depended on considerable secondary legislation in the form of regulations. Throughout Scotland, while local government officers were legally obliged to introduce the Act, their local political employers were opposed to the tax. This was bound to test member-officer relations in Scottish Regional Councils to an extent previously unknown. The increased number of demands for the poll tax as compared with domestic rates inevitably involves more work as with the establishment of mechanisms for more rebates and more defaulters. While far simpler in principle, the poll tax is far more complex in operation than domestic rates. With the added and unpredictable dynamic of strong Scottish political opposition in a climate of a revived Scottish nationalism this radical gamble on the part of the Conservatives seems rash indeed. The threat to Conservative support because of this most important symbol of their fightback has, ironically, been in the highly unusual shape of a major policy which the Scottish Office has initiated and which will operate north of the border first.

Contemporary Conservatism:
From Dependency to Enterprise?

Much debate has taken place in recent years on the nature of contemporary Conservatism, focusing particularly on the changes which have occurred under Margaret Thatcher's leadership. The term 'Thatcherism' has become part of the currency of political discourse as have associated ideas, approaches and policies as 'privatisation', 'conviction politics', 'wets' and 'dries', 'dependency culture' and 'enterprise culture'. Presented by many proponents and opponents alike of the 'new right', they appear coherent and intellectually founded. But closer examination suggests otherwise. There is an interesting Scottish dimension to the debate on Thatcherism, both intellectually and practically. Scottish enlightenment philosophers and Scottish traditions have been cited by the Prime Minister, no less, as the basis of her policies; in practical terms, Scotland has stubbornly rejected the policies of the Thatcher government. Scots have also been criticized by government supporters for their excessive dependence on the state.

Why should Thatcherism have emerged when it did? Why should Scotland remain so unwilling to accept Thatcherite prescriptions? And what precisely is Thatcherism? These questions require consideration in the conclusion to a study of Conservatism in Scotland. Whether 'Thatcherism' will outlive Thatcher and what is left of the distinctive Scottish dimension is considered in answering these questions.

THE INTELLECTUAL PRETENSIONS OF THATCHERISM

In two major speeches in Scotland, given within nine days of each other in May 1988, the Prime Minister set out her views. In her 'Sermon on the Mound,' an address to the General Assembly of the Church of Scotland, she liberally, and all too literally, quoted from the bible which she claimed provided a 'proper attitude to work, and the principles to shape economic and social life'.[1] She quoted St Paul's letter to the Thessalonians, 'If a man will not work he shall not eat', though her interpretation differed from theologians who note the context of the letters involving, as they did, St Paul chastising parasitic preachers living off those who were least well off,[2] A. L. Moore encapsulates the arguments made by a number of other writers on the Pauline Epistles:

> the emphasis is upon 'will not' and designates that persons whose inclination is against earning his living and who prefers to burden others. It certainly does not refer to those who cannot, through incapacity, work nor those for whom no work is available.[3]

Having listened to the Prime Minister, though only after five Kirk Ministers had objected to her presence, the Moderator presented her with copies of two reports, 'Housing Scotland's People' and 'Just Sharing'. Both were highly critical of Government policies and involved a radically different interpretation of the social and economic meaning of Biblical texts. The Kirk did not respond to the speech itself for nine months. In February 1989 the Moderator, the Rt Rev Professor James Whyte, noted that in the *Sermon on the Mound* and in other speeches made subsequently he 'heard much about the importance of the individual, a little about the family, but nothing at all about these other communities which give us our sense of where we belong'.[4] The response from the Conservatives included Nicholas Fairbairn's suggestion that Professor White was a 'socialist animal, totally uninterested in Christian duty'.[5] The problem for the Conservatives was that Mrs Thatcher had mixed politics with religion when she invited herself to the General Assembly. They could not complain when the Church decided to respond.

The week before the *Sermon on the Mound* Mrs Thatcher had invoked her secular mentors at the Scottish Tory party conference.[6] Scotland, she argued, had 'invented Thatcherism' long before she was thought of. The values of 'hard work, self-reliance, thrift, enterprise – the relishing of challenges, the seizing of opportunities' were what the Tories stood for and what Scotland stood for. Four nineteenth-century Scottish entrepreneurs were cited: Andrew Carnegie, James Watt, John McAdam and Alexander Graham Bell. These were strange names for Mrs Thatcher to cite. Each of them had benefited from a public education in Scotland and each had found *laissez-faire* Scotland insufficiently attractive to spend his most productive years in the country. Carnegie and Bell went to the United States and Watt to the English Midlands. John McAdam, too, spent considerable time outside Scotland, including some time in the United States. McAdam had been impoverished by his work and in 1820 had petitioned Parliament and received the substantial sum of £2,000 in 1825 and was appointed to the public office of surveyor-general of metropolitan roads in 1827. The examples of these four might suggest two enduring features of Scottish life – the importance of the public sector and the long history of Scottish emigration – as much as Thatcherite values which were certainly evident in Carnegie's attitude towards trade unions.

Adam Ferguson, David Hume and Adam Smith were also claimed as early Thatcherites. Each is worth considering briefly, as certain values associated with them will be returned to later. Though relatively unrecognized in his own country, Adam Ferguson has been described as the 'father of sociology'.[7] Ferguson recognised the 'fact of society, of the dependence of the individual upon the group, of the need of viewing man in society to understand his life at all'.[8] Margaret Thatcher's assertion that there is no such thing as society[9] simply cannot be squared with her claim to the legacy of Adam Ferguson. Additionally, Ferguson's critique of the consequences of the division of labour and the implications of untrammelled capitalist development is apposite today:

> Manufactures prosper most, where the mind is least consulted, and where the workshop may, without any great effort of imagination, be considered, as an engine, the parts of which are men ... And thinking itself, in this age of separations, may become a peculiar craft.[10]

Ferguson's comments were not, of course, intended as a prescription but a warning – a point well understood by Karl Marx who quoted the passage in his famous attack on Proudhon, and later in *Capital*.[11]

Hume's major contribution to philosophy was his *Treatise on Human Nature*. In this he maintained that politics 'consider men as united in society, and dependent on each other'.[12] His was not an individualist philosophy. Hume's philosophical scepticism might be seen as essentially conservative, though debate continues as to the relationship between his philosophical convictions and his political outlook.[13] Certainly, Quinton has emphasised the importance of scepticism within English conservatism.[14] But though scepticism may with justification be regarded as part of the conservative tradition it would be a fallacy to assume that scepticism predicates conservatism. The absence of scepticism from contemporary Conservatism is particularly noteworthy, though a number of traditionalists such as Ian Gilmour would still see it as essential. Notably, the most distinguished twentieth century sceptical conservative, Michael Oakeshott, has been disowned by thinkers associated with Thatcherite values. Norman Barry for example argues that it is erroneous to associate Oakeshott with the Conservative Party.[15] So too does W. H. Greenleaf, though more of an admirer of Oakeshott.[16] Oakeshott appears to be a twentieth century Humean sceptic and, interestingly, opposed to rationalism in politics and is temperamentally disinclined to being partisan in a very Humean way. There is little in the way of scepticism in 'conviction politics'.[17] The absence of scepticism from contemporary Conservatism has been a most significant development that has been evident, particularly in speeches by Mrs Thatcher.

The absurdity of the Prime Minister citing David Hume, infamous atheist in his day, at the Scottish Conservative Party conference only a week before she visited the Church's General Assembly, where she claimed Christianity as essential to her philosophy, seems to have been missed by commentators. Hume's atheism caused the rejection of his application for the Professorship of Moral and Pneumatic Philosophy at Edinburgh University, the institution within which Mrs Thatcher delivered her lecture to the General Assembly. His atheism and philosophy were strongly attacked by that arch-Conservative Edmund Burke.[18] Echoes of the philosopher's contempt for the 'barbarians who inhabit the Banks of the Thames' and his extreme distaste for the anti-Scottish sentiment he encountered in London in the 1760s have their parallels with Scottish attitudes today.[19]

Adam Smith is generally associated with modern right-wing thinking largely due to the Manchester School and, latterly, the activities of the Adam Smith Institute. His best known work, if little read, is *The Wealth of Nations* but he regarded his *Theory of Moral Sentiments* published in 1759 as his most important one. His moral philosophy was greatly influenced by his friend David Hume. Wealth acquisition, the devotion to arduous labour to amass a fortune is described contemptuously by Smith. Wealth and greatness, he writes, 'are often regarded with the respect and admiration which are due only to wisdom and virtue'.[20] His *Theory of Moral Sentiments* has a sociological component, a sociology of sympathy or empathy. Heilbroner has stated that in its largest focus it is a book,

> about the socialization of men and women who have emerged from the straitjacket of a traditional, often dogmatic social order, and must create a workable system of morality and social order in a new condition of 'perfect' liberty. Smith shows us that the liberty is not perfect.[21]

His theory rejects the possibility of a morality based on individualist principles, of 'perfect liberty' and is founded in his conception of human nature as is explicit in the opening sentence of the book:

> How selfish soever man may be supposed, there are evidently some principles in his nature, which interest him in the fortune of others, and render their happiness necessary to him, though he derives nothing from it except the pleasure of seeing it.[22]

Smith's notion of the 'hidden hand' appears in the *Theory of Moral Sentiments*, meaning deistic intervention, and clearly is antagonistic to Mandeville's belief that 'private vices are public benefits',[23] This is far removed from the crude caricature of Smith as the economistic individualist so often portrayed. As many authorities on Smith have pointed out, his works are both subtle and complex.[24]

Selective quotation from Smith's work is common. In an *Adam Smith Institute* publication, Douglas Mason argued the case for the introduction of the poll tax and included a quotation from Smith at the front of the work:

Capitation taxes are levied at very little expense, and, where they are rigorously exacted, afford a very sure revenue to the state.[25] But Mason failed to quote the very next sentence:

It is upon this account that in countries where the ease, comfort, and security of the inferior ranks of people are little attended to, capitation taxes are very common.[26]

Book Five of *The Wealth of Nations* includes a section on taxation which makes clear Smith's antipathy to capitation taxes and amongst four maxims he sets for taxation are that 'subjects of every state ought to contribute towards the support of the government, as nearly as possible, in proportion to their respective abilities'.[27] The poll tax is undeniably regressive and thereby fails to meet this maxim, The fourth maxim was that every tax should be 'so contrived as both to take out and to keep out of the pockets of the people as little as possible over and above what it brings into the public treasure of the state' and refers to different ways in which this could occur; by a 'great number of additional officers', by 'subjecting the people to the frequent visits and the odious examination of the tax-gatherers, it may expose them to much unnecessary trouble, vexation, and oppression'.[29] The poll tax also fails to meet this maxim.

Adam Smith's views must be interpreted in the historical context in which they were set. The Adam Smith Institute and Margaret Thatcher portray a deracinated caricature of Adam Smith and other Enlightenment thinkers. Smith's writing is more often assumed to be the basis of the New Right than is actually demonstrated to be so. Attempts to find some ideological coherence and intellectual justifications based in the Scottish Enlightenment for the policies of the Thatcher years have been made. But on close examination, 'Thatcherism' is seen to be tawdry, far from coherent and fails to measure up to the traditions and values of the Scottish Enlightenment.

A SCOTTISH DEPENDENCY CULTURE?

The Adam Smith Institute (established in 1977) and Institute of Economic Affairs (established in 1955) have been the main platforms for New Right thinking in Britain. Scant attention has been paid to Scotland *per se* by the New Right. This is partly because the territorial dimension is seen as contingent. The hegemony of a radical, quasi-socialist culture in Scotland is thought to be infertile ground for market-oriented ideas. Allan Massie wrote in 1984 of the strong support for massive state involvement in the Scottish Left and the numb-minded response of the Scottish Right, who 'said nothing that was intellectually challenging. It just dug itself into a trench'.[29]

The notion of dependency cultures is an American import. In Britain there has been no systematic intellectual thesis produced of the kind that has appeared in the United States. Neither the polemical work of George Gilder[30] nor the more academically rigorous work of

Charles Murray[31] has found its equivalent in this country. In the preface to his later work, Gilder acknowledged his debt to supply-side economics and to politicians on the Republican Right such as David Stockman, Jack Kemp and Ronald Reagan.[32]

The American 'New Right' have maintained that the effort and resources poured into helping the least well off have been wasted; state support leads to dependence whereas the market encouraged self-sufficiency. The war on poverty programme inaugurated by President Johnson has been the major focus of these critics; it is criticized as ineffective and deemed to have undermined personal and family responsibilities. According to Charles Murray, American social policy since 1964 has ignored three basic premises which has 'thereby created much of the mess we are in':

Premise 1: People respond to incentives and disincentives. Sticks and carrots work.

Premise 2: People are not inherently hard-working or moral. In the absence of countervailing influences, people will avoid work and be amoral.

Premise 3: People must be held responsible for their actions. Whether they *are* responsible in some ultimate philosophical or biochemical sense cannot be the issue if society is to function.[33]

It is asserted that the provision of state support, however well-intentioned, ineluctably results in the stifling entrepreneurial talents, leads to indolence, and any prospect of individual responsibility is lost. According to its proponents, the dependency thesis owes much to classical economists, including Adam Smith. As there was no welfare state in existence during Adam Smith's period and state intervention was of a minimal kind, Smith's comments on dependency are non-existent, and anything said about his views must be extrapolated from his commentary on his world. Perhaps the nearest comments he made which might justify New Right claims to his legacy, in terms of dependency at least, are to be found in Book Three of *The Wealth of Nations* and his *Lectures on Justice, Police, Revenue and Arms*. In the former he argues that the rural population have been set free from servile dependency on overlords and have become wage earners more or less independent of the landowner class. While the free market has been the liberator from the servility of feudalism it cannot also be the liberator from itself. In his *Lectures* he maintains that

it is not so much the police that prevents the commission of crimes as the having as few persons as possible to live upon others. Nothing tends so much to corrupt mankind as dependence, while independence still increases the honesty of the people. The establishment of commerce . . . is the best police for preventing crimes. The common people have better ages in this way than in any other, and in consequence of this a general probity of manners takes place through the whole country.[34] That servility and dependence is to be deplored is not the same as deploring those who find themselves servile and dependent, a point already made regarding Thatcher's misunderstanding of the Pauline Epistles. It can equally be maintained, in Smithian style, that employment is the best means of avoiding dependence; dependence is the consequence not the cause of the problem which requires to be addressed. If neither the state nor the free market successfully tackles the problem – and the free market right must take some responsibility for both in contemporary Britain – it does not appear to be in the tradition of Adam Smith to blame those who are dependent.

The nearest coherent application of the dependency thesis to Scotland has emerged from the Adam Smith Institute in its *Omega Report on Scottish Policy* and in Michael Fry's *Patronage and Principle*. Journalistic support for these views has been provided by Allan Massie in columns in the press. The *Omega Report* set out a programme of radical reforms which amounted to a manifesto for minimal government. The Scottish Development Agency, Highlands and Islands Development Board and regional assistance would all go. Public housing would be further privatised and parents, pupils and employers would have greater powers over education. The free market would reign supreme, and Scotland would prosper. In praising these proposals, Massie saw them as returning Scotland to eighteenth-century benign neglect. His comments on Glasgow were notable:

> Glasgow is well known as the epicentre of Scotland's economic disaster. It is ironic to recall that the city's motto is 'Let Glasgow Flourish'; it is something that has been abandoned; the policy for the last 50 years has been 'Make Glasgow Flourish', not the same thing. The original motto appeals to the ebullience of natural forces; the revised one asserts the superior wisdom of imposed rationalism.[35]

The strict division of the world into public and private arenas has been a feature of New Right thinkers, with the former castigated for stifling entrepreneurial talents and the latter praised, if not worshipped. Massie's comments on Glasgow typify the response, but also raise a problem for contemporary Scottish Conservatives who divide the world in this way.

The development of Glasgow is an interesting case. The city's renaissance has been widely acclaimed in recent years. The new self-confidence of Glasgow certainly conflicts with Massie's comments. Much of the debate on the regeneration of the city concerns the roles of the public and private sectors. Government spokesmen can hardly maintain that regeneration has simply been the consequence of market forces, given the traditional and continuing levels of public sector involvement. Also, that would imply that central

government played no part. In fact, government spokesmen have
articulated a more sophisticated explanation, arguing that central
government has created the conditions and opportunities for regeneration. However, overwhelming evidence exists to demonstrate the
importance of the public sector in regenerating the city, and the
desparate need for much more public support in some of the most
neglected areas.[36] Keating demonstrated that Glasgow city centre's
revival was 'largely due to the efforts of public policy', not a *laissez-
faire* régime, and that the neglected peripheral estates require public
investment.[37]

Studies of regeneration in other parts of Britain confirm the importance of public policy and public investment in regeneration. The
development of the 'high-tech corridor' along the M4 motorway from
West London to Bristol has been described as 'Sunrise Strip', and the
place where the 'recession passed almost unnoticed'.[38] Far from this
area having benefited from the market, it is clear that active public
policy measures over many years have been vitally important. Defence research establishments 'played a crucial role' as did military
procurement generally with the consequence of 'counteracting and
swamping the effects of conventional regional development expenditure'.[39] Additional public sector policies were important, even if this
'occurred by accident'. Transport planning priorities since the war,
including the siting of Heathrow Airport, the development of the M4
motorway and British Rail's high speed trains all served to provide an
'excellent communications infrastructure' and thereby helped the
area attract investment and employment.[40] Other factors were important, but there can be no doubt that public policy and public
expenditure ensured that the economic boom occurred in this
favoured area.

THE CORPORATE STATE

Michael Fry's challenging work *Patronage and Principle* is a piece of
secondary history. The work's strength lies in its critique of modern
Scotland and Scottish historiography, but its weakness is its insist-
ence on replacing myths (of which he disposes effectively) with
dubious alternatives. In his concluding remarks, Fry describes Scottish government as,

conducted behind closed doors. Debates are predictable and
lifeless. Policies are geared to institutions and interests either
themselves adjuncts of the bureaucracy or else unconcerned with
any but their own fixed demands. All this has been reflected, too,
in the quality of those attracted to public life, marked by stolid
orthodoxy rather than flamboyance or vision, the sort of people,
moreover, who do not generally expect to be questioned or enjoy
it if they are. The consensus, however well-meaning, inevitably
turns inert, inflexible and hostile to novelty. Perpetual friction

there may be, but it is of the sort which grinds down rather than produces bursts of flame. Against the power of patronage, principle stands little chance.[41] The criticisms of collectivism and bureaucratic sclerosis in Scotland in *Patronage and Principle* are convincing up to a point. In identifying patronage in its twentieth-century form as stultifying and the bureaucratic style as unimaginative and lacking in innovation, Fry ignores the major constraint on radical initiatives, which comes not from within the Scottish polity but is externally imposed by the Treasury and Whitehall. He also implies that secrecy is a particular problem of government in Scotland when it is general to British politics. Indeed, the general thesis that a bureaucratic style of policy-making dominates Scottish politics might well apply to Britain as a whole, as has been argued by Jeremy Richardson and Grant Jordan.[42] The Scottish Office was not created to be an initiator policy, nor even to respond to Scottish demands. Its establishment and its history has been one of applying plans and programmes in a Scottish setting with few opportunities for departures from the Whitehall/Westminster approach. Finance is the major constraining factor but the degree to which the Scottish Office has discretion depends on factors such as whether distinctive Scottish circumstances already prevail, whether there will be any consequential demands south of the border, the extent of pressure exerted by the 'Scottish political community', and whether additional public expenditure is involved. The Scottish Office, as we have seen, developed to create the impression of Scottish control of Scottish affairs but, in reality, is greatly constrained within Westminster and Whitehall in what it can do.

Fry fails to spell out any reforms for the government of Scotland in the book and ends despondently. Elsewhere, for example as one of the author's of the *Omega Report*, Fry has articulated a free market response. Interestingly, he has also been a staunch supporter of Scottish Home Rule – describing this position as 'about as significant in the affairs of the country in our day as the Auld Licht Burghers were in theirs'.[43] This seems strange, given that the free market position has rarely been associated with Home Rule, particularly in recent years. Alan Massie's association of Home Rule with increased state intervention has been a more common view. The explanation for Fry's view seems to lie in his perception of the lack of vitality and scrutiny in public life and his understandable view that Home Rule would provide this. Fry's is thus a more coherent outlook than others of the 'New Right' who adopt an almost nihilistic attitude to public affairs; whereas Fry shares the desire to reduce the role of government he, at least, desires greater democratic control over remaining matters.

The argument that Scotland suffers from bureaucratic sclerosis and lack of vitality has much force. The stark choice which appears increasingly to be offered is the Conservative Government's attempt, selectively, to turn back the clock by limiting the extent and nature of the state, continuation of the old bureaucratic styles criticized by Fry or a participatory alternative involving comprehensive reforms. Conservatives are largely divided between those who wish one of the first two ideals with few arguing for the third. Fry's uniqueness is that he desires a combination of the first and last option.

CONTEMPORARY CONSERVATISM

The debate on contemporary Conservatism is often conducted in terms of whether Thatcherism will outlive Thatcher. Yet, contemporary Conservatism developed in a specific context which will endure. That context might be dated from the decline of Britain after the last war. Britain not only lost an Empire and failed to find a role. Domestically, Britain's decline had far-reaching implications. It was an insidious process which received a fateful jolt with the economic crises of the 1970s. Maintaining the notion of being a significant power in a country suffering from stagflation, appalling industrial relations conflicts, rising unemployment was the context in which Thatcherism developed.

The rise of the newly industrialized countries (some former colonies amongst them) and major developments in communications increased international competition. The products of traditional industries such as steel and shipbuilding, remained in demand, but strong competition came from technologically more advanced countries such as Sweden and West Germany, and from those countries where labour costs gave them an edge such as South Korea and Spain.

But in addition to the problems which have had to be faced by all West European states, Britain has another burden, making it difficult to come to terms with the modern world. British 'greatness' is an essential ingredient of British nationalism, so closely related to British Conservatism. The essence of Thatcherism is not free market economics, privatisation, public expenditure cuts, anti-Europeanism and anti-trade unionism. These are the artefacts of Thatcherism. The essence is the myth of British greatness. In order to maintain the myth that Britain is some kind of international power it was necessary that parts of the post-war consensus would have to be dispensed with. Sir Geoffrey Howe's piece in the publication marking ten years of Tory rule is interesting:

> Our status within the international community has been transformed within just ten years of Conservative Government, from that of a middling – and declining – world power into that of a major influence upon international affairs.[44]

However much these sentiments exaggerate the situation, the importance lies in what is perceived by the British public, at least a sizeable section of them. Putting the Great back in Britain allowed unemployment to soar.

Attacking enemies abroad and enemies within was the language of British nationalism which appealed to a section of the population willing to make sacrifices – or have others make them – to regain the lost senes of national destiny. Correlli Barnett's book *Audit of War* is probably far closer to Margaret Thatcher's perceptions of Britain's decline than anything else. A major area of disagreement no doubt would be Barnett's identification of the Second World War as the foundation of decline – a high point in British history in Thatcher's view. In the book, Barnett catalogues the complacency which permeated British industry and condemns the illusions which were shattered one by one. His conclusion is stark:

As that descent took its course the illusions and the dreams of 1945 would fade one by one – the imperial and Commonwealth role, the world-power role, British industrial genius, and, at the last, New Jerusalem itself, a dream turned to a dank reality of a segregated, subliterate, unskilled, unhealthy and institutionalized proletariat hanging on the nipple of state materialism.[45]

Thatcherism involved the lowering of expectations in order ultimately to regain lost glory – unemployment would have to rise, trade union power curbed, state assets sold off, public provision of services reined back. Britain could no longer afford these 'luxuries'. A wartime mentality was fostered. A 'war', conveniently, was provided by the dictatorship of General Galtiera in Argentina. The South Atlantic conflict was a high point for Thatcherism. The Falklands Factor was really the British Nationalist factor. Extremely bombastic, British nationalism harked back to the days of Empire, to Churchill and to British Greatness. The alternative was presented by the Conservatives – and evidently confirmed by the Labour Party – as weak leadership, schisms, trade union militancy, the 'British disease'.

Scotland presented two problems for the Thatcherite experiment. A high proportion of Scots were recipients of state welfare benefits. State involvement in many industries and a tradition of public provision in education made it less likely that Thatcherite prescriptions of regaining British Greatness by 'rolling back the state' would be attractive. Secondly, a dual nationality – Scots and British – operated in Scotland, whereas south of the border 'English' and 'British' were seen as synonymous. Scots were only too willing to embrace their British identity when they perceived it to be in their interests, but with the demise of 'Great Britain' the Scottish dimension became increasingly important. During the 1970s the discovery of oil made Scottish identity even more attractive. Economically, Scots found that British Greatness in the 1980s was very different from the days of Empire, when individual Scots and the Scottish economy had benefited enormously from being part of Great Britain. In England there was not the alternative receptacle for national identity. Conservatism or Unionism in Scotland today is of a quite different kind from that of only twenty years ago. The social and cultural meaning of Unionism, concerned with Presbyterianism, is now largely irrelevant, though occasional attempts are made to tap the remnants of sectarianism in Scotland by fringes of the Party. The one enduring feature of Unionism is Parliamentary sovereignty. However much Mrs Thatcher claims to believe in the popular will against state rights, the place of Parliament remains paramount in Conservative thinking. A Scottish Assembly will not be contemplated unless *Realpolitik* demands it. Any serious threat to the Anglo-Scottish Union might well be met with an attempt to appease the Scots with some measure of legislative devolution, though this seems improbable under Mrs Thatcher. The nature of such a scheme would be a limited type, with Parliament retaining the right to abolish an Assembly, that is, leaving Parliamentary sovereignty intact.

'Certain features of Thatcherism are novel – some of which will prove transitory while others are more permanent. There are also those aspects which are in the tradition of Conservatism which have been dispensed with during the premiership of Margaret Thatcher, and others which will no doubt return to the lexicon and substance of Conservatism. The permanent features are related to the context in which Thatcherism emerged. The new consensus created by Thatcher – on trade unions, privatisation, increased home ownership and share ownership – are likely to prove permanent. These changes are features of contemporary Britain: Thatcherism in this sense has been embraced by the Labour Party. It is conceivable that the permanent features of Conservatism will prove permanent features of British politics, and that the transitory features may prove as temporary to the Conservative Party as to Britain.

Much of what passes for Thatcherism is rhetoric and style which seem certain to disappear regardless of who replaces Mrs Thatcher. The scepticism mentioned earlier which is a feature of traditional Conservatism is likely to return. This may make the Conservatives more amenable to ideas of Scottish legislative devolution. Scepticism is related to pluralist styles, as it doubts the certainty of any one solution. This too makes a distinctive approach in Scotland more likely. Likely too is a less strident form of British nationalism. The increasingly important European dimension will likely play its part in this. However, the anti-European rhetoric of Thatcherism has been a persistent feature of British nationalism, and seems bound to continue to exist and bombastic British nationalism has proved a useful device at times of domestic difficulties.

'One nation' Conservatism has not disappeared and, no doubt, there are many Conservatives awaiting the day when it will come to the fore within the party and government. In Scotland there was considerable support for this aspect of Conservatism during the twentieth century, Scottish Conservatives have permanently lost the old coalition of support which gave them more votes than any other party. Partly, this coalition was held together in the past by such people as Walter Elliot, Noel Skelton and John Buchan who articulated a distinctively Scottish dimension, stressed the 'one nation' aspect of Conservatism and deliberately set out to appeal to the Presbyterian working class. The working-class Protestant vote no longer functions as a block, and with a leader who sees herself as an English nationalist and is perceived by many Scots to be anti-Scottish, the party have great problems. A new Unionist coalition requires to be forged, but in the present circumstances there appear insurmountable difficulties for the Tories.

CONCLUSION

In the introduction to this book it was argued that a distinctive Scottish dimension to citizenship exists. The sense of national identity in contemporary Scotland with the developed welfare state relates closely with ideas of citizenship. The distinctive nature of education and housing provision in Scotland and the relationship with Scottish political culture have proved important in understanding Scotland's position within the United Kingdom. The emergence and development of the Scottish Office proved important in this. That these aspects of citizenship in Scotland have been perceived to be under attack may explain why the bundle of policies and ideas referred to as New Right or Thatcherism has met with hostility north of the border. It has been easy for opponents of the Conservatives to portray Mrs Thatcher's years as marked by an anti-Scottish bias. That these developments pre-dated Margaret Thatcher's premiership has not helped the Tories particularly given their infatuation with an ideology stressing rolling back the state.

The increased importance of the Scottish aspect of the dual nationality operating north of the border makes it essential for all parties to have a highly distinctive Scottish dimension. In the past, advocacy of increased administrative devolution allowed the Conservatives to appear 'more Scottish' than the Labour Party, but today legislative devolution is the principal yardstick by which the Scottishness is measured. Unless the Conservatives can change the agenda of politics – either by making the British dimension more important in Scotland or by dominating in a distinctive non-Home Rule area of Scottish politics – it seems destined to languish in the polls.

Notes

Introduction

1. *Scotsman/Glasgow Herald*, 10 September 1987.
2. Lucien Pye, 'Political Culture' *International Encyclopedia of Social Sciences* Vol. 12, p. 218.
3. T. H. Marshall, *Citizenship and Social Class.*
4. Anthony Giddens, *Profiles and Critiques and Social Theory*; John Goldthorpe, 'Social inequality and social integration in modern Britain' in D. Wedderburn (ed), *Poverty, Inequality and Class Structure*; Bryan Turner, *Citizenship and Capitalism – The Debate Over Reformism*, Ralf Dahrendorf, *Class and Class Conflict in Industrial Society*; Rheinhold Bendix, *Nation-Building and Citizenship*; M. Mann 'Ruling class strategies and citizenship' in *Sociology* Vol. 21, 1987; J. M. Barbalet, *Citizenship.*
5. Ian Levitt, 'The Scottish Poor Law and Unemployment, 1890–1929' in T. C. Smout (ed), *The Search for Wealth and Security.*
6. T. C. Smout, *A Century of the Scottish People, 1830–1950* (1986), pp. 241–242.
7. James G. Kellas, *The Scottish Political System*, 4th edition.
8. Michael Keating, Arthur Midwinter and James Mitchell, *Government and Politics in Scotland.*
9. Rod Hague and Martin Harrop, *Comparative Government and Politics: An Introduction*, p. 71.
10. Iain Maclean, *The Legend of Red Clydeside*; James D. Young, *The Rousing of the Scottish Working Class.*
11. R. A. Anderson, *Education and Opportunity in Victorian Scotland.*
12. Hansard, Commons, 3rd Series, Vol. 300, August 3, 1885, col. 937.
13. George Elder Davie, *op cit* pp. 75, 286–7, 289. Walter Elliot, *A Scotsman's Heritage.*
14. Charles A. Cooper, *An Editor's Retrospect*, 1896, p. 166.

Chapter One: Conflicts Within Conservatism in Scotland

1. Robert Nisbet, *Conservatism* p. viii.
2. T. S. Eliot, *The Literature of Politics*, p. 22.
3. Vernon Bogdanor, in Zig Layton-Henry (ed.), *Conservative Party Politics*, p. 89.
4. Anthony Quinton, *The Politics of Imperfection*, p. 40.
5. Russell Kirk, *The Conservative Mind*, ch. 4.
6. J. G. Lockhart, *The Life of Sir Walter Scott*, Vol. 11, pp. 284–285.
7. Edwin Muir, *Scott and Scotland*, pp. 90–91.

8. Allan Massie, *Ibid.*, Introduction, p. xvii.
9. David Daiches, *Scott and Scotland* p. 42.
10. P. H. Scott, preface to *The Letters of Malagathi Malagrowther*.
11. P. H. Scott, 'The Malachi Episode', *ibid.*, p. xxvi.
12. P. H. Scott, 'The Politics of Sir Walter Scott', in J. H. Alexander and David Hewitt (eds), *Scott and His Influence*.
13. John Buchan, *Sir Walter Scott*, p. 48.
14. John Buchan, 'We have never objected to things anomolous and logically indefensible, provided they work,' Hansard, Commons, Vol. 208, July 6, 1927, col. 1312.
15. Elliot Papers, Acc. 6721, No. 45; *News Chronicle* August 19, 1952.
16. Colin Coote, *A Companion of Honour*, p. 249.
17. Walter Elliot, *Toryism and the Twentieth Century*, p. 4.
18. *Ibid*, p. 135.
19. Anthony Quinton, *op cit*, p. 16.
20. It could be argued that the Treaty of Union of 1707 is such an entrenched, formal written element. See T. B. Smith, 'The Union of 1707 As Fundamental Law', in *Public Law*, Summer 1957, pp. 99–121.
21. Henry Craik, 'The Cabinet Secretariat', *The Nineteenth Century and After*, p. 215.
22. George Elder Davie, *The Democratic Intellect*.
23. Michael Oakeshott, 'On Being Conservative', in *Rationalism In Politics* pp. 172–173.
24. Sir Ian Gilmour, *Inside Right – A Study of Conservatism*, p. 127.
25. Robert Michels, *Conservatism*, p. 252.
26. Michael Oakeshott, *Rationalism in Politics*, p. 6.
27. *Ibid.*, p. 22.
28. James Kellas, *The Liberal Party in Scotland, 1885–95*, p. 11; Derek Urwin, *Politics and the Development of the Unionist Party in Scotland*, p. 27.
29. G. S. Pryde, *Scotland from 1603 to the Present Day*, p. 209.
30. James Kellas, *op. cit*, p. 405.
31. Derek Urwin, *op. cit*, p. 67.
32. Sydney and Olive Checkland, *Industry and Ethos: Scotland 1832–1914*, p. 83.
33. *Glasgow Herald*, October 22, 1927; speech at 50th anniversary of Scottish Conservative Club, Princes Street, Edinburgh.
34. Urwin, *op. cit*, p. 92 refers to Orange Order actively campaigning in Bothwell for the Unionists as reported in the *Scotsman*, 24 October 1931.
35. Callum Brown, *The Social History of Religion in Scotland*, p. 202.
36. Walter Elliot Papers, National Library of Scotland, Acc. 6721, Box 14.
37. Ian Budge and D. W. Urwin, *Scottish Political Behaviour – A Case Study in British Homogeneity*, p. 62.
38. J. M. Bochel and D. T. Denver, 'Religion and voting: a critical review and a new analysis', *Political Studies* Vol. 18.
39. Anna McCurley, 'Winning back in Scotland', *Reformer – The Journal of the Tory Reform Group*, Autumn 1987.
40. Sir Henry Craik, *A Century of Scottish History*, Vol. I, p. 451
41. *Ibid*, Vol. II, p. 427.

42. D. G. Boyce, 'Dicey, Kilbrandon and Devolution', *Political Quarterly* July–Sept 1975, p. 292.
43. R. S. Rait, 'Dicey', *Dictionary of National Biography, 1922–1930* p. 260.
44. T. B. Smith, 'The Union of 1707 as Fundamental Law', *Public Law*, Summer 1957, p. 99.
45. G. Maher, 'The Identity of the Scottish Legal System', *Juridical Review*, 1977.
46. Hans Kelsen, *General Theory of Law and State*.
47. T. B. Smith, *op. cit.*
48. A. V. Dicey and R. S. Rait, *Thoughts on the Union between England and Scotland*, pp. 244–245.
49. William Keegan, 'The Hi-jacking of a political party', in *Mrs Thatcher's Economic Experiment*; Sir Ian Gilmour, 'The Post-War Years and How Monetarism Captured the Conservatives', in *Britain Can Work*: Dennis Kavanagh, *Thatcherism and British Politics: The End of Consensus?*, p. 248.
50. Norman Barry, *The New Right*, p. 94.
51. *Ibid.*, p. 97.
52. Roger Scruton, *The Meaning of Conservatism*, p. 186.
53. In a paper presented to the Annual Political Studies Association conference in Aberdeen in April 1986, Scruton failed to take into account that many of his assumptions relating to British nationalism were founded in English traditions rather than a British tradition. This was pointed out to him by an American.
54. Desmond King, *The New Right*.
55. Robert Michels, *Conservatism*, p. 230.
56. Samuel Huntington, *Conservatism as an Ideology*, pp. 457–458.
57. Clinton Rossiter, *Conservatism*, p. 294.

Chapter Two: Conservatives and Scottish Administration

1. H. J. Hanham, *Scottish Nationalism*, p. 73.
2. Quoted in H. J. Hanham, *Elections and Party Management: Politics In The Time of Disraeli and Gladstone*, p. 161.
3. H. J. Hanham, *The Creation of the Scottish Office, 1881–87*, pp. 210–11.
4. Gerald Warner, *The Scottish Tory Party*, p. 166.
5. Lord Rosebery is usually credited with having been most active, but his motives were questioned by Gladstone and others. See H. J. Hanham *The Creation of the Scottish Office, 1881–87*; Robert Rhodes James, *Rosebery*, pp. 113–118; Roy Jenkins, *Sir Charles Dilke*, p. 146.
6. *Ibid.*, Salisbury to Richmond and Gordon, August 7, 1885, p. 229.
7. *Ibid.*, August 13 1885, p. 230.
8. H. J. Hanham, *The Development of the Scottish Office*, p. 51.
9. Hansard, Commons, Vol. 62, May 15, 1914, cols. 1547–1548.
10. Report of the Royal Commission on the Civil Service (MacDonnell), 1914, Fourth Report, Cd. 7338, Ch. 9, pp. 77–79, paras. 67–71.
11. Report of the Machinery of Government Committee (Haldane), Cd. 9230, 1918, p. 11, para. 31.
12. Geoffrey Marshall, *Constitutional Conventions*, pp. 54–55.
13. Hansard, Commons, Vol. 195, May 7 1926, col. 611.
14. *Ibid.*, col. 616.
15. *Ibid.*, Vol. 192, February 28, 1928, col. 266.
16. *Ibid.*, Vol. 204, March 23, 1927, col. 474.

17. *Ibid.*, Vol. 192, March 5, 1928, col. 869.
18. *Ibid.*, Vol. 204, March 23 1927, col. 482.
19. *Ibid.*, Vol. 192, February 28 1928, col. 272.
20. *Ibid.*, Vol. 272, November 24, 1932, col. 251.
21. Gilmour Papers, GD 383/61/1, 68/2, 68/4, 68/5, 68/7x, 68/8, 68/9, 68/11x, for correspondence between Gilmour and Collins and Elliot.
22. Report of the Committee on Scottish Administration (Gilmour), Cmd. 5563, October 1937.
23. Sir Reginald Coupland, *Welsh and Scottish Nationalism*, p. 404.
24. Christopher Harvie, *Scottish Nationalism*, p. 51.
25. H. J. Hanham, *The Development of the Scottish Office*, pp. 67–68.
26. *Ibid.*, p. 67.
27. R. H. Campbell, 'The Committee of Ex-Secretaries of State for Scotland and Industrial Policy, 1941–1945' *Scottish Industrial History*, Vol. 2, 1979.
28. Tom Johnston, *Memories*, p. 150.
29. *Ibid.*, p. 164.
30. Sir Norman Chester, *The Nationalisation of British Industry, 1945–51*, p. 432.
31. *Ibid.*, p. 674.
32. *Scotsman*, May 21, 1949.
33. Elliot papers, Acc. 6721, Box 9.
34. *Ibid.*
35. The committee consisted of James Stuart MP (chairman), Lord Clydesmuir, Col. A. Gomme Duncan MP, Walter Elliot MP, Cdr. T. D. Galbraith MP, G. I. Clark Hutchison MP, W. S. Morrison MP, W. McNair-Snadden MP, Sir Basil Neven Spence MP, Sir Arthur Young MP, Col. P. J. Blair, Mrs. Stirling Brown, Charles G. Connell, Mrs. Chriton, Ian Dickson, Col. William Forbes, J. J. Craik Henderson, Capt. J. H. F. McEwen, Cllr. J. Logan Strang, G. A. Williamson, Major Iain MacLeod (secretary), *Scotsman* November 29, 1949.
36. *Scotsman*, November 29, 1949.
37. *Scotsman*, November 30, 1949.
38. James A. A. Porteous, *Unionist Policy for Scotland – A Criticism*, pp. 8–9.
39. Sir Norman Chester, *The Nationalization of British Industry, 1945–51*, p. 1031.
40. Lord Home, *The Way The Wind Blows*, p. 103.
41. Kenneth Young, *Sir Alec Douglas Home*, p. 82.
42. Hansard, Commons, Vol. 493, November 6, 1951, cols. 62–63.
43. *Ibid.*, November 21, 1951, col. 486.
44. Anthony Seldon, *op. cit.*, p. 133.
45. *Ibid.*, Vol. 493, November 8, 1951, col. 397.
46. Mackenzie Committee Report, 1962, Cmnd, 1859.
47. Committee on Scottish Financial and Trade Statistics (Catto Report), July 1952, Cmd. 8609.
48. Hansard, Commons, Vol. 504, July 24, 1952, col. 768.
49. Anthony Seldon, *Churchill's Indian Summer – The Conservative Government, 1951–55*.
50. James Stuart, *Within The Fringe*, pp. 69, 161.
51. John P. Mackintosh, *The British Cabinet*, p. 504.

52. Report of the Committee on Scottish Financial and Trade Statistics (Catto), July 1952, Cmd. 8609.
53. Gilmour Papers, GD 383/43/118, October 6, 1932.
54. Hansard, Commons, Vol. 504, July 24, 1952, cols. 768.
55. John MacCormick, *The Flag In The Wind*, pp. 185–186.
56. Report of the Royal Commission on Scottish Affairs, 1952–54, July 1954, Cmd. 9212, p. 12, para. 13.
57. The Committee consisted of Walter Elliot, J. H. R. Hutchison, J. S. Maclay, Col. Alan Gomme-Duncan, R. Brooman-White.
58. *Glasgow Herald*, December 23, 1954.
59. Christopher Harvie, *No Gods and Precious Few Heroes*, pp. 48–52.
60. *Employment Policy*, 1944, Cmd. 6527.
61. Gavin McCrone, *Scotland's Economic Progress, 1951–60*, p. 131.
62. Barry Moore and John Rhodes, 'Regional Economic Policy and the Movement of Manufacturing Firms to Development Areas' in *Economica* Vol. 43 (1976), pp. 17–31.
63. Charles Oakley, *Scottish Industry Today*, (1937)
64. A. D. Campbell, *Changes in Scottish Income, 1924–49*, p. 233.
65. Gavin McCrone, *op. cit.* p. 21, Tables I, II, pp. 31–32.
66. *The Next Five Years*, Conservative Party Manifesto, 1959.
67. *Glasgow Herald*, May 12, 1956.

Chapter Three: Unionist Opposition to Scottish Home Rule

1. Hansard, Lords, Vol. 262, June 13, 1881, col. 320.
2. I. G. C. Hutchison, *A Political History of Scotland, 1832–1924*, p. 171.
3. Gordon Donaldson, 'Scottish Devolution – The Historical Background in J. N. Wolfe, *Government and Nationalism in Scotland*, p. 9.
4. John E. Kendle, *The Round Table Movement And Imperial Union*, p. 154.
5. *Ibid.*, p. 140.
6. Sir Reginald Coupland, *Welsh And Scottish Nationalism*, p. 314.
7. *Times*, April 16, 1918. Letter signed by Laurence Hardy, J. F. Mason, A. Shirley Benn, J. W. Hills, G. R. Lane-Fox, Leslie Wilson, Waldorf Astor, Edward Wood, George Lloyd.
8. *Scotsman*, November 27, 1918.
9. *Hansard*, Commons, Vol. 116, June 3, 1919, cols. 1873–1974, June 4, 1919, cols. 2063–2129.
10. *Ibid.*, Hugh Edwards MP, June 4, col. 2122.
11. H. J. Hanham, *Scottish Nationalism*, p. 107.
12. Hansard, Commons, Vol. 173, May 9, 1924, cols. 848–850.
13. *Ibid.*, cols. 802–803.
14. Balfour's in October 1927 on the 'Ideals of Unionism' in Edinburgh is an example. *Glasgow Herald*, October 22, 1927.
15. John Malcolm McEwen, *Unionist and Conservative Members of Parliament, 1914–1939*, p. 172.
16. Hansard, Commons, Vol. 272, Nov. 24, 1932, col. 245.
17. Michael Keating and David Bleiman, *Labour and Scottish Nationalism*, p. 30.
18. Hansard, Commons, Third Series, Vol. 335, April 9, 1889, cols. 98–99.
19. *Ibid.*, col. 110.
20. Keating and Bleiman, *op. cit.*, p. 46.

21. *Ibid.*, p. 62.
22. *The Spectator*, June 23, 1928.
23. *Daily Express*, December 6, 1929.
24. Gilmour Papers, GD 383/29/32–33, July 12, 1929.
25. S. B. Chrimes, *The General Election in Glasgow, February 1950*, p. 81.
26. Hansard, Commons, Vol. 189, May 26, 1908.
27. Walter Elliot, *The Devolution Report, circa*, 1920, amongst newspaper cuttings in Elliot papers, Acc. 6721, No. 11.
28. *Glasgow Herald*, October 26, 1932.
29. *Times*, November 15, 1932. The signatories included the Dukes of Buccleuch, Argyll, Richmond and Gordon, and Atholl; Lords Ailsa, Linlithgow, Morton, Caithness, Moray, Mar and Kellie, Dunedin, Lovat, Elphinstone, Lamington, Sempill, Glentanar, and Weir.
30. *Times*, November 21, 25, 1932.
31. *Glasgow Herald*, December 1, 1932.
32. Montrose, MacEwen, McDowell, Sir Henry Keith, Sir D. M. Stevenson, Sir W. E. Whyte, Sheriff J. R. N. McPhail, Sir Robert Wright, Prof. A. Berriedale Keith, Messrs. W. E. Bosomworth Andrew Dewar Gibb, J. F. Stewart, John Ritchie, E. Rosslyn Mitchell, W. Kelvin Thomson, Ernest Glen, Harold Alexander, Mrs. Burnett Smith, *Glasgow Herald* December 6, 1932.
33. *Glasgow Herald*, December 6, 1932.
34. *Ibid.*, February 1, 1933.
35. Hansard, Commons, Vol. 272, November 24, 1932, col. 261.
36. John MacCormick, *The Flag In the Wind*, pp. 120–121.
37. Christopher Harvie, *No Gods and Precious Few Heroes*, p. 107.
38. *Scotsman*, February 15, 1950.

Chapter Four: The Adoption of Legislative Devolution

1. *Scotsman*, April 24, 1965.
2. N. M. Kelly, D. Bogie, D. Murdie, W. Reid, *Devolution: A New Appraisal*, p. 4.
3. *Ibid.*, p. 5.
4. *Ibid.*, p. 8.
5. A. Pollock, N. Asprey and M. Ancram, *Scottish Education – A Time for Decision*, Thistle Group Paper No. 2, p. 11.
6. Resolution submitted by the Thistle Group to Scottish Conservative and Unionist Association Conference, May 13–15, 1971: from Conference Handbook.
7. Edward Taylor, 'Inside Look at Scottish Tories', *New Outlook*, November 1969.
8. John Ramsden. *The Making of Conservative Party Policy*, p. 264.
9. *Ibid.*, pp. 264–265.
10. *Crossman Diaries*, Vol. 2, pp. 550–551.
11. Geoffrey Smith, 'The Conservative commitment to devolution', in *The Spectator*, February 19, 1977.
12. *Times*, July 8, 1968.
13. Hansard, Commons, January 15, 1976, Vol. 903, col. 623.
14. *Scotland's Government*, para. 104, p. 29.
15. *Ibid.*, para. 287, p. 64.
16. *Ibid.*, para. 264, p. 62.
17. *Ibid.*, para. 273, p. 63.

18. *Ibid.*, pp. 71–72.
19. John P. Mackintosh, *The Devolution of Power*, pp. 169–170.
20. A. W. Bradley, 'Some Constitutional Aspects of Scottish Development' in J. N. Wolfe (ed.), *Government and Nationalism in Scotland*, p. 45.
21. *Scotsman*, June 10, 1970.
22. Hansard, Commons, Vol. 803, 2 July 1970, col. 48.
23. Geoffrey Smith, 'Devolution and not saying what you mean', *The Spectator*, February 26, 1977.
24. John P. Mackintosh, 'The Report of the Royal Commission on the Constitution, 1969–73', originally in *Political Quarterly* 1974, also in Henry Drucker (ed.) *John P. Mackintosh on Scotland*, p. 86.
25. *The Spectator*, February 19 and 26, 1977.
26. Vernon Bogdanor, *Devolution* (1979), p. 111.
27. Kenneth J. Button, 'Spatial Economic Policy' in W. P. J. Maunder, *The British Economy in the 1970s*, p. 174.
28. *Scotsman*, May 13, 1971.
29. *Ibid.*, May 11, 1973.
30. *Ibid.*
31. Geoffrey Smith, *op. cit.*
32. *Scotsman*, May 11, 1973.
33. Written evidence 9, Royal Commission on the Constitution, 1972. Submitted by six members of the Bow Group.
34. Oral evidence from Scottish Chamber of Commerce to Royal Commission on the Constitution. Minutes of Evidence IV, Scotland, July 20, 1970; p. 139, para. 621.
35. Written evidence from Scottish Council of the CBI to the Royal Commission on the Constitution. Minutes of Evidence IV, Scotland, p. 74, para. 4.
36. Oral evidence from the Scottish Council of the CBI to the Royal Commission on the Constitution. Minutes of Evidence IV, Scotland, May 5, 1970, p. 86, paras, 401–407.
37. *Scotsman*, November 8, 1973.
38. *Freedom for all the people; a charter for Scotland*, Conservative Party Scottish Manifesto, October 1974.

Chapter Five: Conservatives in Opposition, 1974–79

1. *Scotsman*, October 7, 1974.
2. Nevil Johnson, *In Search of the Constitution*, pp. 76, 218–219.
3. Ian Lang and Barry Henderson, *The Scottish Conservatives – A Past and A Future*.
4. *'Q'*, November 1, 1975.
5. *Scotsman*, November 12, 1975.
6. *Ibid.*
7. *Ibid.*, October 26, 1976.
8. *Ibid.*, February 21, 1975.
9. *Ibid.*, January 12, 1976.
10. Tam Galbraith, Betty Harvie Anderson, Teddy Taylor and Iain Sproat were Scottish members of the committee. The other members were Maurice Macmillan, Winston Churchill, Nicholas Ridley, Nigel Lawson, Timothy Renton, Hugh Dykes, David Walder, Ian Gow, Peter Morrison and Peter Rees.

11. *Scotsman*, May 15, 1976.
12. John Biffen, *A Nation in Doubt*.
13. Michael Keating and David Bleiman, *Labour and Scottish Nationalism*, p. 186.
14. Grant Jordan, 'The Committee Stage of the Scotland and Wales Bill, 1976–77', Waverley Papers, No. 1. Those who were in favour of the three-line whip against the Bill were Joseph, Davies, Taylor, Heseltine, Maude, Neave, Peyton, Thorneycroft and Whitelaw. Those against were Gilmour, Pym, Prior, Howe, St John Stevas, King and Thatcher.
15. *Ibid*.

Chapter Six: The Scotland Act and Referendum

1. Letter to author, February 3, 1982.
2. Letter to author, February 22, 1982.
3. Allan Macartney, 'The Protagonists' in John Bochel, David Denver and Allan Macartney, *The Referendum Experience*, p. 16.
4. *Scotsman*, September 12, 1977.
5. Balsom and McAllister, 'The Scottish and Welsh Referenda of 1979: Constitutional change and popular choice', *Parliamentary Affairs*, Vol. 32, 1979.
6. Quoted in John Bochel, David Denver and Allan Macartney, *The Referendum Experience*, pp. 22–23.
7. *Scotsman*, January 17, 1979.
8. Letter to author, March 9, 1982.
9. Hansard, Lords, Vol. 390, 11 April 1978, col. 499.
10. Bochel, Denver and Macartney, *op. cit.*, 169–70.
11. *Scotsman*, February 19, 1979.
12. James Callaghan, *Time and Chance*, p. 560.

Chapter Seven: The Thatcher Years

1. Peter Riddell, *The Thatcher Government*, p. 59.
2. Geoffrey Maynard, *The Economy Under Mrs Thatcher*, p. 43.
3. David Smith, *The Rise and Fall of Monetarism*.
4. Godfrey Barker, 'Lame ducks in a grouse moor sanctuary', *Daily Telegraph*, 21 March 1984.
5. Hugo Young and Anne Sloman, *The Thatcher Phenomenon*, p. 43.
6. House of Commons Paper 413, June 1982, Select Committee on Scottish Affairs, Scottish Aspects of 1982–85 Public Expenditure White Paper, Minutes of Evidence, p. 44, para. 10.
7. *Glasgow Herald*, 22 September 1986.
8. *Scotsman*, 15 December 1967.
9. *Ibid*.
10. Neal Ascherson, *Don't be afraid – and don't steal*, p. 3.
11. Quoted in Wayne Parsons. *The Political Economy of British Regional Policy*, p. 187.
12. *Bank of England Quarterly Bulletin*, August 1988, p. 374.
13. *The Economist*, 19 May 1979; Nick Bosanquet, 'Sir Keith Joseph's Reading List' *Political Quarterly*, Vol. 52, 1981.
14. Hugo Young and Anne Sloman, *op. cit.*, p. 69.

15. Brian Hogwood, 'Recent Developments in British Regional Policy', *Strathclyde Papers on Government and Politics*, No. 51, 1987.
16. Wayne Parsons, *op. cit.*, p. 200.
17. *Ibid.*, p. 193.
18. Hansard, Commons, 13 December 1983, Vol. 50, col. 844.
19. Cm. 278, January 1988, p. 2, para, 1, 13.
20. Hansard, Commons, Vol. 33, 1 December 1982.
21. *Scotsman/Glasgow Herald*, 13 November 1982.
22. *Ibid.*, 9 December 1982.
23. 'The Proposed Closure of BSC Gartcosh', *Scottish Affairs Select Committee, 1985–86 Session*, 18 December 1985, Parliamentary Papers 154.
24. Brian Ashcroft, 'Using our own devices', *Scottish Business Insider*, July 1988, p. 63.
25. *Scotsman*, 17 October 1980.
26. C. Robinson and E. Marshall, *Oil's Contribution to UK Self-Sufficiency*.
27. Geoffrey Maynard, *op. cit.*, pp. 52–53.
28. *Conservative Manifesto for Scotland*, p. 24.
29. Hansard, Commons, Vol. 973, 7 November 1979, cols. 234–235.
30. *Ibid.*, Vol. 6, 16 June 1981, col. 968.
31. *Glasgow Herald*, 30 April 1986.
32. Donald Dewar, 'The Select Committee on Scottish Affairs', *Scottish Government Yearbook 1981*, p. 25.
33. Notes for speech by George Younger addressing Royal Institute of Public Administration, City Chambers, Edinburgh, 29 October 1982.
34. H. Drucker and J. G. Kellas, 'The Scottish Affairs Committee' in Gavin Drewry (ed), *The New Select Committees: a study of the 1979 reforms*, p. 228.
35. *Ibid.*, p. 235.
36. *Glasgow Herald*, 25 July 1987.
37. Hansard, Commons, Vol. 125, 13 January 1988, col. 397.
38. *Glasgow Herald*, 22 June 1987.
39. *Glasgow Herald*, 15 August 1987.
40. 'Waiting in the wings: an interview with Brian Meek', *Radical Scotland* No. 29, Oct/Nov 1987, pp. 10–12.
41. J. Ross Harper, *Devolution*.
42. Michael Ancram, *Devolution – Why Not?*
43. *Scotsman*, 19 November 1987.
44. John Davidson, 'Unwilling to go it alone', *Scottish Business Insider* Vol. 5, No. 6, June 1988, pp. 20–22.
45. *Glasgow Herald*, 12 May 1988.
46. *Scotsman* and *Glasgow Herald*, 13 May 1988.
47. *Ibid.*
48. *Scotsman*, 1 March 1988.
49. *Glasgow Herald*, 9 May 1988.
50. *Q*, 1 November 1975.
51. *Glasgow Herald/Scotsman*, 24 November 1987.
52. *Sun*, 24 November 1987.
53. Hansard, Vol. 124, 9 December 1988, cols. 439–454.
54. *Ibid.*, Vol. 120, 22 July 1987, cols 233–234.
55. *Scotsman*, 5 September 1988.

56. CM, 242, November 1987.
57. *Housing Scotland's People*, p. 45.
58. Duncan Forrester and Danus Skene (eds). *Just Sharing*, pp. 12–13.
59. Michael Keating, *Glasgow: the city that refused to die*, p. 160.
60. *Scotsman*, 16 January 1981.
61. *Financial Times*, 5 November 1981.
62. COSLA, *Central/Local Government Relations: a time to listen – a time to speak out*, p. 31, para. 71.
63. Michael Forsyth, *The case for a poll tax*; Douglas Mason, *Revising the rating system*.
64. Cmnd. 9714, January 1986.
65. *Paying for Local Government*, p. 24, para. 3, 35.
66. Abolition of Domestic Rates (Scotland) Act 1987, Part IV, clause 24.
67. *Paying for Local Government*, Annex J.
68. Arthur Midwinter and Colin Mair, *Rates Reform: Issues, Arguments and Evidence*.
69. *Ibid.*, ch. 4.
70. Hansard, Commons, Vol. 115, 5 May 1987, col. 573.
71. 'The Poll Tax: Fair and Workable?', *Weekend World*, 11 October 1987.

Chapter Eight: Contemporary Conservatism: From Dependency to Enterprise?

1. *Glasgow Herald/Scotsman*, 23 May 1988.
2. Hans-Andreas Egenolf, 'The Second Epistle to the Thessalonians' in John L. McKenzie (ed), *New Testament for Spiritual Reading*, pp. 157, 159; F. F. Bruce, *1 & 2 Thessalonians, World Biblical Commentary*, Vol. 45, p. 206; E. J. Bicknell, *The First and Second Epistle to the Thessalonians*, p. 93; William Neil, *The Epistle of Paul to the Thessalonians*, p. 194.
3. A. L. Moore, *1 & 2 Thessalonians*, p. 118.
4. *Glasgow Herald*, 18 February 1989.
5. *Ibid*.
6. *Glasgow Herald/Scotsman*, 14 May 1989.
7. H. E. Barnes, 'Sociology before Comte', *American Journal of Sociology*, p. 32; Duncan Forbes, 'Introduction' to *An Essay On The History Of Civil Society*, p. xiii.
8. W. C. Lehmann, *Adam Ferguson and the Beginnings of Modern Sociology*, p. 48.
9. Margaret Thatcher asserted on 1 November 1987. 'There is no such thing as society. There are individual men and women and there are families.' A report by Robert Harris in the *Sunday Times*, 23 July 1989, stated that Mrs Thatcher had edited a speech by Kenneth Clarke, her Health Minister, and removed the word 'society' whenever it appeared.
10. Adam Ferguson, *An Essay On The History Of Civil Society*, pp. 182–183.
11. Karl Marx, *The Poverty of Philosophy*, p. 145; *Capital*, pp. 382–383.
12. David Hume, *A Treatise of Human Nature*, Vol. I, p. 5.
13. See for example David Miller, *Hume's Political Thought* on the one hand; and Bertrand Russell, 'A Reply to my Critics', Geoffrey Marshall, 'David Hume and Political Scepticism' and Duncan Forbes, *Hume's Philosophical Politics* on the other.
14. Anthony Quinton, *The Politics of Imperfection*.

15. Norman Barry, *The New Right*, p. 94.
16. W. H. Greenleaf, *Oakeshott's Philosophical Politics*, p. 81.
17. Dennis Kavanagh, *Thatcherism and British Politics*, p. 7.
18. Ernest Mossner, *The Life of David Hume*, p. 394.
19. *Ibid.*, ch. 28.
20. Adam Smith, *Theory of Moral Sentiments*, pp. 61–62.
21. Robert L. Heilbroner, *The Essential Adam Smith*, p. 62.
22. Adam Smith, *Theory of Moral Sentiments*, p. 9.
23. Bernard Mandeville, *The Fable of the Bees, or Private Vices, Public Benefits*.
24. A. L. Macfie, 'The Moral Justification of Free Enterprise', *Scottish Journal of Political Economy*, Vol. 14; E. R. Seligman, 'Introduction', 1910 edition *Wealth of Nations*; J. Viner, 'Adam Smith and Laissez-faire', *Journal of Political Economy*, Vol. 35; L. Robbins, *The Theory of Economic Policy in English Classical Political Economy*; Andrew Skinner, *A System of Social Science: Papers relating to Adam Smith, Adam Smith and the role of the state* and 'Adam Smith and Economic Liberalism', *Hume Occasional Paper* 9.
25. Douglas Mason, *Revising the Rating System*, p. iii.
26. Adam Smith, *An Enquiry into the Nature and Causes of the Wealth of Nations*, Book V, ch. II, Art IV, p. 399.
27. *Ibid.*, p. 350.
28. *Ibid.*, p. 352.
29. *The Spectator*, 14 January 1984.
30. George Gilder, *Wealth and Poverty*.
31. Charles Murray, *Losing Ground: American Social Policy, 1950–1980*.
32. G. Gilder, *Wealth and Poverty*.
33. Charles Murray, *op. cit.*, p. 146.
34. Adam Smith, 'Lectures on Justice, Police, Revenue and Arms' in H. W. Schneider (ed.), *Adam Smith's Moral and Political Philosophy*, II, i, i.
35. *Ibid.*, 21 January 1984.
36. Michael Keating, *Glasgow: the City that Refused to Die*; M. Keating and J. Mitchell, 'Urban Change and Public Policy in Glasgow', *Scottish Government Yearbook 1987* and *Easterhouse: An Urban Crisis*.
37. Michael Keating, *op. cit.*, p. 196, ch. 6.
38. *The Economist*, 30 January 1982; A. Neil, 'The Information Revolution' *The Listener*, 23 June 1983; Peter Hall *et. al.*, *Western Sunrise*, p. 3.
39. Peter Hall *et. al.*, *op. cit.*, p. 176.
40. *Ibid.*, p. 178.
41. Michael Fry, *Patronage and Principle*, pp. 255–256.
42. J. J. Richardson and A. G. Jordan, *Governing Under Pressure* and *British Politics and the Policy Process*.
43. M. Fry *op. cit.*, p. 5.
44. Conservative Party, *The First Ten Years*, p. 31.
45. Correlli Barnett, *The Audit of War*, p. 304.

Bibliography

This bibliography contains articles, books and official publications consulted. Various other publications, including numerous Conservative Party publications were consulted. Selected newspaper articles are referenced.

Newspapers and periodicals:
Daily Record, Daily Telegraph, Economist, Financial Times, Glasgow Herald, Observer, Q, Radical Scotland, Scotsman, Scottish Business Insider, Spectator, Sunday Times, Times

Private and public collections of papers held in Aberdeen University Library, Bodleian Library, Oxford, Churchill College Library, Cambridge, National Library of Scotland, Scottish Records Office, Edinburgh:
Sir Henry Craik Papers, National Library of Scotland, Edinburgh.
Walter Elliot Papers, National Library of Scotland, Edinburgh.
Sir John Gilmour Papers, Scottish Records Office, Edinburgh.
Tom Johnston Papers, National Library of Scotland, Edinburgh.
Sir Archibald Sinclair (Thurso) Papers, Churchill College Archive Centre, Cambridge.

Books and articles
Ancram, Michael (1988), *Devolution – Why Not?*, (London: Aims of Industry).
Anderson, R. D. (1983), *Education and Opportunity in Victorian Scotland* (Oxford: Oxford University Press).
Ascherson, Neal (1986), *Don't be afraid – and don't steal*, (Edinburgh: SNP publications).
Ashcroft, Brian (1988), 'Using our own devices', *Scottish Business Insider* Vol. 5.
Bain, Dougie (1978), 'Scotland: The Referendum Campaign and Beyond', *Marxism Today*, August.
Balfour (chairman) (1954), *Report of Royal Commission on Scottish Affairs* Cmnd. 9212.

Balsom, Denis and McAllister Ian (1979), 'The Scottish and Welsh Devolution Referenda of 1979: Constitutional Change and Popular Choice', *Parliamentary Affairs* Vol. 32.

Barbalet, J. M. (1988), *Citizenship* (Milton Keynes: Open University Press).

Barker, Geoffrey (1984), 'Lame ducks in a grouse moor sanctuary', *Daily Telegraph*, 21 March.

Barnes, H. E. (1917), 'Sociology Before Comte', *American Journal of Sociology*, Vol. 23.

Barnett, Correlli (1986), *The Audit of War* (London: Macmillan).

Barrow, G. W. S. (1980). *The Extinction of Scotland*, Inaugural lecture on appointment to Sir William Fraser Chair of Scottish History, Edinburgh University, December 11 (Stirling: Scots Independent).

Barry, Norman (1987), *The New Right* (London: Croom Helm).

Bendix, Rheinhold (1964), *Nation-building and Citizenship* (New York: John Wiley and Sons).

Berridge, John and Kellas, James G. (1973), 'The Mechanism of Scottish Government – A Description and Commentary with some suggestions for reform', *Research Paper 5 for the Royal Commission on the Constitution* (London: HMSO).

Bicknell, E. J. (1932), *The First and Second Epistle to the Thessalonians* (London: Methuen).

Biffen, John (1977), *A Nation in Doubt* (London: Conservative Political Centre).

Birch, Anthony (1977), *Political Integration and Disintegration* (London: Allen and Unwin).

Bochel, J. and Denver, D. T. (1970), 'Religion and voting: a critical review and a new analysis' *Political Studies* Vol. 18.

Bochel, John, Denver, David and Macartney, Allan (1981), *The Referendum Experience* (Aberdeen: Aberdeen University Press).

Bogdanor, Vernon (1979), *Devolution* (Oxford: Oxford University Press).

Bogdanor, Vernon (1980), 'Devolution' in Layton-Henry, Zig (ed.), *Conservative Party Politics* (London: MacMillan).

Bogdanor, Vernon (1980), 'The 40 Per Cent Rule' *Parliamentary Affairs* Vol. 33.

Boothby, Lord (1962), *My Yesterday, Your Tomorrow* (London: Quality Book Club).

Bosanquet, Nick (1981), 'Sir Keith Joseph's Reading List', *Political Quarterly*, Vol. 52.

Bosanquet, Nick (1983), *After the New Right* (London: Heinemann).

Boyce, D. G. (1975), 'Dicey, Kilbrandon and Devolution', *Political Quarterly* Vol. 46.

Bradley, A. W. (1969), 'Some Constitutional Aspects of Scottish Development' in Wolfe, J. N. (ed), *Government and Nationalism in Scotland* (Edinburgh: Edinburgh University Press).

Bradley, A. W. (1985), *Constitutional and Administrative Law*, 10th edition (London: Longman)

Brand, Jack (1978), *The National Movement in Scotland* (London: Routledge & Kegan Paul).

Brown, Callum (1987), *The Social History of Religion in Scotland* (London: Methuen)

Bruce, F. F, (1982), *1 & 2 Thessalonians*, World Biblical Commentary Vol. 45 (Texas: World Books).

Buchan, John (1912), 'What the Home Rule Bill Means', speeches of Buchan when Unionist Candidate for Peebles and Selkirk, National Library of Scotland.

Buchan, John (1929), 'Conservatism and Progress,' *The Spectator*, November 23.

Buchan, John (1939), *Sir Walter Scott* (London: Cassell).

Budge, Ian and Unwin, D. W. (1966), *Scottish Political Behaviour: a Case Study in British Homogeneity* (London: Longman).

Burke, Edmund (1969 edition), *Reflections on the Revolution in France* (London: Penguin).

Button, Kenneth J (1980), 'Spatial Economic Policy' in Peter Maunder (ed.), *The British Economy in the 1970s* (London: Heinemann Educational Books).

Cairncross, A. K. (ed.), (1954), *The Scottish Economy* (Cambridge: Cambridge University Press).

Callaghan, James (1988), *Time and Chance* (London: Fontana).

Calvert, Harry (ed.) (1975), *Devolution* (London: Professional Books).

Campbell, R. H. (1979), 'The Committee of Ex-Secretaries of State for Scotland and Industrial Policy, 1941–45' *Scottish Industrial History* Vol. 2.

Campbell, A. D. (1955), 'Changes in Scottish Incomes 1924–49' *The Economic Journal* Vol. 65.

Catto (chairman), (1952), *Report on Scottish Financial and Trade Statistics*, Cmd. 8609.

Checkland, Sydney and Checkland, Olive (1984), *Industry and Ethos: Scotland 1832–1914* (London: Edward Arnold).

Chester, Sir Norman (1975), *The Nationalisation of British Industry, 1945–1951* (London: HMSO).

Chester, Sir Norman (editor) (1957), *The Organisation of British Central Government, 1914–56* (London: Allen & Unwin).

Chrimes, S. B. (ed) (1950), *The General Election in Glasgow, February 1950* (Glasgow: Jackson, Son & Co.).

Church and Nation Committee (1980), *Church and Nation Committee Report to the General Assembly* (Edinburgh: Church of Scotland).

Church of Scotland (1988), *Housing Scotland's People* (Edinburgh: Saint Andrew Press).

Cockburn, Henry Lord (1910 edition), *Memorials of His Time* (Edinburgh: T. N. Foulis).

Cooper, Charles (1896), *An Editor's Retrospect* (London: Macmillan).

Coote, Sir Colin (1965), *A Companion of Honour – The Story of Walter Elliot* (London: Collins).

COSLA (1982), *Central-Local Government Relations: A Time To Listen – A Time To Speak Out* (Edinburgh: COSLA).

Coupland, Sir Reginald (1954), *Welsh and Scottish Nationalism: A Study* (London: Collins).

Craig, F. W. S. (1975), *British General Election Manifestos 1900–1974* (London: Macmillan).

Craig, F. W. S. (1982), *Conservative and Labour Party Conference Decisions, 1945–1981* (Chichester: Parliamentary Research Services).

Craik, Sir Henry (1922), 'The Cabinet Secretariat', *The Nineteenth Century and After*, Vol. 91.

Craik, Sir Henry (1901), *A Century of Scottish History*, Vols. I and II (Edinburgh: Wm. Blackwood & Sons).

Crick, Bernard (1982), *In Defence of Politics*, second edition, (London: Penguin).

Crossman, Richard (1977), *Diaries of a Cabinet Minister* (London: Hamish Hamilton).

Daiches, David (1973), 'Scott and Scotland' in Alan Bell (ed.) *Scott Bicentenary Essays* (Edinburgh: Scottish Academic Press).

Dahrendorf, Ralf (1959), *Class and Class Conflict in Industrial Society* (London: Routledge and Kegan Paul).

Dalyell, Tam (1977), *Devolution: the End of Britain?* (London: Jonathan Cape).

Davidson, John (1988), 'Unwilling to go it alone', *Scottish Business Insider* Vol. 5.

Davie, George E. (1961), *The Democratic Intellect: Scotland and Her Universities in the Nineteenth Century* (Edinburgh: Edinburgh University Press).

Dewar, Donald (1980), 'The Select Committee on Scottish Affairs', *Scottish Government Yearbook 1981* (Edinburgh: Paul Harris Publishing).

Dicey, A. V. (1973), *England's Case Against Home Rule* (Richmond: Richmond Publishing) (first published in 1886).

Dicey, A. V. and Dicey, R. S. (1920), *Thoughts on the Union Between England and Scotland* (London: Macmillan).

Donaldson, Gordon (1969), 'Scottish Devolution – the historical background' in J. N. Wolfe (ed.) *Government and Nationalism in Scotland* (Edinburgh: Edinburgh University Press).

Drucker, H. M. (ed.) (1982), *Mackintosh on Scotland* (London: Longman).

Drucker, H. M. and Brown, Gordon (1980), *The Politics of Nationalism and Devolution*, (London: Longman).

Drucker, H. M. and Kellas, J. G. (1985), 'The Scottish Affairs Committee' in Gavin Drewry (ed) *The New Select Committees: a study of the 1979 reforms* (Oxford: Oxford University Press).

Edwards, G. E. (1972), 'The Scottish Grand Committee 1958–70' *Parliamentary Affairs* Vol. 25.

Egenolf, Hans-Andreas (1969), 'The Second Epistle to the Thessalonians' in John L. Mackenzie (ed.), *New Testament for Spiritual Reading* (London: Burns and Oates).

Eliot, T. S. (1955), *The Literature of Politics* (London: Conservative Political Centre).

Elliot, Walter (1934), 'The Endless Adventure', Aberdeen University Rectorial Address, January 18, 1934. (Aberdeen: Aberdeen University).

Elliot, Walter (1943), *Long Distance* (London: Constable & Co.).

Elliot, Walter (1932), 'The Scottish Heritage in Politics', Duke of Atholl *et. al., A Scotsman's Heritage* (London: MacLehose).

Elliot, Walter (1927), *Toryism and the Twentieth Century* (London: Philip Allen & Co.).

Ferguson, Adam (1966 edition), *An Essay On The History Of Civil Society* (Edinburgh: Edinburgh University Press).

Forbes, Duncan (1966), 'Introduction' to Adam Ferguson, *An Essay On The History Of Civil Society* (Edinburgh: Edinburgh University Press).

Forbes, Duncan (1975), *Hume's Philosophical Politics* (Cambridge: Cambridge University Press).

Forbes, Duncan (1977), 'Hume's Science of Politics' in G. P. Morice (ed.), *David Hume: Bicentenary Papers* (Edinburgh: Edinburgh University Press).

Forrester, Duncan and Skene, Danus (eds.) (1988), *Just Sharing* (London: Epworth Press).

Forsyth, Michael (1985), *The Case for the Poll Tax* (London: Conservative Political Centre).

Fry, Michael (1987), *Patronage and Principle* (Aberdeen: Aberdeen University Press).

Gibson, John (1985), *The Thistle and the Crown* (Edinburgh: HMSO).

Giddens, Anthony (1982), *Profiles and Critiques and Social Theory* (London: Macmillan).

Gilder, George (1982), *Wealth and Poverty* (London: Buchanan and Enright).

Gilmour, Sir Ian (1977), *Inside Right – A Study of Conservatism* (London: Hutchinson).

Gilmour, Sir Ian (1983), *Britain Can Work* (Oxford: Martin Robertson).

Gilmour (chairman) (1937), *Report of the Committee on Scottish Administration* Cmd, 5563 (Edinburgh: HMSO).

Goldthorpe, John (1974), 'Social inequality and social integration in modern Britain' in D. Wedderburn (ed.) *Poverty, Inequality and Class Structure* (London: Cambridge University Press).

Greenleaf, W. H. (1966), *Oakeshott's Philosophical Politics*, (London: Longman).

Gunn, Lewis and Lindley, Peter (1977), 'Devolution – Origins, Events and Issues', *Public Administration Bulletin*, No. 25.

Hague, Rod and Harrop, Martin (1987), *Comparative Government and Politics: An Introduction*, second edition (London: Macmillan)

Haldane (chairman) (1918), *Report of the Machinery of Government Committee* HMSO, Cmd. 9230.

Peter Hall *et. al.* (1987), *Western Sunrise* (London: Allen and Unwin).

Hanham, H. J. (1965), 'The Creation of the Scottish Office, 1881–87', in *Juridical Review*.

Hanham, H. J. (1969), 'The Development of the Scottish Office' in Wolfe, J. N. (ed.) *Government and Nationalism in Scotland* (Edinburgh: Edinburgh University Press).

Hanham, H. J. (1959), *Elections and Party Management: Politics in the time of Disraeli and Gladstone* (London: Longmans, Green and Co.).

Hanham, H. J. (1967), 'Mid Century Scottish Nationalism: Romantic and Radical' Robson, Robert (editor), *Ideas and Institutions of Victorian Britain* (London: Bell).

Hanham, H. J. (1969), *Scottish Nationalism* (London: Faber and Faber).

Harper, J. Ross (1988), *Devolution* (Society of Scottish Conservative Lawyers).

Harvie, Christopher (1983), 'Elliot and the politics of adventure', *The Scotsman*, April 9.

Harvie, Christopher (1981), *No Gods and Precious Few Heroes* (London: Edward Arnold).

Harvie, Christopher (1977), *Scotland and Nationalism – Scottish Society and Politics, 1707–1977*, (London: George Allen and Unwin).

Harvie, Christopher (1981), 'Tom Johnston: A Patriot's Progress', *The Scotsman*, May 16.

Heald, David (1980), 'Territorial Equity and Public Finances: Concepts and Confusion', *Centre for the Study of Public Policy* No. 75.

Hetherington, Peter (1979), 'The 1979 General Election Campaign in Scotland', *Scottish Government Yearbook 1980* (Edinburgh: Paul Harris Publishing).

Hill, C. W. (1976, *Edwardian Scotland* (Edinburgh: Scottish Academic Press).

Hogwood, Brian (1987), 'Recent Developments in British Regional Policy', *Strathclyde Papers on Government and Politics* No. 51. (Glasgow: Strathclyde University).

Hogg, Quinton (1947), *The Case for Conservatism* (London: Penguin).

Hogg, Quintin (1978), *The Dilemma of Democracy: Diagnosis and Prescription* (London: Collins).

Home, Sir Alec Douglas (Lord Home) (1976), *The Way the Wind Blows* (London: Collins).

Home, Sir Alec Douglas (chairman) (1970), *Scotland's Government: the Report of the Scottish Constitutional Committee* (Edinburgh: Scottish Constitutional Committee).

Hoover, Kenneth and Plant, Raymond (1989), *Conservative Capitalism in Britain and the United States* (London: Routledge).

Hume, David (1911), *A Treatise of Human Nature* Vols. I & II (London: J. M. Dent & Sons).

Huntington, Samuel P. (1957), 'Conservatism as an ideology', *American Political Science Review* Vol. 51

Hutchison, I. G. C. (1986), *A Political History of Scotland, 1832–1924: Parties, Elections and Issues*, (Edinburgh: John Donald).

Innes, A. Taylor (1885), 'Why I Am A Liberal', Reid, Andrew (ed.), *Why I Am A Liberal* (London).

James, Robert Rhodes (1963), *Rosebery* (London: Weidenfeld and Nicolson).

Jaensch, Dean (1976), 'The Scottish Vote, 1974: A Realigning Party System?' *Political Studies*, Vol. 24.

Jenkins, Roy (1965), *Sir Charles Dilke: A Victorian Tragedy*, (London: Collins).

Johnston, Nevil (1974), 'The Royal Commission on the Constitution', *Public Administration* Vol. 52.

Johnston, Nevil (1981), 'Select Committees as Tools of Parliamentary Reform: Some Further Reflections', Walkland, S. A. and Ryle, Michael (eds.), *The Commons Today* (London: Fontana).

Johnston, Nevil (1980), *In Search of the Constitution* (London: Methuen).

Johnston, Tom (1952), *Memories* (London: Collins).

Jordan, Grant (1979), 'The Committee Stage of the Scotland and Wales Bill (1976–77)' *Waverley Papers* No. 1 (Edinburgh: Edinburgh University Politics Department).

Jordan, A. G. and Richardson J. J. (1987), *British Politics and the Policy Process* (London: Allen and Unwin).

Kavanagh, Dennis (1987), *Thatcherism and British Politics* (Oxford: Oxford University Press).

Keating, Michael (1976), 'Administrative devolution in practice: the Secretary of State for Scotland and the Scottish Office', *Public Administration* Vol. 54.

Keating, Michael (1975), *The Role of the Scottish MP in the Scottish Political System, in the UK Political System and in the Relationship Between the Two* (Ph.D, CNAA).

Keating, Michael (1979), 'Scotland in Parliament: Options for Reform'

Studies in Public Policy No. 45 (Glasgow: Centre for the Study of Public Policy).

Keating, Michael (1988), *The City That Refused to Die* (Aberdeen: Aberdeen University Press).

Keating, Michael and Bleiman, David (1979), *Labour and Scottish Nationalism* (London: Macmillan).

Keating, Michael and Lindley, Peter (1981), 'Devolution: The Scotland and Wales Bill' *Public Administration* No. 37.

Keating, Michael and Midwinter, Arthur (1983), *The Government of Scotland* (Edinburgh: Mainstream).

Keating, Michael, Midwinter, Arthur and Mitchell, James (1990, forthcoming), *Government and Politics in Scotland* (London: Macmillan).

Keating, Michael and Mitchell, James (1988), 'Urban Change And Public Policy', in *Scottish Government Yearbook, 1987* (Edinburgh: Unit for the Study of Government in Scotland).

Keating, Michael and Mitchell, James (1987), 'Easterhouse: An Urban Crisis', *Strathclyde Papers on Politics and Government* (Glasgow: University of Strathclyde).

Keegan, William (1984), *Mrs Thatcher's Economic Experiment* (London: Allen Lane).

Kellas, James G. (1961), *The Liberal Party in Scotland, 1885–95* (University College London, Ph.D.)

Kellas, James G. (1980), *Modern Scotland*, 2nd edition, (London: George Allen and Unwin).

Kellas, James G. (1984), *The Scottish Political System*, 3rd edition, (Cambridge: Cambridge University Press).

Kelsen, Hans (1961), *General Theory of Law and State* (New York: Russell and Russell).

Kelly, N. M., Bogie, D., Hurdie, D. and Reid, W. (n.d.), *Devolution: A New Appraisal*, Thistle Group Paper No. 2 (Edinburgh: Michael Ancram).

Kendle, John E. (1975), *The Round Table Movement and Imperial Union* (Toronto: University of Toronto Press).

Kerr, John (1977), 'The Failure of the Scotland and Wales Bill', *Scottish Government Yearbook 1978* (Edinburgh: Paul Harris Publishing).

Kilbrandon (chairman) (1973), *Report of the Royal Commission on the Constitution, 1969–73, With Evidence*, Cmnd. 5460 (London: HMSO).

King, Desmond (1987), *The New Right* (London: Macmillan).

Kirk, Russell (1954), *The Conservative Mind* (London: Faber & Faber).

Laing, James F. (1982), 'The Scottish Office and Nationalised Industries', *Acton Society Trust Occasional Papers* (London: Acton Society Trust).

Lang, Ian and Henderson, Barry (1975), *The Scottish Conservatives: A*

Past and a Future (Edinburgh: Scottish Conservative and Unionist Association).

Layton-Henry, Zig (ed.) (1982), *Conservative Politics in Western Europe* (London: Macmillan).

Lehmann, W. C. (1930), *Adam Ferguson and the Beginnings of Modern Sociology* (New York: Columbia University Press).

Lenman, Bruce (1977), *An Economic History of Modern Scotland, 1660– 1976* (London: Batsford).

Levitt, Ian (1979), 'The Scottish Poor Law and Unemployment, 1890– 1929', in Smout, T. C. (ed.), *The Search for Wealth and Security* (London: Macmillan).

MacCormick, John (1955), *The Flag in the Wind* (London: Gollancz)

MacCormick, Neil (1970), *The Scottish Debate* (Oxford: Oxford University Press).

McCrone, Gavin (1965), *Scotland's Economic Progress, 1951–1960* (London: Allen and Unwin).

McCurley, Anna (1987), 'Winning Back in Scotland', *Reformer – the Journal of the Tory Reform Group*.

MacDonald, Mary and Redpath, Adam (1979), 'The Scottish Office, 1954–79', *The Scottish Government Yearbook 1980* (Edinburgh: Paul Harris Publishing).

MacDonnell (chairman) (1914), *Report of the Royal Commission on the Civil Service* Cmd. 7338 (London: HMSO).

McEwen, John Malcolm (1959), *Unionist and Conservative Members of Parliament, 1914–1939* (University of London, Ph.D.).

Macfie, A. L. (1967), 'The Moral Justification of Free Enterprise', *Scottish Journal of Political Economy* Vol. 14.

Mackenzie (chairman) (1962), *Report of the Committee on the Generation and Distribution of Electricity in Scotland* Cmd. 1859 (London: HMSO).

Mackintosh, John P. (1977), *The British Cabinet*, third edition (London: Stevens and Stevens).

Mackintosh, John P. (1968), *The Devolution of Power* (London: Penguin).

Mackintosh, John P. (1964), 'Regional Administration: has it worked in Scotland?' *Public Administration*, Vol. 42.

Mackintosh, John P. (1974), 'The Report of the Royal Commission on the Constitution, 1969–73' *Political Quarterly*, Vol. 45.

Mackintosh, John P. (1977), 'Will boredom kill the devolution bill?' *The Scotsman*, September 12.

MacLean, Colin (editor) (1979), *The Crown and the Thistle* (Edinburgh: Scottish Academic Press).

MacLean, Iain (1983), *The Legend of Red Clydeside* (Edinburgh: John Donald).

Maher, G. (1977), 'The Identity of the Scottish Legal System', *Juridical Review*.

Marshall, Geoffrey (1954), 'David Hume and Political Scepticism', *Philosophical Quarterly*.

Mandeville, Bernard (1989), *The Fable of the Bees, or Private Vices, Public Benefits* (London: Penguin).

Mann, M. (1987), 'Ruling Class Strategies and Citizenship', *Sociology* Vol. 21.

Marshall, Geoffrey (1984), *Constitutional Conventions* (Oxford: Clarendon).

Marshall, T. H. (1950), *Citizenship and Social Class* (Cambridge: Cambridge University Press).

Marx, Karl (1928), *Capital: A Critique of Political Economy*, Book One (London: Allen and Unwin).

Marx, Karl (1956), *The Poverty of Philosophy* (London: Lawrence and Wishart).

Mason, Douglas (1985), *Revising the Rating System* (London: Adam Smith Institute).

Massie, Alan (1984), 'Scotland – Omega One', *The Spectator*, 14 January.

Massie, Alan (1984), 'Towards Economic Self-Rule?' *The Spectator*, 21 January.

Maynard, Geoffrey (1988), *The Economy under Mrs Thatcher* (Oxford: Blackwell).

Mercer, John (1978), *Scotland: The Devolution of Power* (London: John Calder).

Michels, Robert (1930), 'Conservatism', *Encyclopaedia of the Social Sciences*, Vol. 4.

Midwinter, Arthur and Mair, Colin (1987), *Rates Reform: Issues, Arguments and Evidence* (Edinburgh: Mainstream).

Miller, David (1985), *Hume's Political Thought* (Oxford: Oxford University Press).

Miller, William (1981), *The End of British Politics?* (Oxford: Oxford University Press).

Miller, William, Brand, Jack and Jordan, Maggie (1981), 'Government Without a Mandate: Its Causes and Consequences for the Conservative Party in Scotland', *Political Quarterly*, Vol. 52.

Miller, William *et. al* (1977), 'The connection between SNP voting and the demand for Scottish self-government', *European Journal of Political Research*, Vol. 5.

Milne, Sir David (1957), *The Scottish Office* (London: Allen and Unwin).

Mitchell, James (1988), 'Central and Local Government' in John English (ed.). *Social Services in Scotland*, second edition (Edinburgh: Scottish Academic Press).

Money, William John (1982), 'Some Causes and Consequences of the Failure of Scottish Conservatism', in Layton-Henry, Zig (ed.), *Conservative Politics in Western Europe* (London: Macmillan).

Moore, A. L. (1969), *1 & 2 Thessalonians* (London: Thomas Nelson and Sons).

Moore, Barry and Rhodes, John (1976), 'Regional Economic Policy and the Movement of Manufacturing Firms to Development Areas', *Economica* Vol. 43.

Mossner, Ernest (1979), *The Life of David Hume* (Oxford: Clarendon).

Muir, Edwin (1982), *Scott and Scotland* (Edinburgh: Polygon).

Murray, Charles (1984), *Losing Ground: American Social Policy, 1950–1980* (New York: Basic Books).

Nisbet, Robert (1986), *Conservatism* (Milton Keynes: Open University Press).

Naughtie, James (1978), 'The Scotland Bill in the House of Commons', *Scottish Government Yearbook 1979* (Edinburgh: Paul Harris Publishing).

Neil, A. (1983), 'The Information Revolution', *The Listener*, 23 June.

Neil, William (1950), *The Epistle to the Thessalonians* (London: Hodder and Stoughton).

Oakeshott, Michael (1962), *Rationalism in Politics* (London: Methuen).

Oakley, Charles (1937), *Scottish Industry Today* (Edinburgh: Moray Press).

O'Sullivan, Noel (1976), *Conservatism* (London: J. M. Dent and Sons).

Peele, Gillian (1978), 'Change, Decay and the British Constitution', *Hull Papers on Politics* No. 1 (Hull, University of Hull).

Perman, Ray (1979), 'The Devolution Referendum of 1979', *Scottish Government Yearbook 1980* (Edinburgh: Paul Harris Publishing).

Pollock, A. Asprey, N. and Ancram, M. (n.d.), *Scottish Education – A Time for Decision*, Thistle Group Paper No. 2 (Edinburgh: Michael Ancram).

Porteous, James A. A. (1950), 'Unionist Policy for Scotland – A Criticism', (Edinburgh: Scottish Convention).

Pottinger, George (1979), *The Secretaries of State for Scotland, 1926–76* (Edinburgh: Scottish Academic Press).

Pryde, G. S. (1962), *Scotland from 1603 to the Present Day* (London: Nelson).

Punnett, R. M. (1983), 'The Anglo-Celtic Partisan Divide: Regional Representation in Parliament, 1868–1983', *Strathclyde Papers on Government and Politics* No. 16 (Glasgow: University of Strathclyde).

Punnett, R. M. (1984), 'Regional Partisanship and the Legitimacy of British Governments, 1868–1983', *Parliamentary Affairs* Vol. 37.

Pye, Lucien (1968), 'Political Culture', *International Encyclopedia of Social Sciences* Vol. 12.

Quinton, Anthony (1978), *The Politics of Imperfection: the Religious and Secular Traditions of Conservative Thought in England from Hooker to Oakeshott* (London: Faber and Faber).

Ramsden, John (1978), 'The Changing Base of British Conservatism', in C. Cook and J. Ramsden (ed.), *Trends in British Politics Since 1945* (London: Macmillan).

Ramsden, John (1980), *The Making of Conservative Party Policy: the Conservative Research Department since 1929* (London: Longman)

Richardson, J. J. and Jordan, A. G. (1979), *Governing Under Pressure* (Oxford: Basil Blackwell).

Riddell, Peter (1985), *The Thatcher Government* (Oxford: Basil Blackwell)

Robbins, L. (1962), *The Theory of Economic Policy in English Classical Political Economy* (London: Macmillan)

Robertson, George (1978), 'Wreckers in the Lords', *The Scotsman*, August 3.

Robinson, C. and Marshall, E. (1984), *Oil's Contribution to UK Self-Sufficiency* (London: Heinemann Educational Books).

Rose, Richard (1978), 'From Steady State to Fluid State: the Unity of the Kingdom Today', *Studies in Public Policy* No. 26 (Glasgow: Centre for the Study of Public Policy).

Rose, Richard (1975), 'The Future of Scottish Politics: a Dynamic Analysis' *Fraser of Allander Institute Speculative Papers*, No. 3 (Glasgow: University of Strathclyde).

Rose, Richard (1982), *Understanding the United Kingdom* (London: Longman).

Rossiter, Clinton (1968), 'Conservatism', *International Encyclopaedia of the Social Sciences* Vol. 3.

Russell, Bertrand (1944), 'A Reply to My Critics' in Schilpp, P. (ed.), *The Philosophy of Bertrand Russell* (Evanston: North-Western University Press).

Schneider, W. H. (editor), *Adam Smith's Moral and Political Philosophy*

Scott, P. H. (1983) 'The Politics of Sir Walter Scott' in J. H. Alexander and David Hewitt (eds.), *Scott and his influence* (Aberdeen: Association of Scottish Literary Studies).

Scott, Sir Walter (1981) *The Letters of Malachi Malagrowther* (Edinburgh: William Blackwood).

Scottish Biographies (1938) (London: E. J. Thurston and Jackson).

Scruton, Roger (1980), *Conservatism* (London: Penguin).

Seldon, Anthony (1981), *Churchill's Indian Summer: the Conservative Government, 1951–1955* (London: Hodder & Stoughton).

Seligman, E. R. (1910), 'Introduction' to 1910 edition of Adam Smith, *The Wealth of Nations* (London: J. M. Dent & Sons).

Skelton, Noel (1924), *Constructive Conservatism* (Edinburgh: Wm. Blackwood).

Skinner, Andrew (1979), *A System of Social Science: Papers relating to Adam Smith* (Edinburgh: David Hume Institute).

Skinner, Andrew (1989), 'Adam Smith and Economic Liberalism' *Hume Occasional Papers* No. 9 (Edinburgh: David Hume Institute).

Smith, Adam (1984), *Theory of Moral Sentiments* (Indianapolis: Liberty Classics).

Smith, Adam (1976), *An Enquiry Into The Nature And Causes Of The Wealth of Nations* (Chicago: University of Chicago Press).

Smith, David (1987), *The Rise and Fall of Monetarism* (London: Penguin).

Smith, Geoffrey (1977), 'The Conservative commitment to devolution', *The Spectator*, February 19.

Smith, Geoffrey (1977), 'Devolution and not saying what you mean', *The Spectator*, February 26.

Smith, Janet Adam (1965), *John Buchan* (London: Rupert Hart-Davis).

Smith, T. B. (1957), 'The Union of 1707 as Fundamental Law', *Public Law*.

Smout, T. C. (1986). *A Century of the Scottish People, 1830–1950* (London: Collins)

Stuart, James (1967), *Within the Fringe* (London: Bodley Head).

Taylor, Edward (1969), 'Inside Look at Scottish Tories', *New Outlook*, November.

Toothill (chairman) (1961), *Report of the Committee of Inquiry into the Scottish Economy, 1960–61* (Edinburgh: Scottish Council (Development and Industry).

Turner, Arthur C. (1952), *Scottish Home Rule* (Oxford: Basil Blackwell).

Turner, Bryan (1986), *Citizenship and Capitalism – The Debate Over Reformism* (London: Allen & Unwin).

Urwin, Derek W. (1963), *Politics and the Development of the Unionist Party in Scotland* (Manchester University, M.A. thesis).

Urwin, Derek W. (1965), 'The Development of the Conservative Organisation in Scotland Until 1912' *Scottish Historical Review*. Vol. 44.

Urwin, Derek W. (1966), 'Scottish Conservatism: a Party Organisation in Transition', *Political Studies* Vol. 14.

Utley, T. E. (1975), 'The Balkanisation of Britain', in Boyson, Rhodes (ed.), *1985: An Escape from Orwell's 1984*, A Conservative Path to Freedom (London: Churchill Press).

Viner, J. (1927), 'Adam Smith and Laissez-Faire', *Journal of Political Economy* Vol. 35.

Waldegrave, William (1978), *The Binding of Leviathan* (London: Hamish Hamilton).

Ward, J. T. (1982), *The First Century: A History of Scottish Tory Organisation, 1882–1982* (Edinburgh: Scottish Conservative and Unionist Association).

Warner, Gerald (1988), *The Scottish Tory Party* (London: Weidenfeld and Nicolson).

Webb, Keith (1977), *The Growth of Nationalism in Scotland* (Glasgow: Molendinar Press).

Webb, Keith and Hall, Eric (1978), 'Explanations of the Rise of Political

Nationalism in Scotland', *Studies in Public Policy* No. 26 (Glasgow: Centre for the Study of Public Policy).

Wolfe, J. N. (1968), *Government and Nationalism in Scotland* (Edinburgh: Edinburgh University Press).

Wright, Esmond (1971), 'Politics' in Glen, Duncan (ed.), *Whither Scotland* (London: Gollancz).

Young, Hugo and Sloman, Anne (1986), *The Thatcher Phenomenon* (London: BBC).

Young, James D. (1979), *The Rousing of the Scottish Working Class* (London: Croom Helm).

Young, Kenneth (1970), *Sir Alec Douglas-Home* (London: J. M. Dent and Sons).

Younger, George (1967), 'A Tory's view of Scotland' *Scotsman*, December 15.

Index